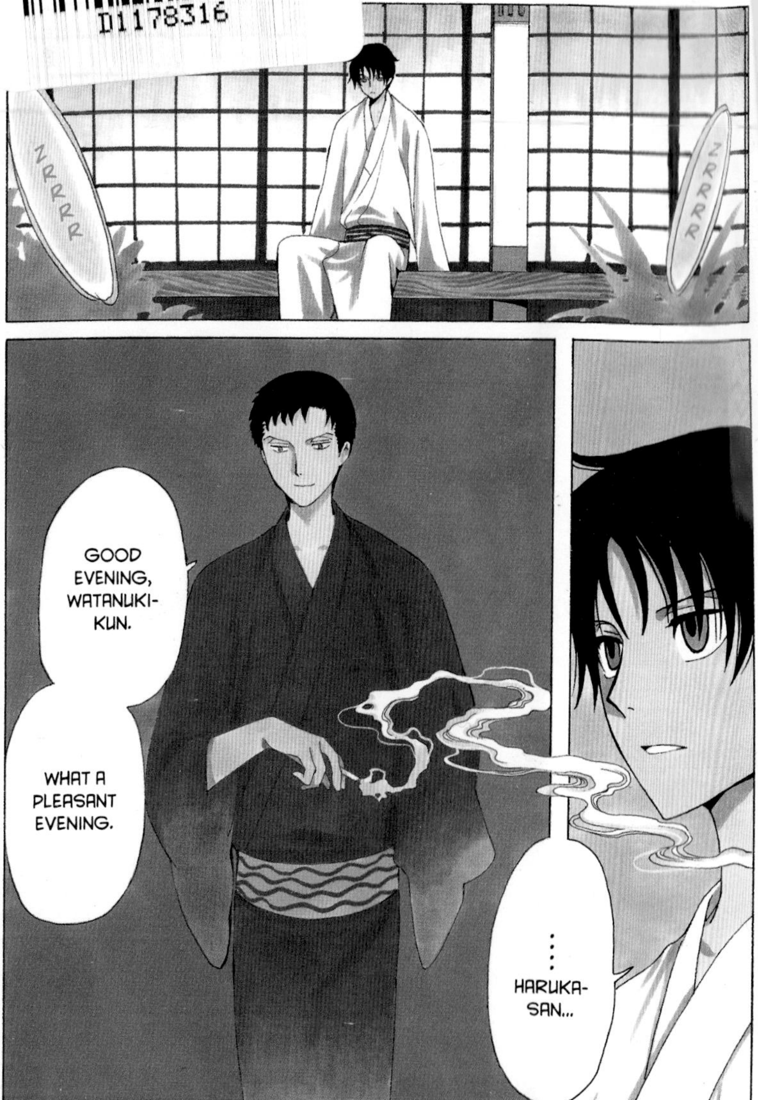
ZRRRR
ZRRRR
.... HARUKA-SAN...
GOOD EVENING, WATANUKI-KUN.
WHAT A PLEASANT EVENING.

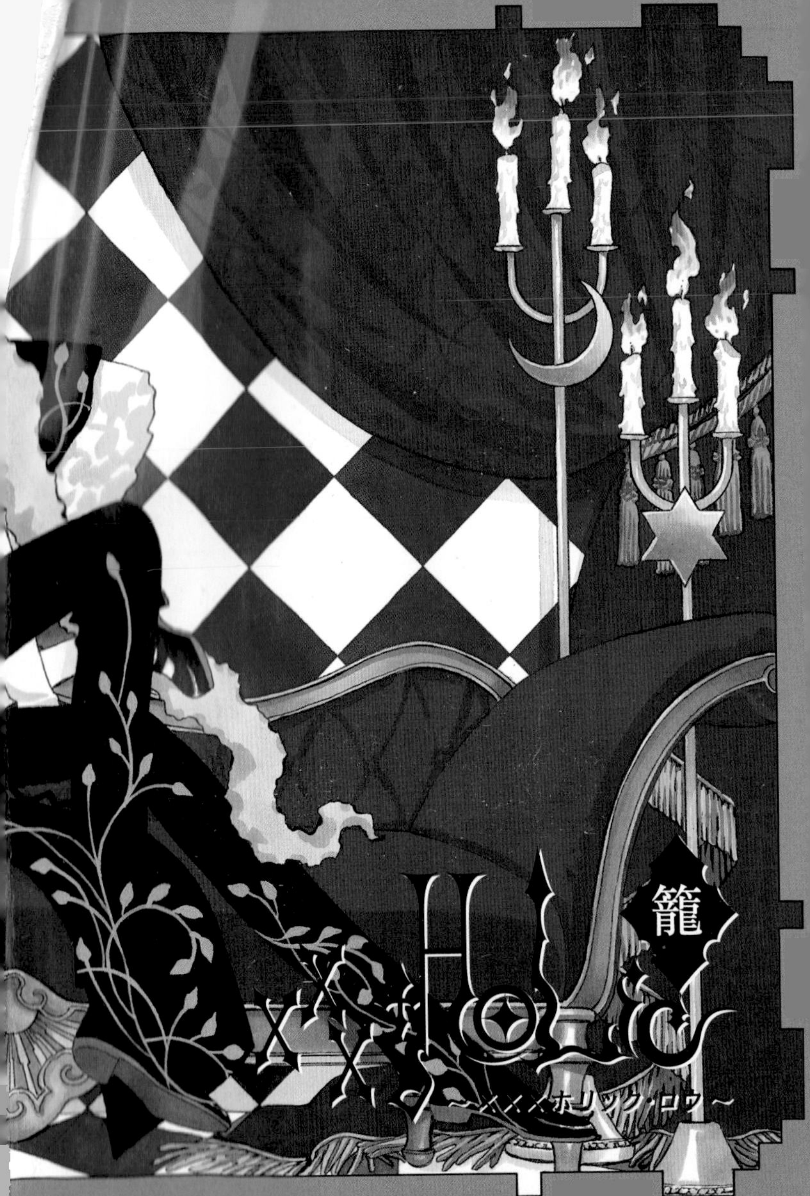
籠
xxxHOLiC
～×××ホリック・ロウ～

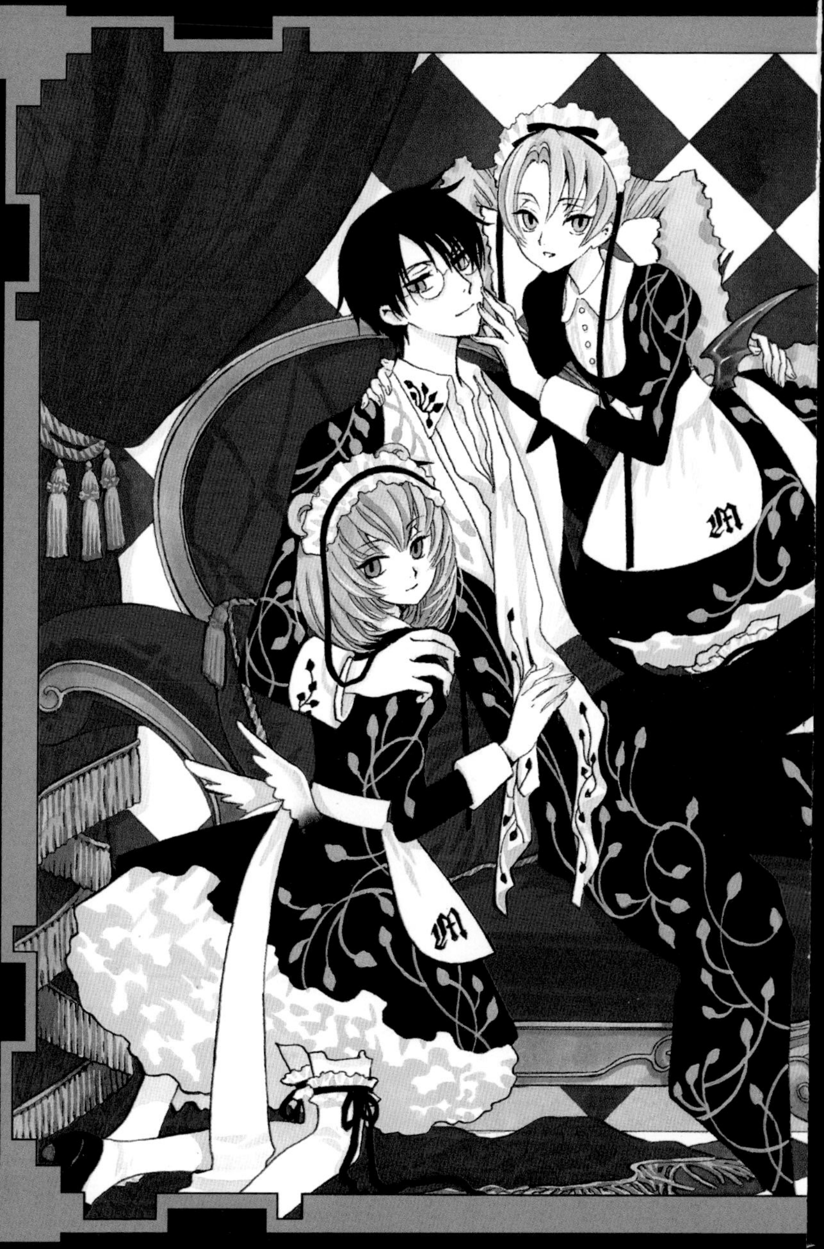

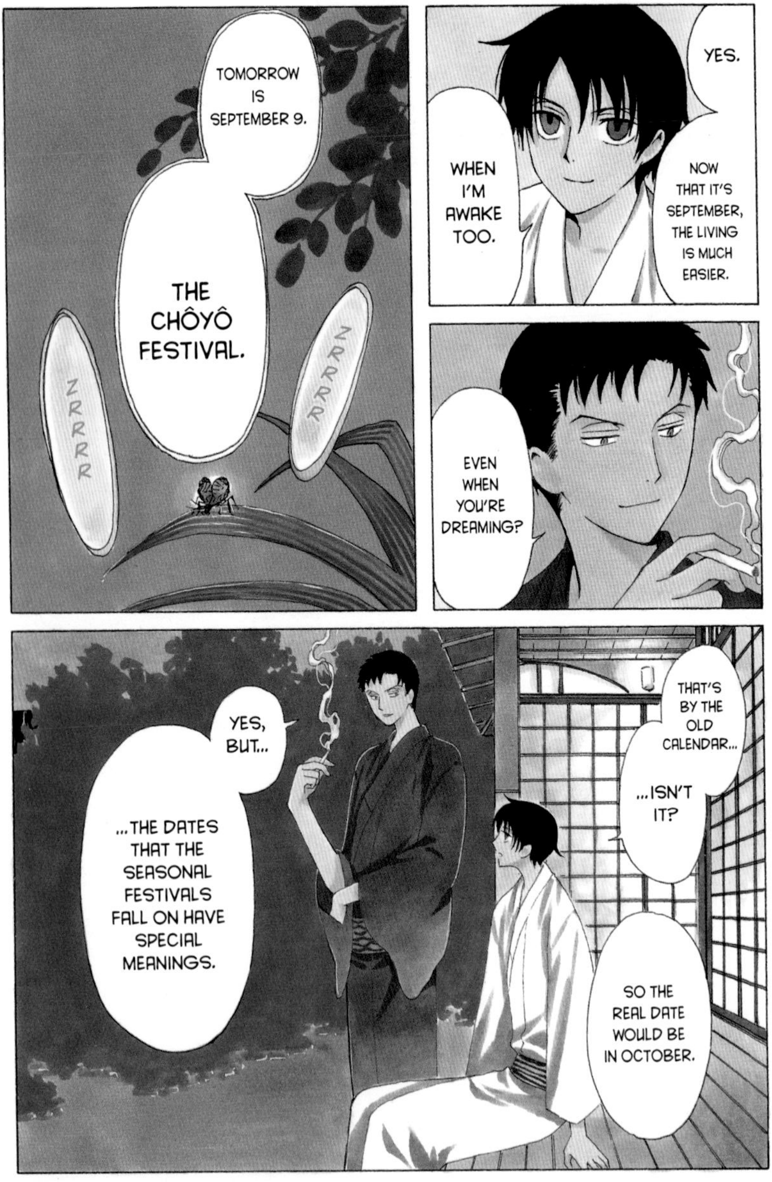
YES.
NOW THAT IT'S SEPTEMBER, THE LIVING IS MUCH EASIER.
WHEN I'M AWAKE TOO.
EVEN WHEN YOU'RE DREAMING?
TOMORROW IS SEPTEMBER 9.
ZRRRR
THE CHÔYÔ FESTIVAL.
ZRRRR
THAT'S BY THE OLD CALENDAR...
...ISN'T IT?
SO THE REAL DATE WOULD BE IN OCTOBER.
YES, BUT...
...THE DATES THAT THE SEASONAL FESTIVALS FALL ON HAVE SPECIAL MEANINGS.

19

CLAMP

WITHDRAWN

TRANSLATED AND ADAPTED BY
William Flanagan

LETTERED BY
North Market Street Graphics

BALLANTINE BOOKS • NEW YORK

xxxHOLiC, volume 19 is a work of fiction. Names, characters, places, and incidents are the products of the author's imagination or are used fictitiously. Any resemblance to actual events, locales, or persons, living or dead, is entirely coincidental.

A Del Rey Manga/Kodansha Trade Paperback Original

Published in the United States by Del Rey, an imprint of The Random House Publishing Group, a division of Random House, Inc., New York.

DEL REY is a registered trademark and the Del Rey colophon is a trademark of Random House, Inc.

Publication rights arranged through Kodansha Ltd.

First published in Japan in 2011 by Kodansha Ltd., Tokyo

ISBN 978-0-345-53126-1

Printed in the United States of America

www.delreymanga.com

9 8 7 6 5 4 3 2 1

Translator and Adapter—William Flanagan
Lettering—North Market Street Graphics

xxxHOLiC crosses over with *Tsubasa*. Although it isn't necessary to read *Tsubasa* to understand the events in *xxxHOLiC*, you'll get to see the same events from different perspectives if you read both series!

Contents

Honorifics Explained

Throughout the Del Rey Manga books, you will find Japanese honorifics left intact in the translations. For those not familiar with how the Japanese use honorifics and, more important, how they differ from American honorifics, we present this brief overview.

Politeness has always been a critical facet of Japanese culture. Ever since the feudal era, when Japan was a highly stratified society, use of honorifics—which can be defined as polite speech that indicates relationship or status—has played an essential role in the Japanese language. When you address someone in Japanese, an honorific usually takes the form of a suffix attached to one's name (example: "Asuna-san"), is used as a title at the end of one's name, or appears in place of the name itself (example: "Negi-sensei," or simply "Sensei!").

Honorifics can be expressions of respect or endearment. In the context of manga and anime, honorifics give insight into the nature of the relationship between characters. Many English translations leave out these important honorifics and therefore distort the feel of the original Japanese. Because Japanese honorifics contain nuances that English honorifics lack, it is our policy at Del Rey not to translate them. Here, instead, is a guide to some of the honorifics you may encounter in Del Rey Manga.

-san: This is the most common honorific and is equivalent to Mr., Miss, Ms., or Mrs. It is the all-purpose honorific and can be used in any situation where politeness is required.

-sama: This is one level higher than "-san" and is used to confer great respect.

-dono: This comes from the word "tono," which means "lord." It is an even higher level than "-sama" and confers utmost respect.

-kun: This suffix is used at the end of boys' names to express familiarity or endearment. It is also sometimes used by men among friends, or when addressing someone younger or of a lower station.

-chan: This is used to express endearment, mostly toward girls. It is also used for little boys, pets, and even among lovers. It gives a sense of childish cuteness.

Bozu: This is an informal way to refer to a boy, similar to the English terms "kid" and "squirt."

Sempai/Senpai: This title suggests that the addressee is one's senior in a group or organization. It is most often used in a school setting, where underclassmen refer to their upperclassmen as "sempai." It can also be used in the workplace, such as when a newer employee addresses an employee who has seniority in the company.

Kohai: This is the opposite of "sempai" and is used toward underclassmen in school or newcomers in the workplace. It connotes that the addressee is of a lower station.

Sensei: Literally meaning "one who has come before," this title is used for teachers, doctors, or masters of any profession or art.

-[blank]: This is usually forgotten in these lists, but it is perhaps the most significant difference between Japanese and English. The lack of honorific means that the speaker has permission to address the person in a very intimate way. Usually, only family, spouses, or very close friends have this kind of permission. Known as *yobisute*, it can be gratifying when someone who has earned the intimacy starts to call one by one's name without an honorific. But when that intimacy hasn't been earned, it can be very insulting.

GOOD EVENING, WATANUKI-KUN.

WHAT A PLEASANT EVENING.

...
HARUKA-SAN...

xxxHOLiC 籠

〜××× ホリック・ロウ〜

TOMORROW IS SEPTEMBER 9.

THE CHÔYÔ FESTIVAL.

ZRRRR

ZRRRR

YES.

WHEN I'M AWAKE TOO.

NOW THAT IT'S SEPTEMBER, THE LIVING IS MUCH EASIER.

EVEN WHEN YOU'RE DREAMING?

YES, BUT...

...THE DATES THAT THE SEASONAL FESTIVALS FALL ON HAVE SPECIAL MEANINGS.

THAT'S BY THE OLD CALENDAR...

...ISN'T IT?

SO THE REAL DATE WOULD BE IN OCTOBER.

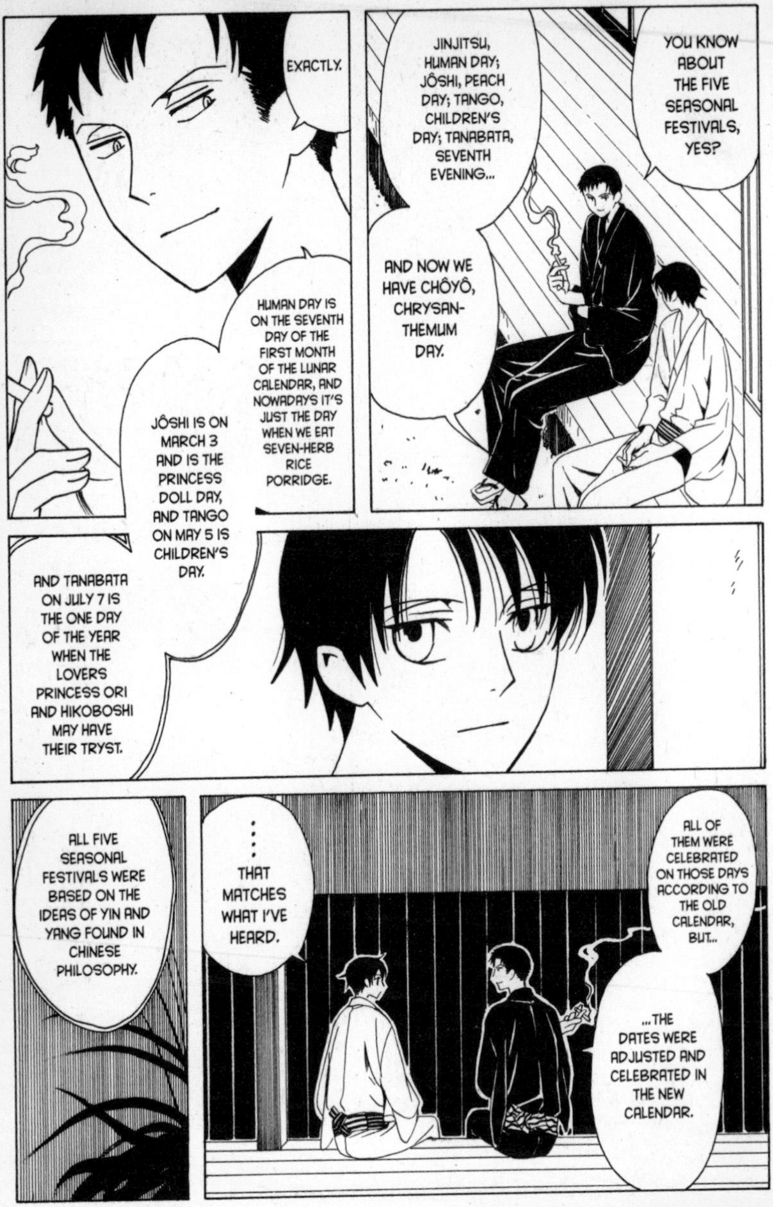
YOU KNOW ABOUT THE FIVE SEASONAL FESTIVALS, YES?
JINJITSU, HUMAN DAY; JÔSHI, PEACH DAY; TANGO, CHILDREN'S DAY; TANABATA, SEVENTH EVENING...
AND NOW WE HAVE CHÔYÔ, CHRYSANTHEMUM DAY.
EXACTLY.
HUMAN DAY IS ON THE SEVENTH DAY OF THE FIRST MONTH OF THE LUNAR CALENDAR, AND NOWADAYS IT'S JUST THE DAY WHEN WE EAT SEVEN-HERB RICE PORRIDGE.
JÔSHI IS ON MARCH 3 AND IS THE PRINCESS DOLL DAY, AND TANGO ON MAY 5 IS CHILDREN'S DAY.
AND TANABATA ON JULY 7 IS THE ONE DAY OF THE YEAR WHEN THE LOVERS PRINCESS ORI AND HIKOBOSHI MAY HAVE THEIR TRYST.
ALL OF THEM WERE CELEBRATED ON THOSE DAYS ACCORDING TO THE OLD CALENDAR, BUT...
...THE DATES WERE ADJUSTED AND CELEBRATED IN THE NEW CALENDAR.
...... THAT MATCHES WHAT I'VE HEARD.
ALL FIVE SEASONAL FESTIVALS WERE BASED ON THE IDEAS OF YIN AND YANG FOUND IN CHINESE PHILOSOPHY.

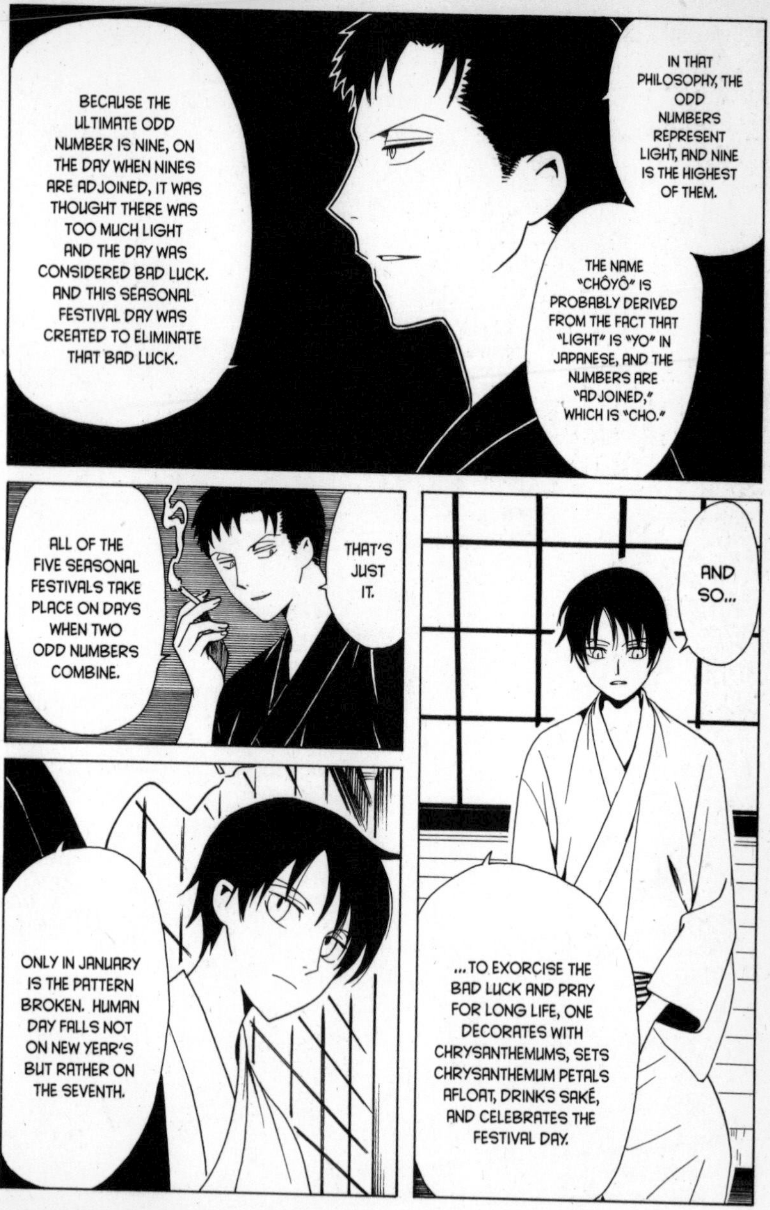
IN THAT PHILOSOPHY, THE ODD NUMBERS REPRESENT LIGHT, AND NINE IS THE HIGHEST OF THEM.
THE NAME "CHÔYÔ" IS PROBABLY DERIVED FROM THE FACT THAT "LIGHT" IS "YO" IN JAPANESE, AND THE NUMBERS ARE "ADJOINED," WHICH IS "CHO."
BECAUSE THE ULTIMATE ODD NUMBER IS NINE, ON THE DAY WHEN NINES ARE ADJOINED, IT WAS THOUGHT THERE WAS TOO MUCH LIGHT AND THE DAY WAS CONSIDERED BAD LUCK. AND THIS SEASONAL FESTIVAL DAY WAS CREATED TO ELIMINATE THAT BAD LUCK.
AND SO...
...TO EXORCISE THE BAD LUCK AND PRAY FOR LONG LIFE, ONE DECORATES WITH CHRYSANTHEMUMS, SETS CHRYSANTHEMUM PETALS AFLOAT, DRINKS SAKÉ, AND CELEBRATES THE FESTIVAL DAY.
THAT'S JUST IT.
ALL OF THE FIVE SEASONAL FESTIVALS TAKE PLACE ON DAYS WHEN TWO ODD NUMBERS COMBINE.
ONLY IN JANUARY IS THE PATTERN BROKEN. HUMAN DAY FALLS NOT ON NEW YEAR'S BUT RATHER ON THE SEVENTH.

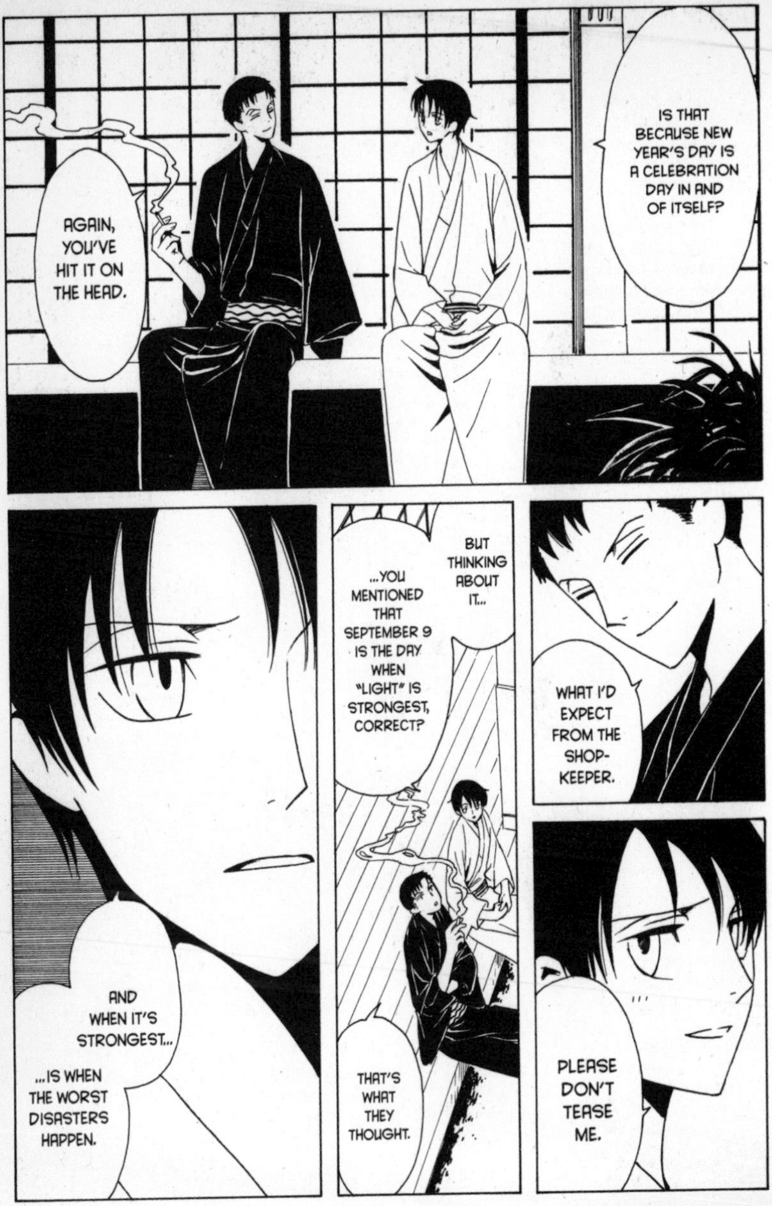
IS THAT BECAUSE NEW YEAR'S DAY IS A CELEBRATION DAY IN AND OF ITSELF?
AGAIN, YOU'VE HIT IT ON THE HEAD.
WHAT I'D EXPECT FROM THE SHOP-KEEPER.
PLEASE DON'T TEASE ME.
BUT THINKING ABOUT IT...
...YOU MENTIONED THAT SEPTEMBER 9 IS THE DAY WHEN "LIGHT" IS STRONGEST, CORRECT?
THAT'S WHAT THEY THOUGHT.
AND WHEN IT'S STRONGEST...
...IS WHEN THE WORST DISASTERS HAPPEN.

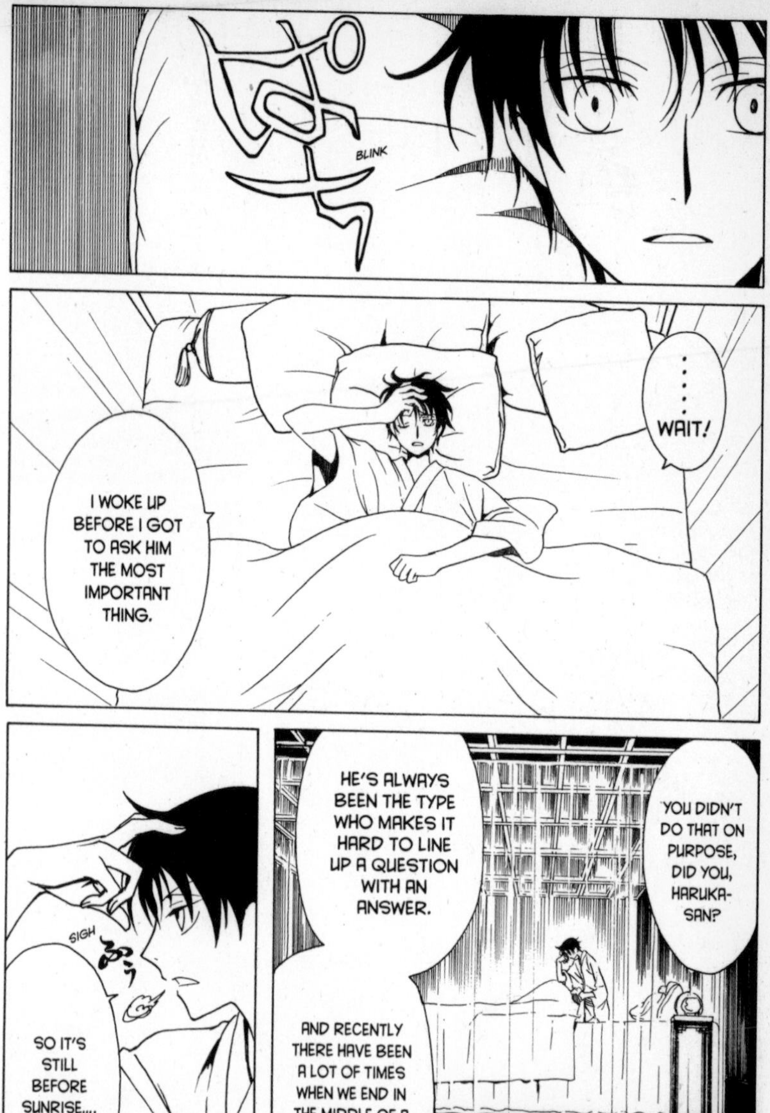
BLINK
...... WAIT!
I WOKE UP BEFORE I GOT TO ASK HIM THE MOST IMPORTANT THING.
YOU DIDN'T DO THAT ON PURPOSE, DID YOU, HARUKA-SAN?
HE'S ALWAYS BEEN THE TYPE WHO MAKES IT HARD TO LINE UP A QUESTION WITH AN ANSWER.
AND RECENTLY THERE HAVE BEEN A LOT OF TIMES WHEN WE END IN THE MIDDLE OF A CONVERSATION.
SIGH
SO IT'S STILL BEFORE SUNRISE....

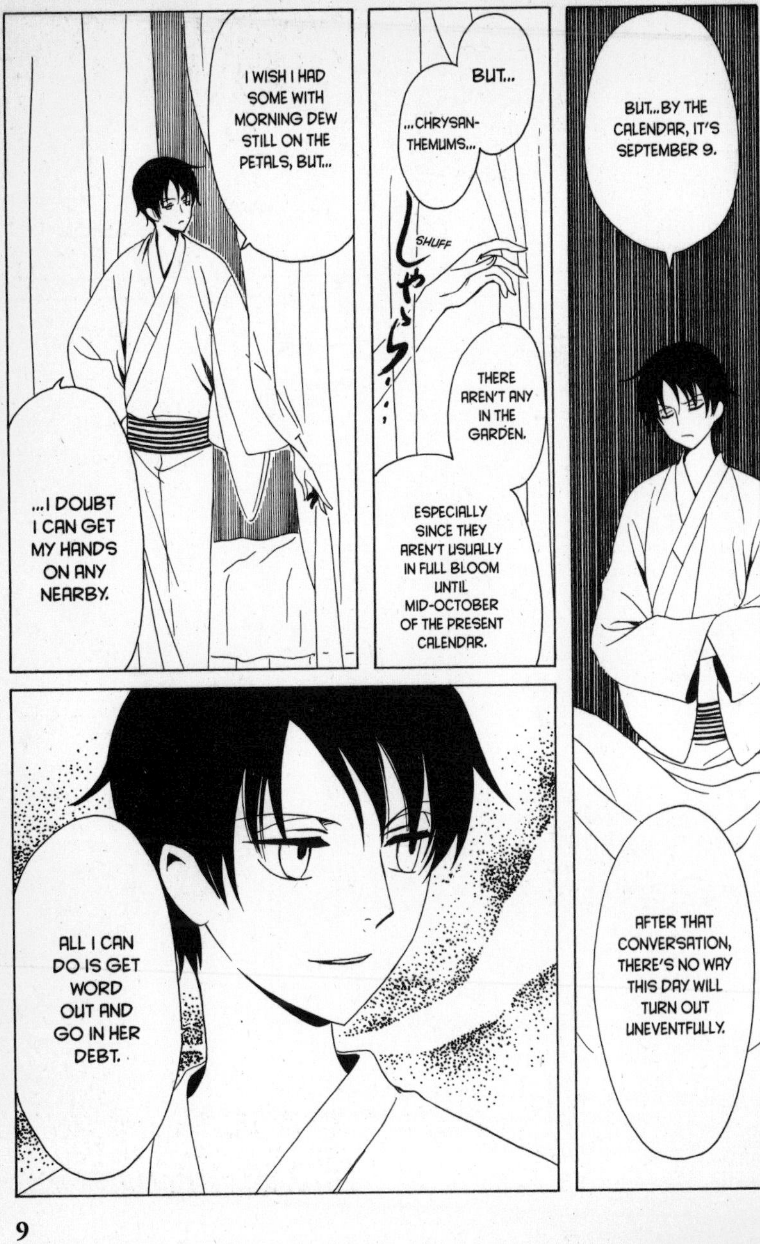
BUT...BY THE CALENDAR, IT'S SEPTEMBER 9.
AFTER THAT CONVERSATION, THERE'S NO WAY THIS DAY WILL TURN OUT UNEVENTFULLY.
BUT...
...CHRYSAN-THEMUMS...
SHUFF
THERE AREN'T ANY IN THE GARDEN.
ESPECIALLY SINCE THEY AREN'T USUALLY IN FULL BLOOM UNTIL MID-OCTOBER OF THE PRESENT CALENDAR.
I WISH I HAD SOME WITH MORNING DEW STILL ON THE PETALS, BUT...
...I DOUBT I CAN GET MY HANDS ON ANY NEARBY.
ALL I CAN DO IS GET WORD OUT AND GO IN HER DEBT.

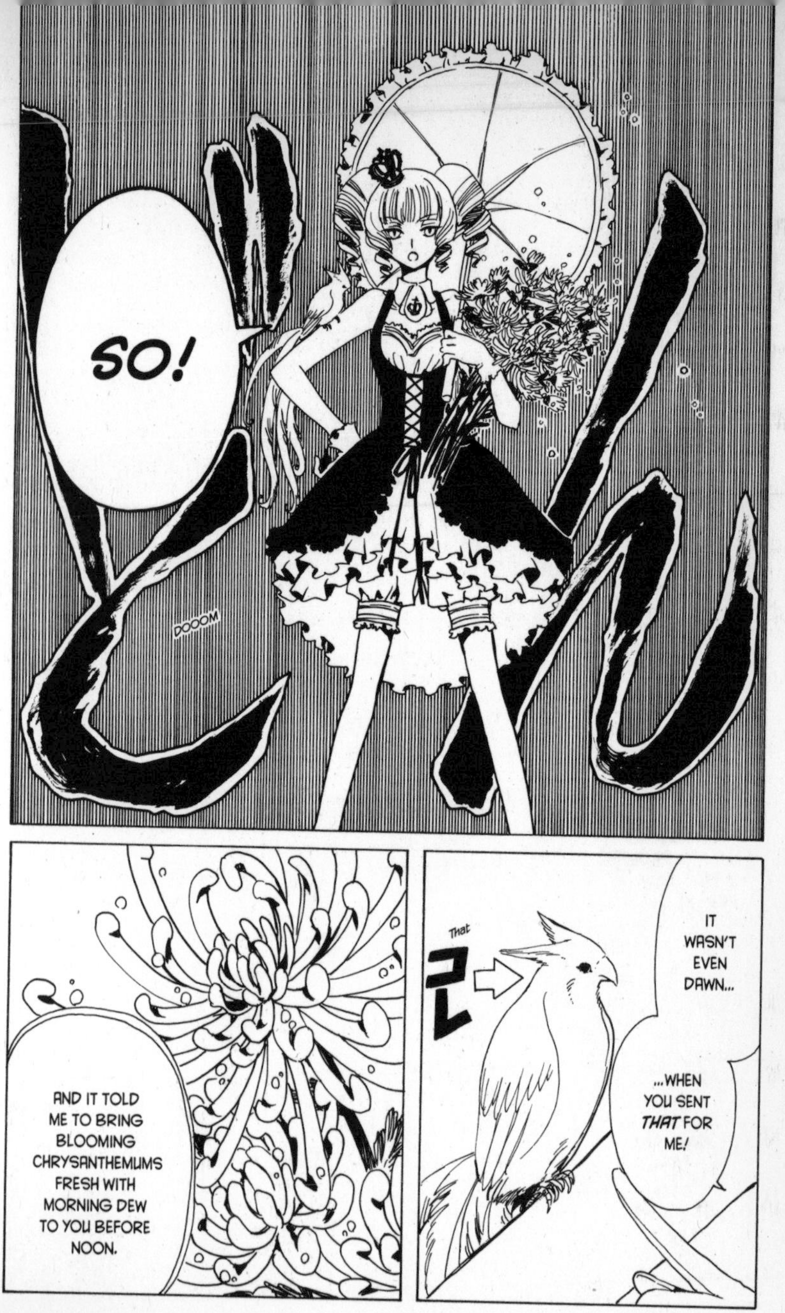
SO!
DOOOM
That
コレ
IT WASN'T EVEN DAWN...
...WHEN YOU SENT *THAT* FOR ME!
AND IT TOLD ME TO BRING BLOOMING CHRYSANTHEMUMS FRESH WITH MORNING DEW TO YOU BEFORE NOON.

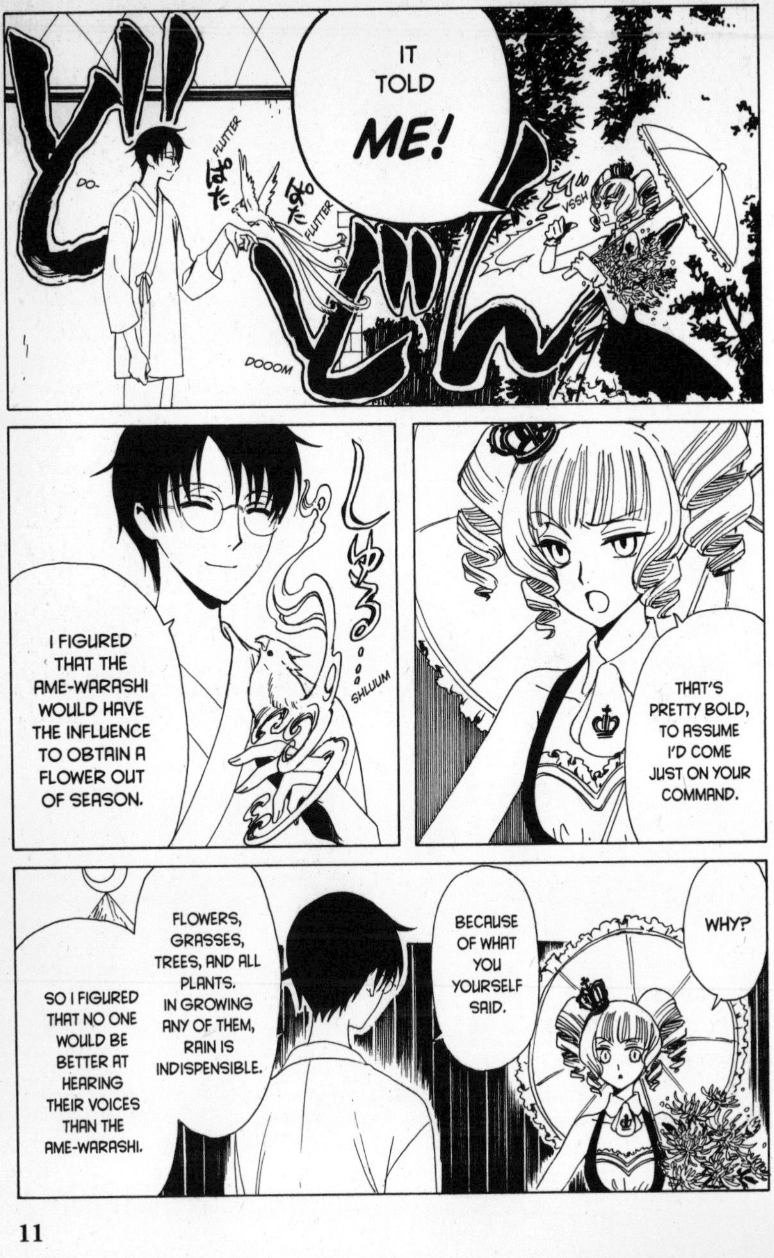
VSSH
IT TOLD ME!
FLUTTER
FLUTTER
DO-
DOOOM
THAT'S PRETTY BOLD, TO ASSUME I'D COME JUST ON YOUR COMMAND.
SHUUM
I FIGURED THAT THE AME-WARASHI WOULD HAVE THE INFLUENCE TO OBTAIN A FLOWER OUT OF SEASON.
WHY?
BECAUSE OF WHAT YOU YOURSELF SAID.
FLOWERS, GRASSES, TREES, AND ALL PLANTS. IN GROWING ANY OF THEM, RAIN IS INDISPENSIBLE.
SO I FIGURED THAT NO ONE WOULD BE BETTER AT HEARING THEIR VOICES THAN THE AME-WARASHI.

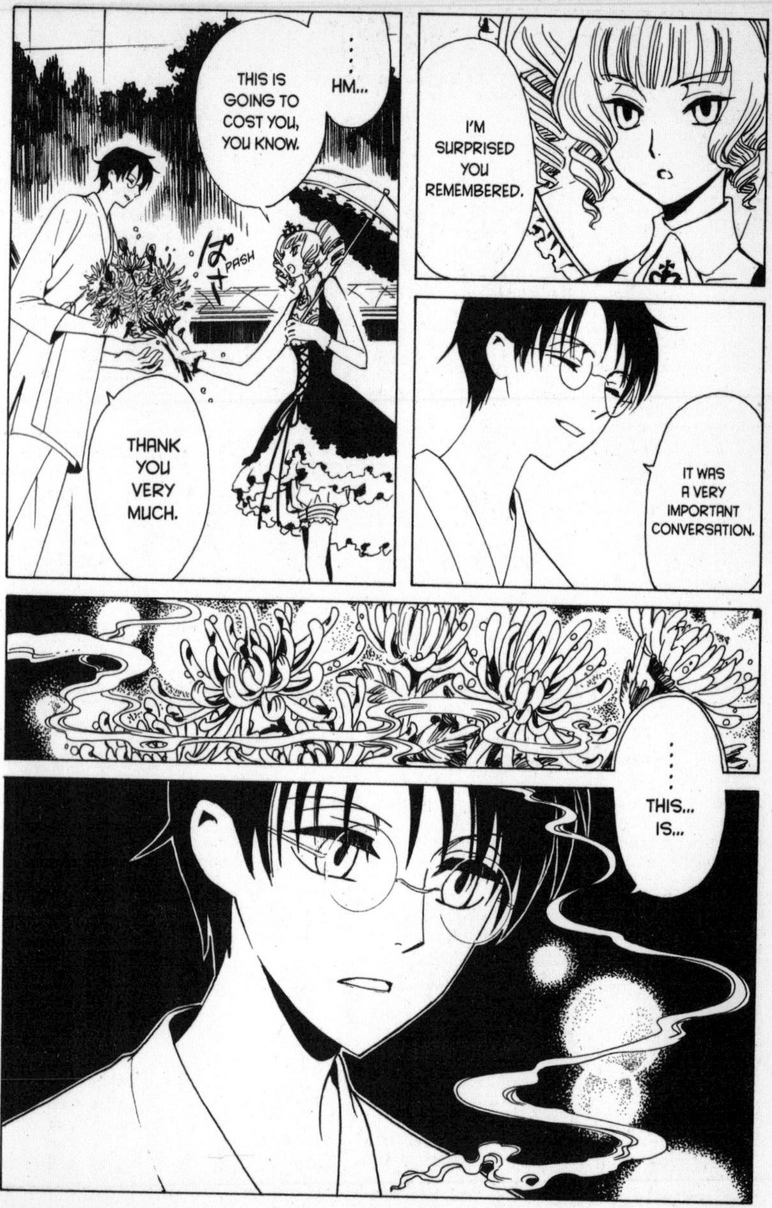
I'M SURPRISED YOU REMEMBERED.
IT WAS A VERY IMPORTANT CONVERSATION.
......HM...
THIS IS GOING TO COST YOU, YOU KNOW.
ぱさ
PASH
THANK YOU VERY MUCH.
......THIS... IS...

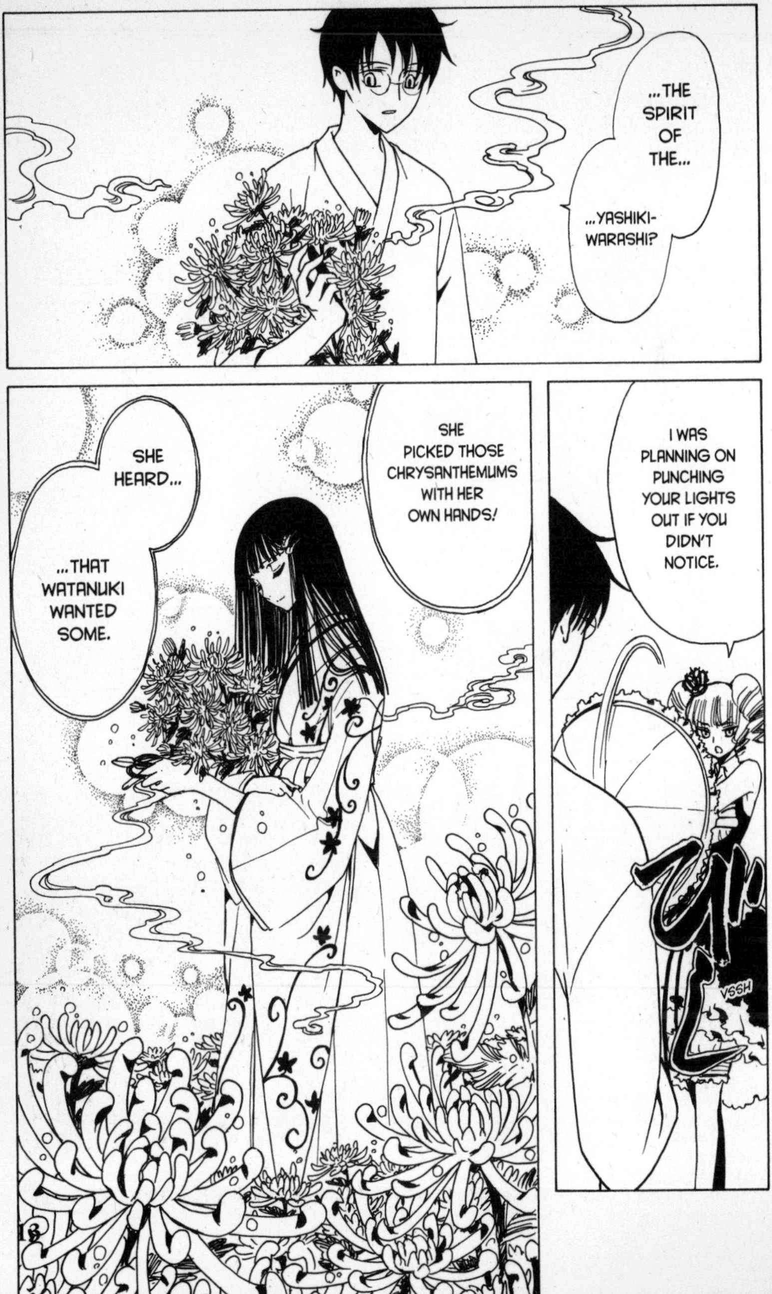
...THE SPIRIT OF THE...
...YASHIKI-WARASHI?
I WAS PLANNING ON PUNCHING YOUR LIGHTS OUT IF YOU DIDN'T NOTICE.
VSSH
SHE PICKED THOSE CHRYSANTHEMUMS WITH HER OWN HANDS!
SHE HEARD...
...THAT WATANUKI WANTED SOME.

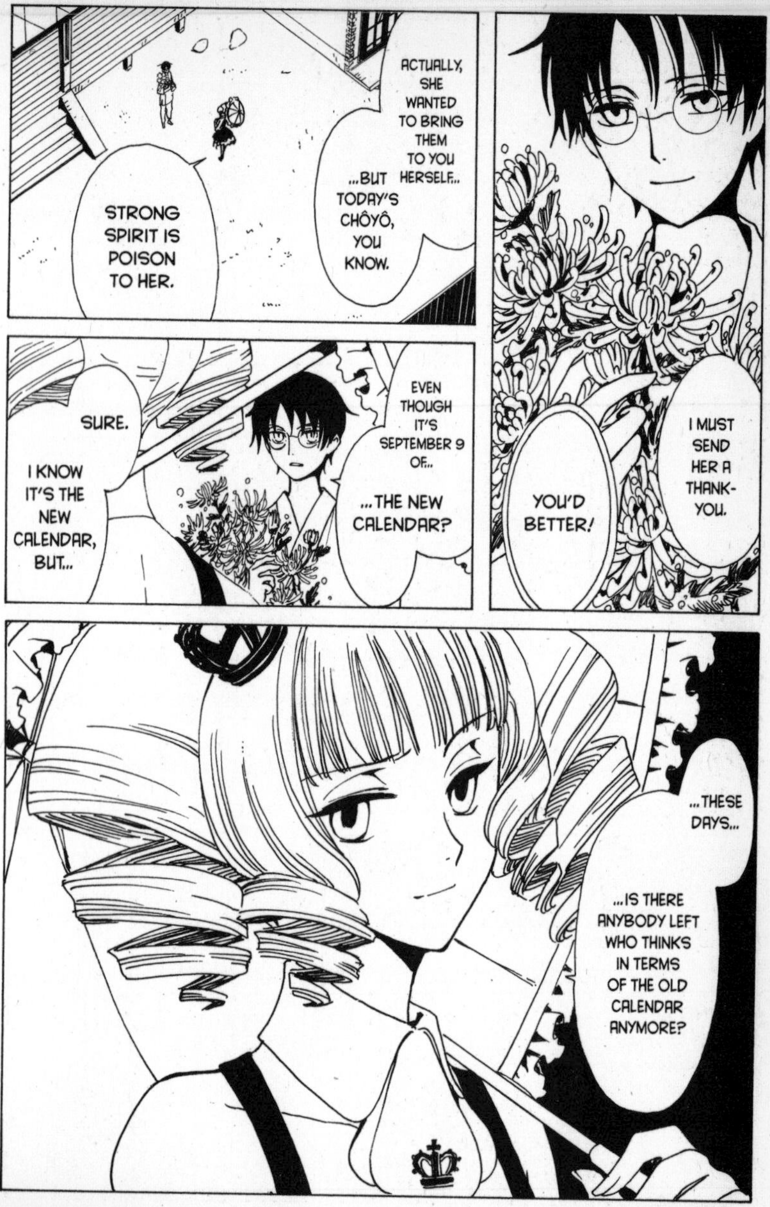
I MUST SEND HER A THANK-YOU.
YOU'D BETTER!
ACTUALLY, SHE WANTED TO BRING THEM TO YOU HERSELF...
...BUT TODAY'S CHÔYÔ, YOU KNOW.
STRONG SPIRIT IS POISON TO HER.
EVEN THOUGH IT'S SEPTEMBER 9 OF...
...THE NEW CALENDAR?
SURE.
I KNOW IT'S THE NEW CALENDAR, BUT...
...THESE DAYS...
...IS THERE ANYBODY LEFT WHO THINKS IN TERMS OF THE OLD CALENDAR ANYMORE?

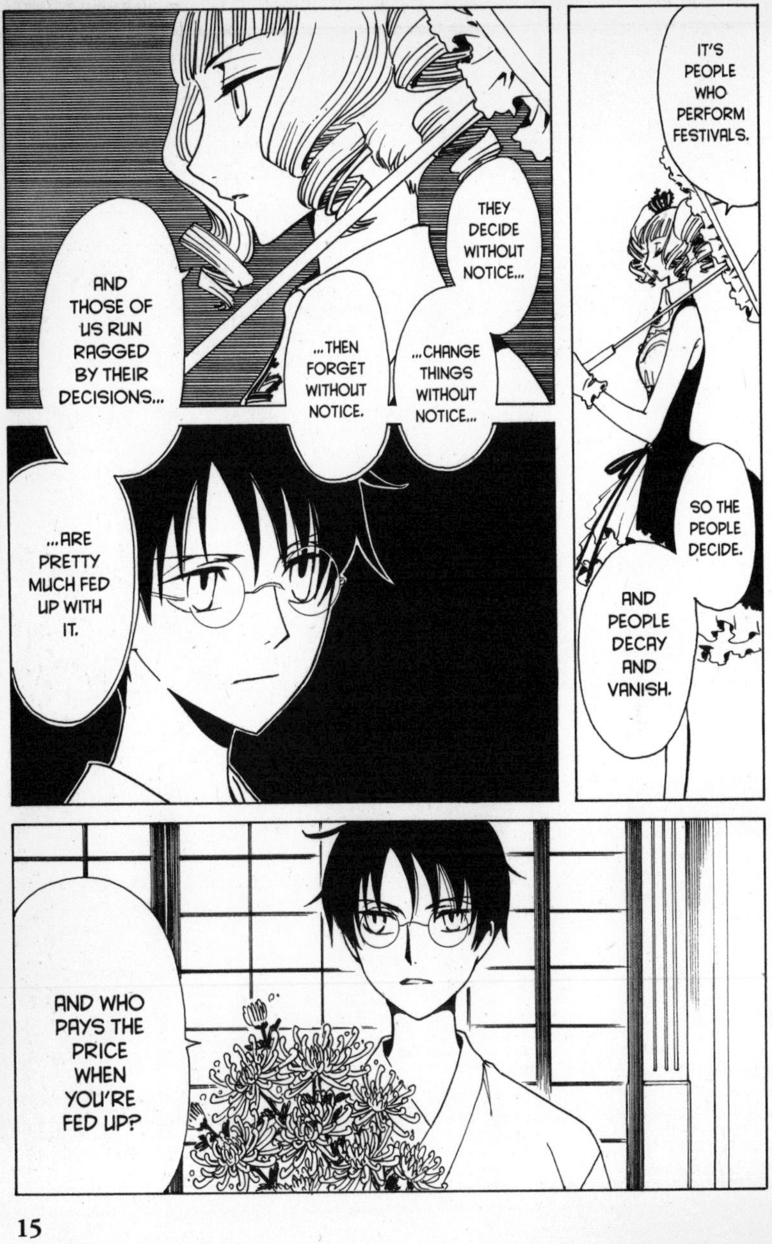
IT'S PEOPLE WHO PERFORM FESTIVALS.
SO THE PEOPLE DECIDE.
AND PEOPLE DECAY AND VANISH.
THEY DECIDE WITHOUT NOTICE...
...CHANGE THINGS WITHOUT NOTICE...
...THEN FORGET WITHOUT NOTICE.
AND THOSE OF US RUN RAGGED BY THEIR DECISIONS...
...ARE PRETTY MUCH FED UP WITH IT.
AND WHO PAYS THE PRICE WHEN YOU'RE FED UP?

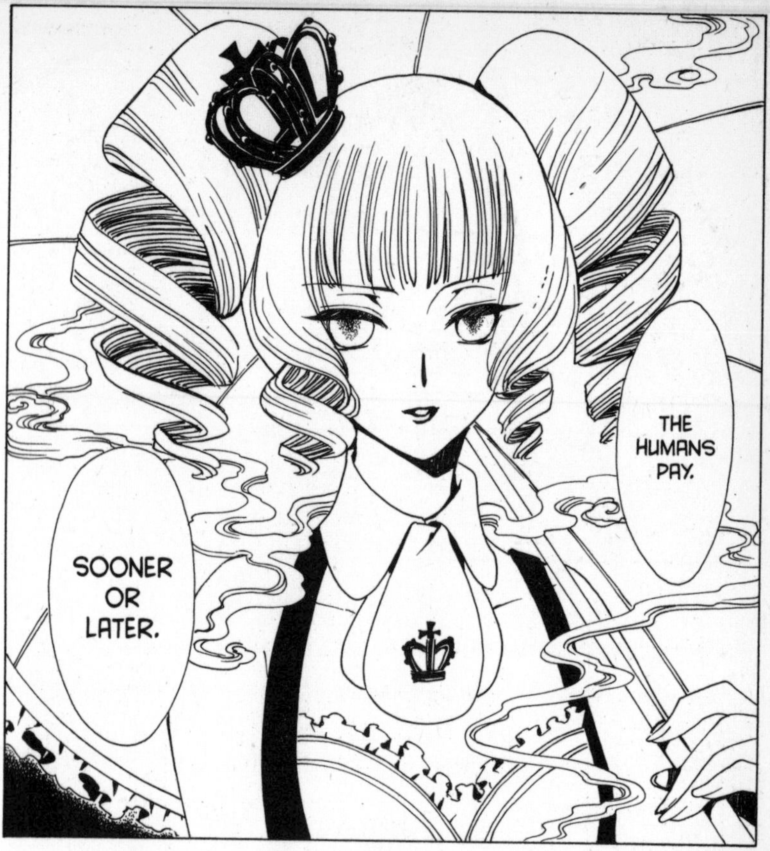
THE HUMANS PAY.
SOONER OR LATER.
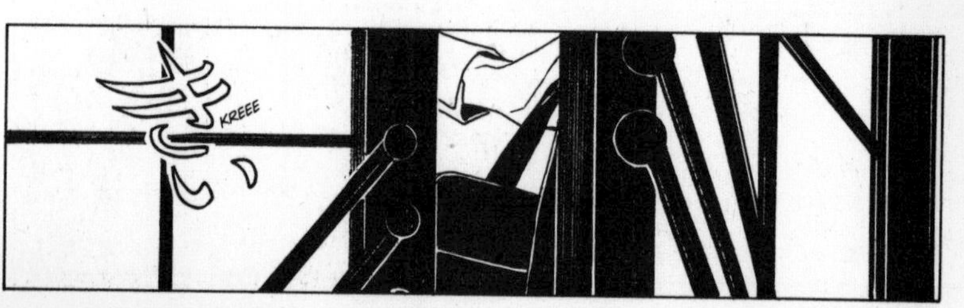
KREEE

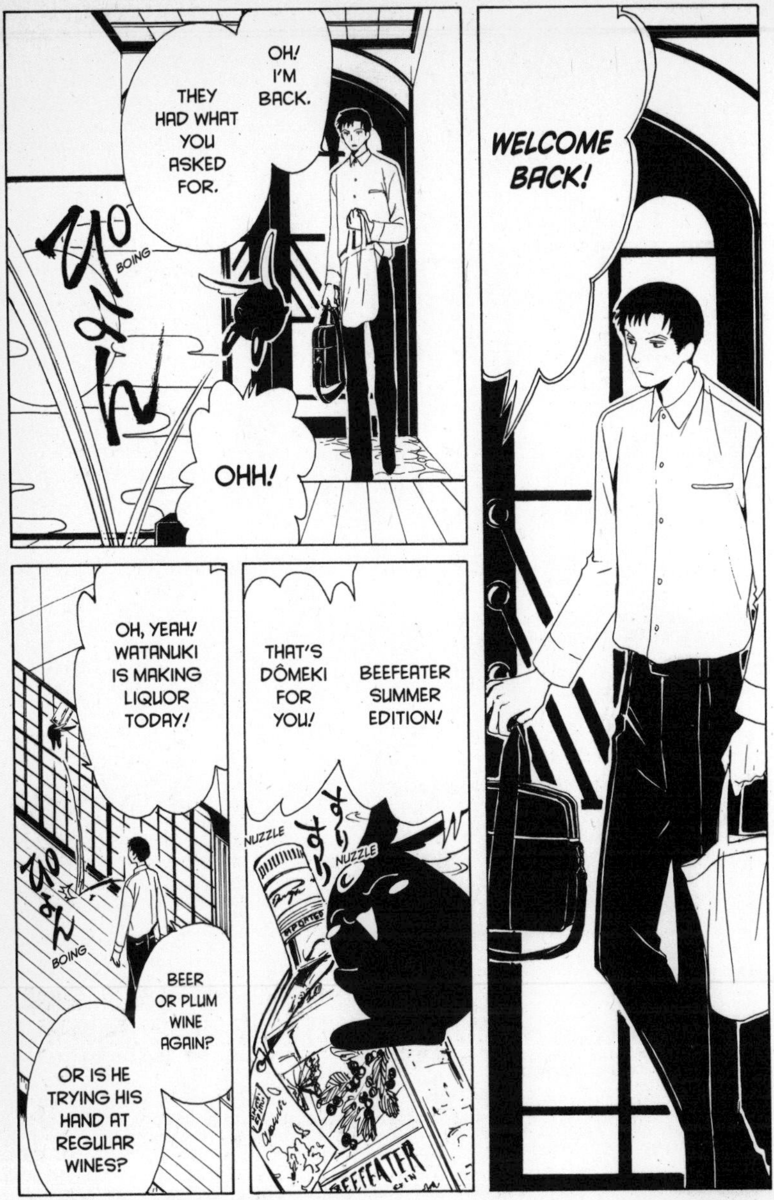
WELCOME BACK!
OH! I'M BACK.
THEY HAD WHAT YOU ASKED FOR.
BOING
OHH!
THAT'S DÔMEKI FOR YOU!
BEEFEATER SUMMER EDITION!
すり すり
NUZZLE
NUZZLE
BEEFEATER
OH, YEAH! WATANUKI IS MAKING LIQUOR TODAY!
BOING
BEER OR PLUM WINE AGAIN?
OR IS HE TRYING HIS HAND AT REGULAR WINES?

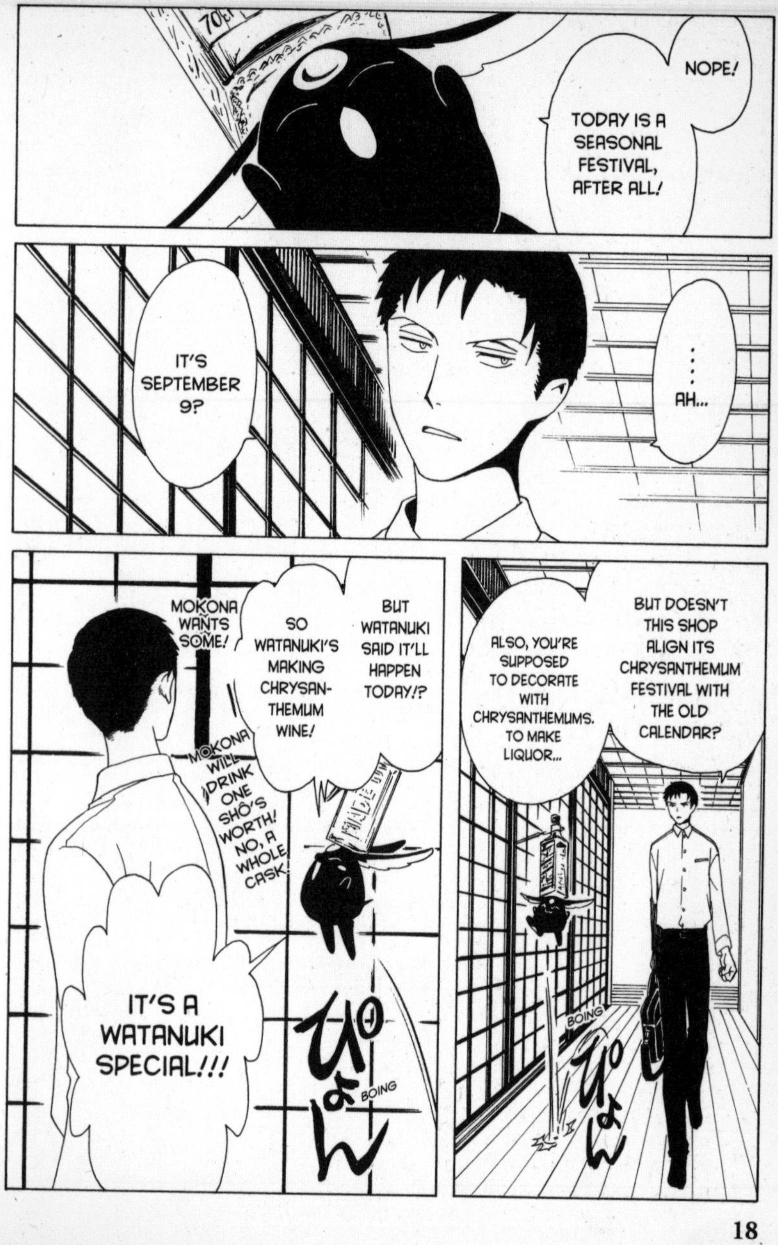
NOPE!
TODAY IS A SEASONAL FESTIVAL, AFTER ALL!
......
AH...
IT'S SEPTEMBER 9?
BUT DOESN'T THIS SHOP ALIGN ITS CHRYSANTHEMUM FESTIVAL WITH THE OLD CALENDAR?
ALSO, YOU'RE SUPPOSED TO DECORATE WITH CHRYSANTHEMUMS. TO MAKE LIQUOR...
BOING
ぴょん
BUT WATANUKI SAID IT'LL HAPPEN TODAY!?
SO WATANUKI'S MAKING CHRYSANTHEMUM WINE!
MOKONA WANTS SOME!
MOKONA WILL DRINK ONE SHÔ'S WORTH! NO, A WHOLE CASK!
IT'S A WATANUKI SPECIAL!!!
ぴょん
BOING

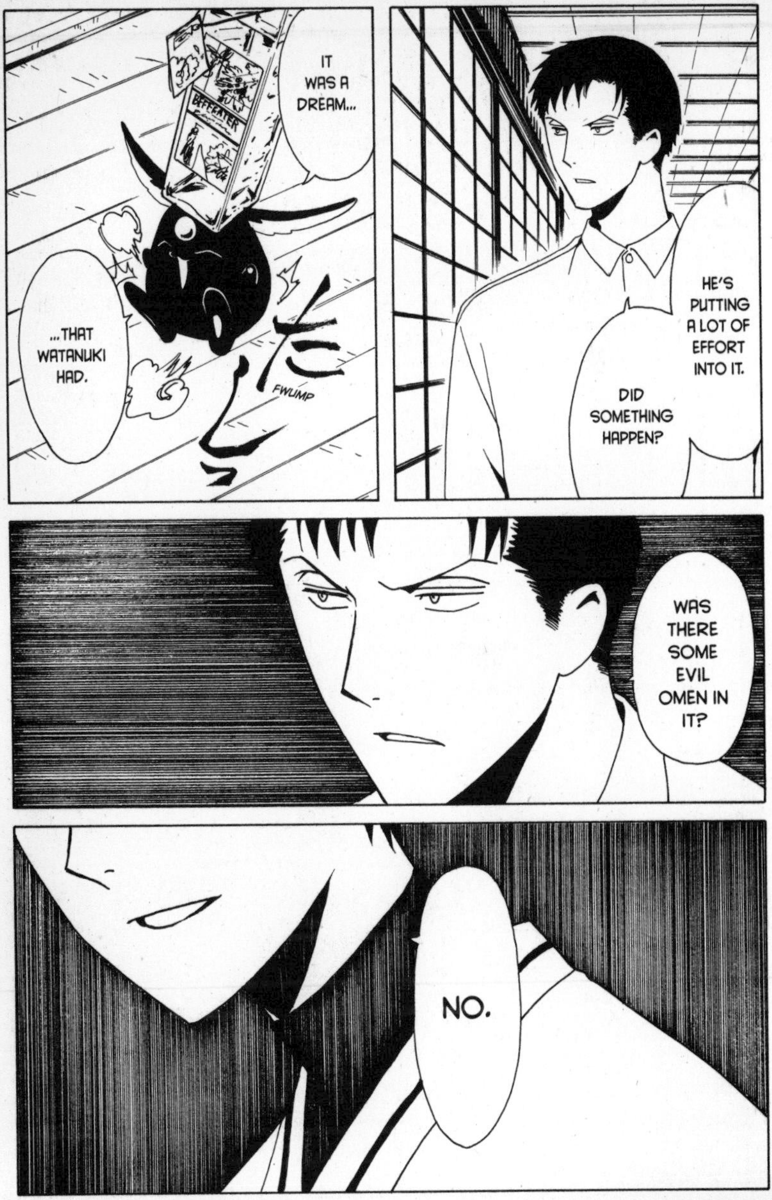
HE'S PUTTING A LOT OF EFFORT INTO IT.
DID SOMETHING HAPPEN?
IT WAS A DREAM...
...THAT WATANUKI HAD.
FWUMP
WAS THERE SOME EVIL OMEN IN IT?
NO.

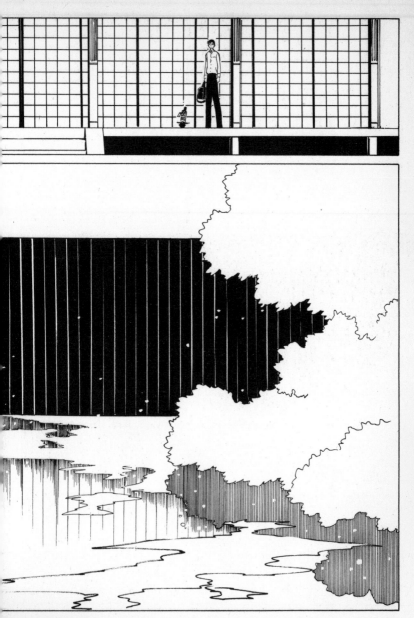

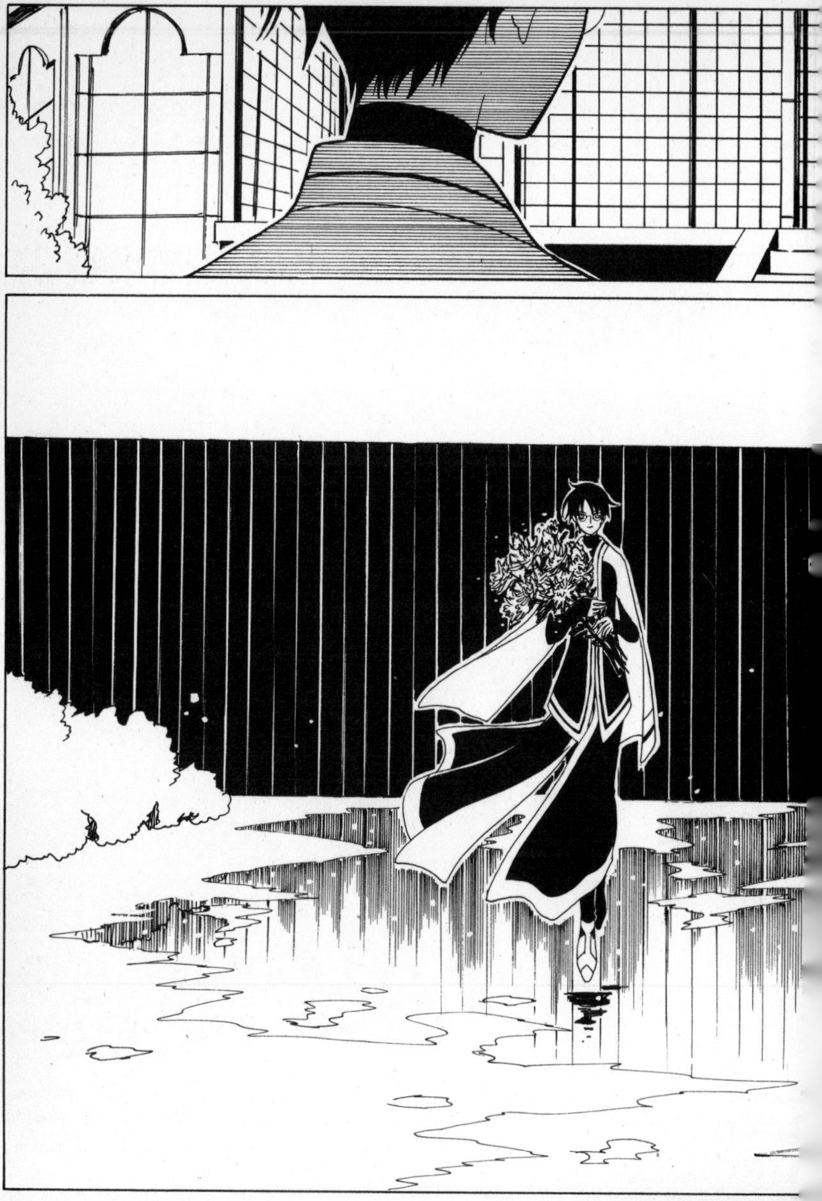

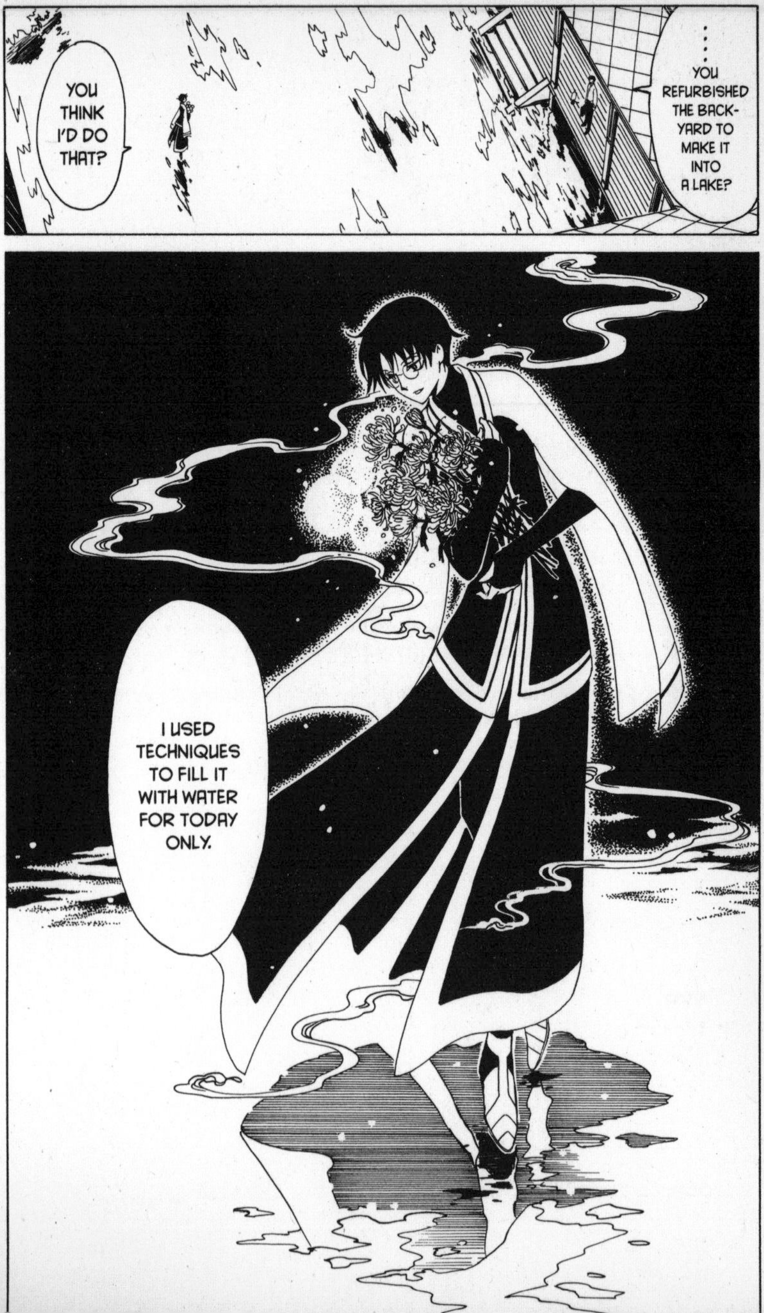

. . . YOU REFURBISHED THE BACK-YARD TO MAKE IT INTO A LAKE?
YOU THINK I'D DO THAT?
I USED TECHNIQUES TO FILL IT WITH WATER FOR TODAY ONLY.

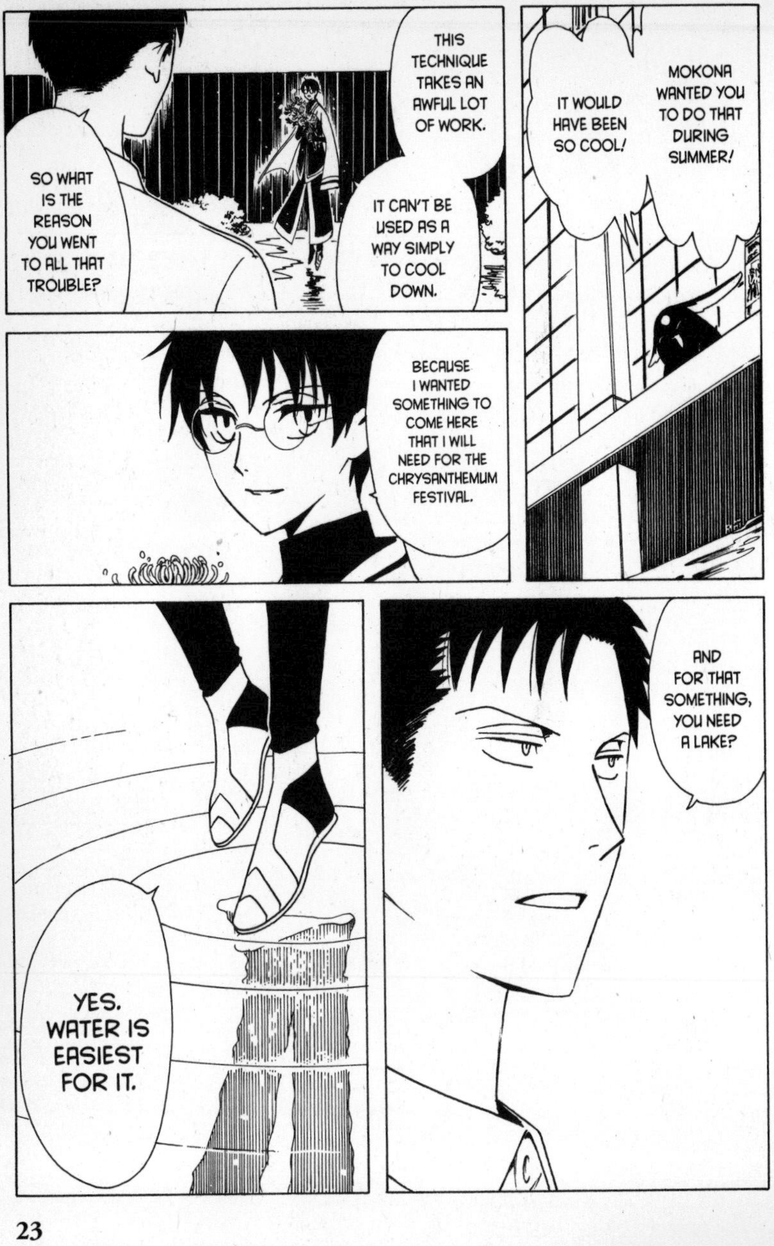
MOKONA WANTED YOU TO DO THAT DURING SUMMER!
IT WOULD HAVE BEEN SO COOL!
THIS TECHNIQUE TAKES AN AWFUL LOT OF WORK.
IT CAN'T BE USED AS A WAY SIMPLY TO COOL DOWN.
SO WHAT IS THE REASON YOU WENT TO ALL THAT TROUBLE?
BECAUSE I WANTED SOMETHING TO COME HERE THAT I WILL NEED FOR THE CHRYSANTHEMUM FESTIVAL.
AND FOR THAT SOMETHING, YOU NEED A LAKE?
YES. WATER IS EASIEST FOR IT.

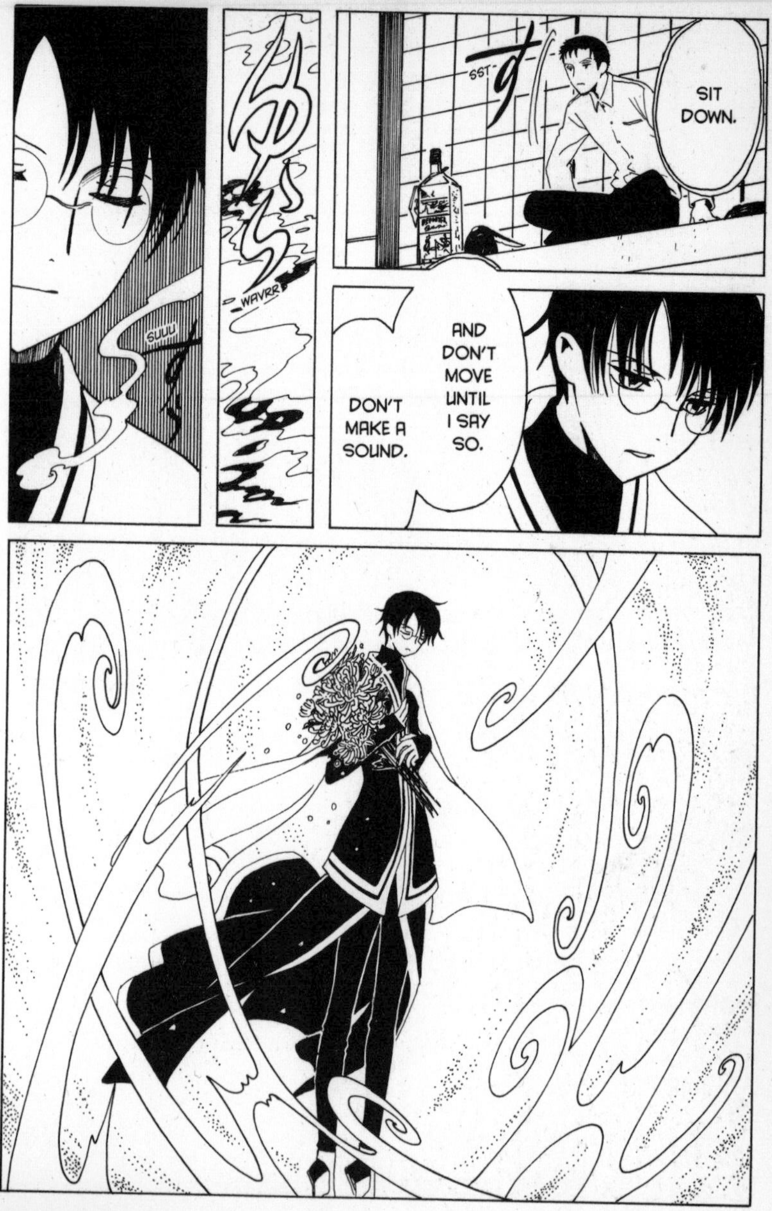
SIT DOWN.
SST
AND DON'T MOVE UNTIL I SAY SO.
DON'T MAKE A SOUND.
WAVRR
SUUU

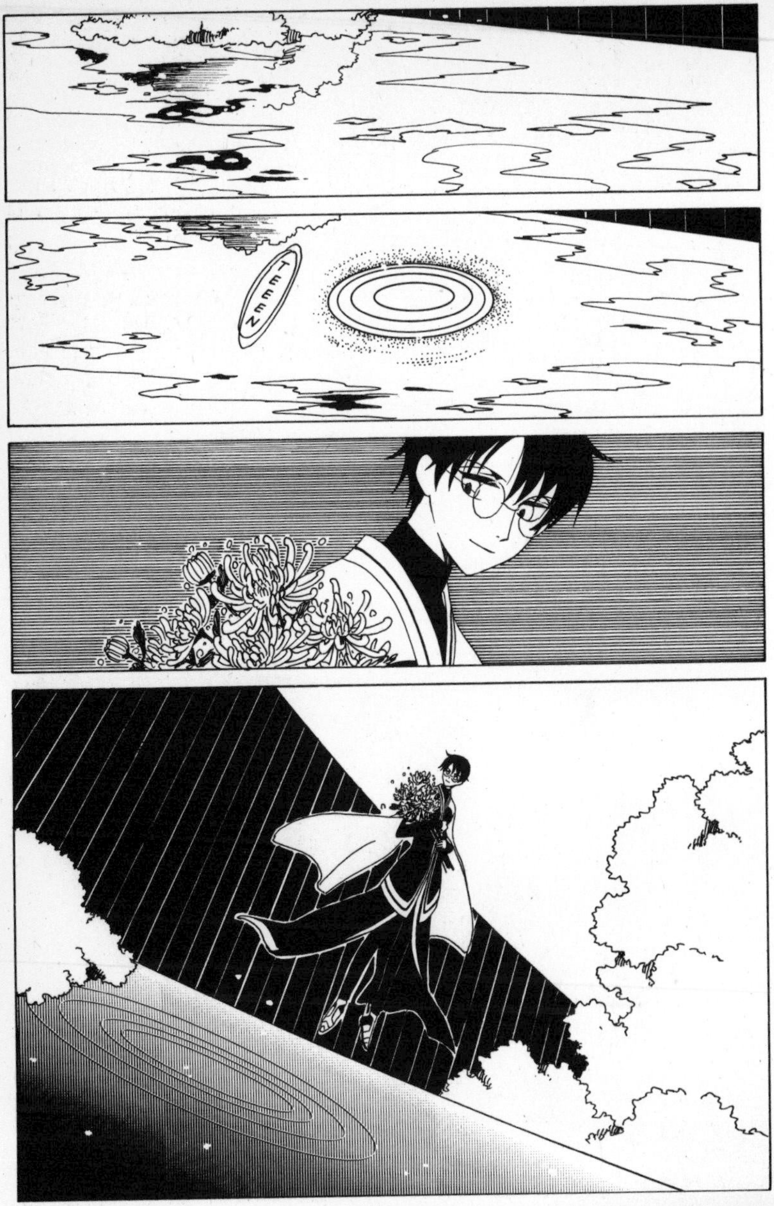
TEEEN

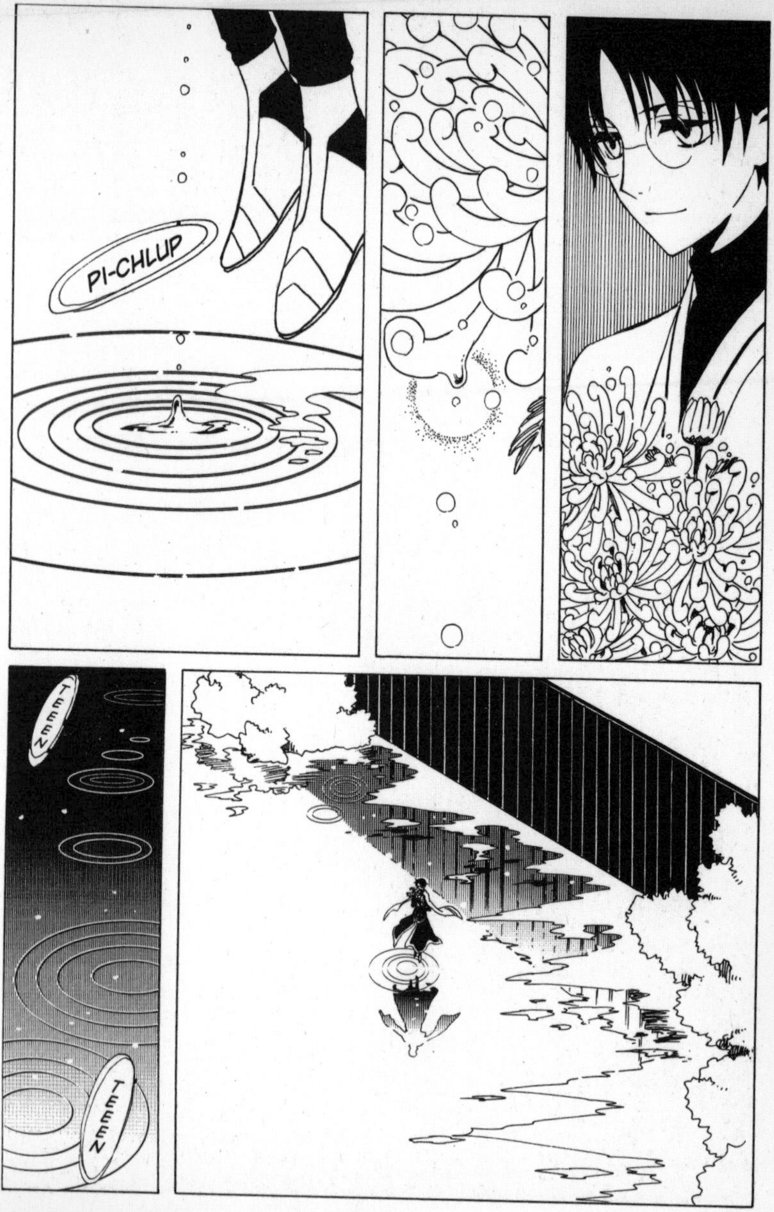
PI-CHLUP
TEEEN
TEEEN

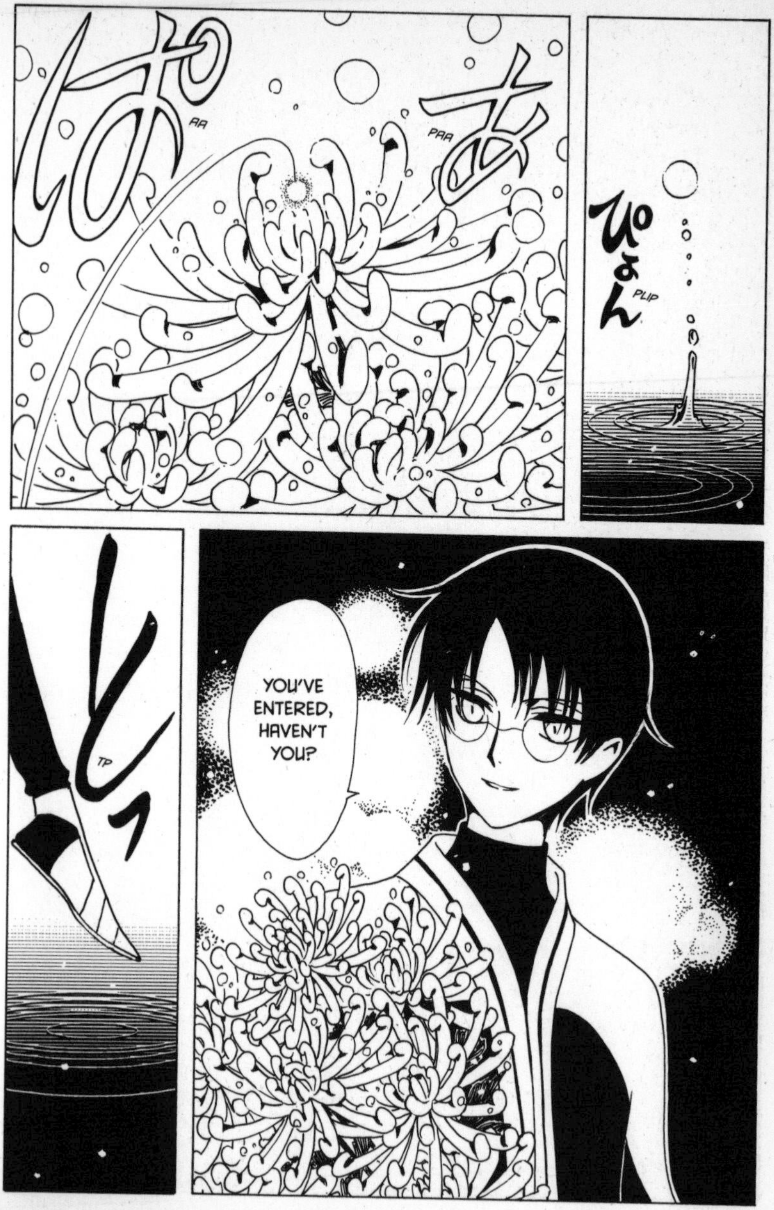
ぴょん
PLIP
ぱあ
AA
PAA
YOU'VE ENTERED, HAVEN'T YOU?
とっ
TP

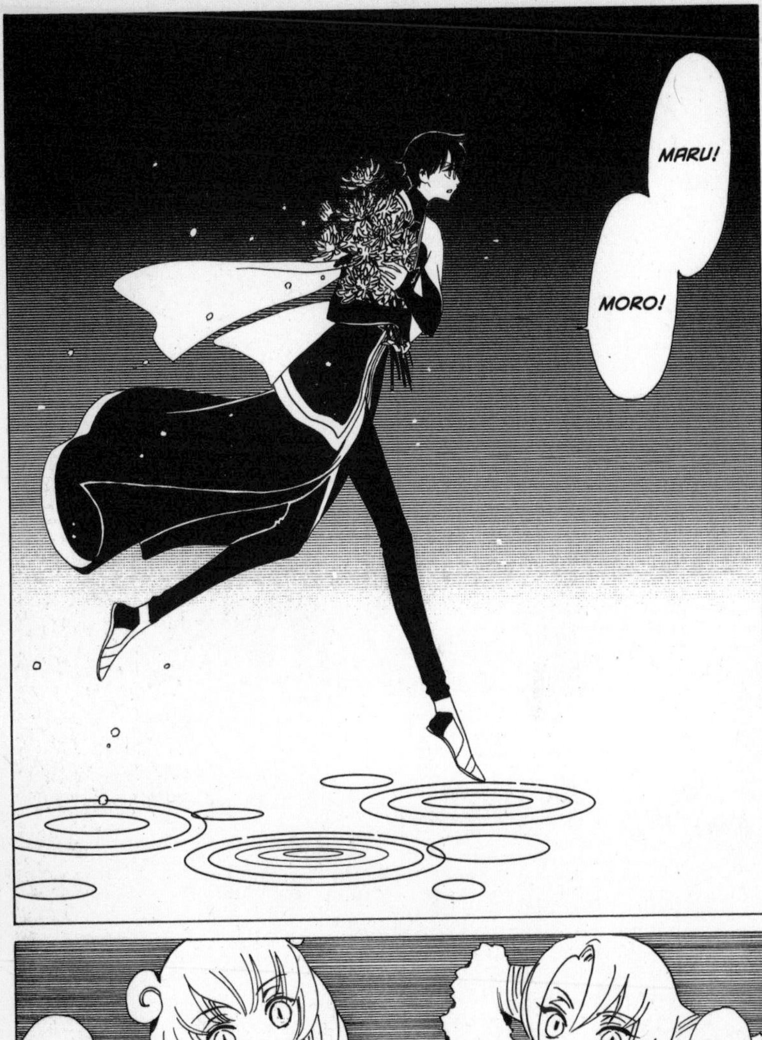
MARU!
MORO!
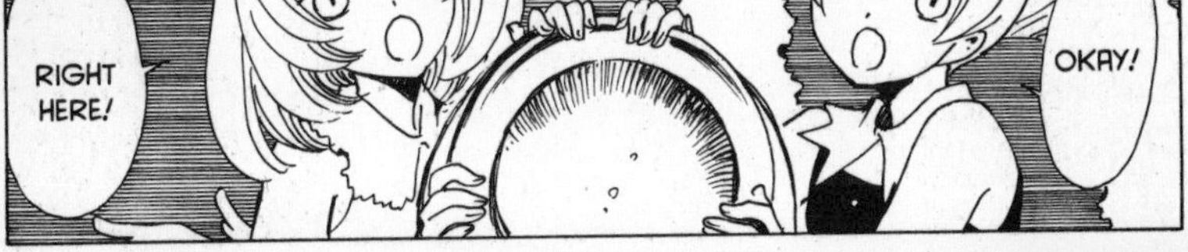
OKAY!
RIGHT HERE!

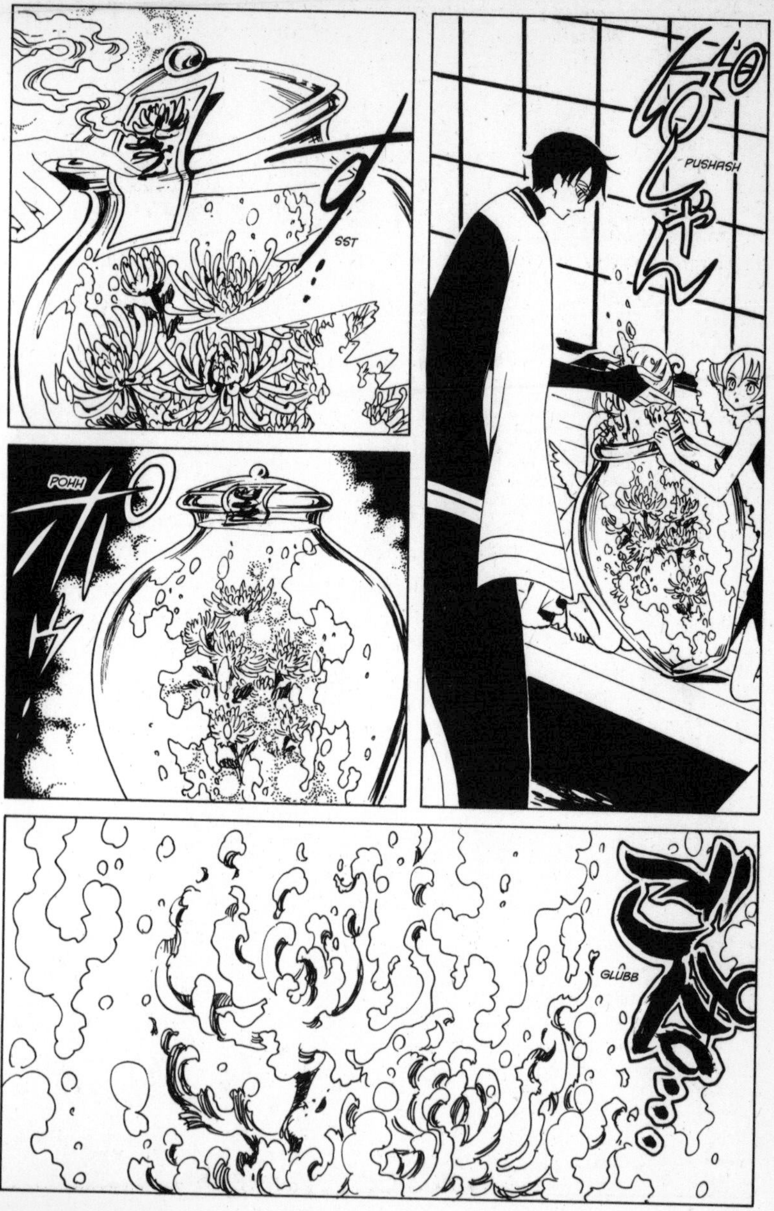
PUSHASH
SST
POHH
GLUBB

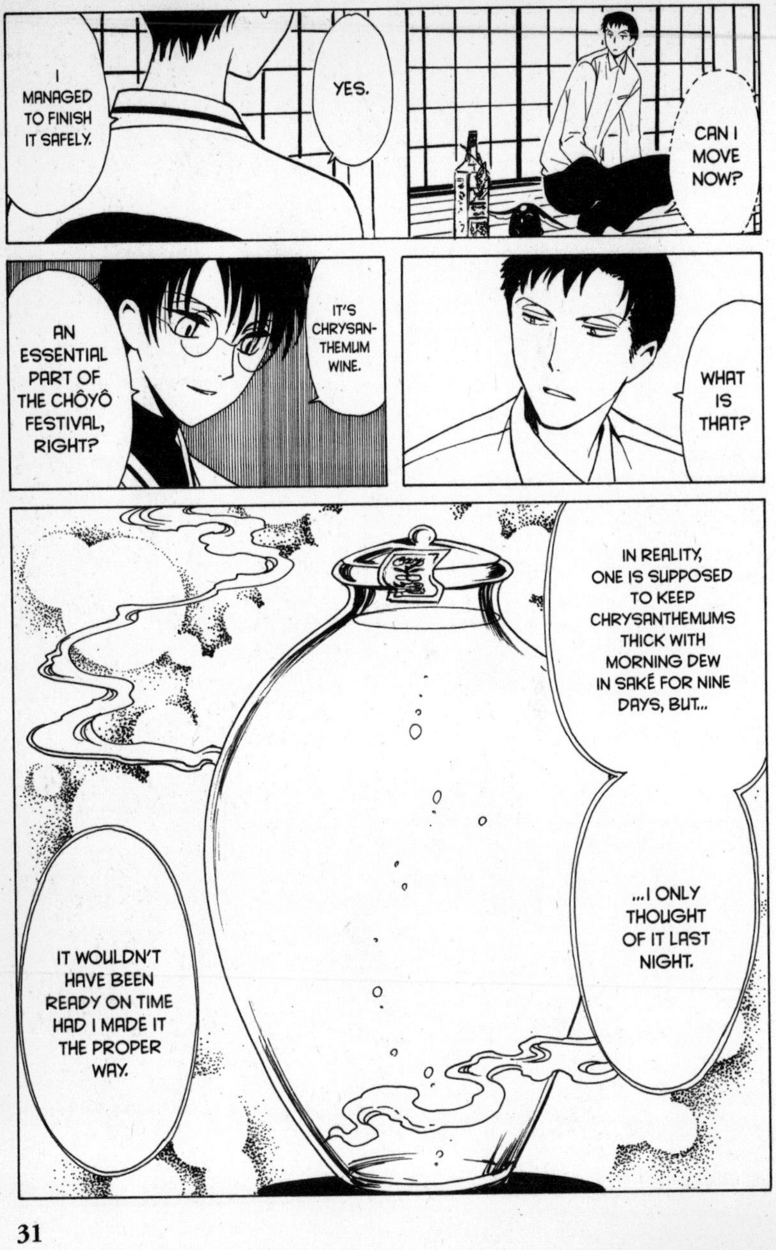
CAN I MOVE NOW?
YES.
I MANAGED TO FINISH IT SAFELY.
WHAT IS THAT?
IT'S CHRYSANTHEMUM WINE.
AN ESSENTIAL PART OF THE CHÔYÔ FESTIVAL, RIGHT?
IN REALITY, ONE IS SUPPOSED TO KEEP CHRYSANTHEMUMS THICK WITH MORNING DEW IN SAKÉ FOR NINE DAYS, BUT...
...I ONLY THOUGHT OF IT LAST NIGHT.
IT WOULDN'T HAVE BEEN READY ON TIME HAD I MADE IT THE PROPER WAY.

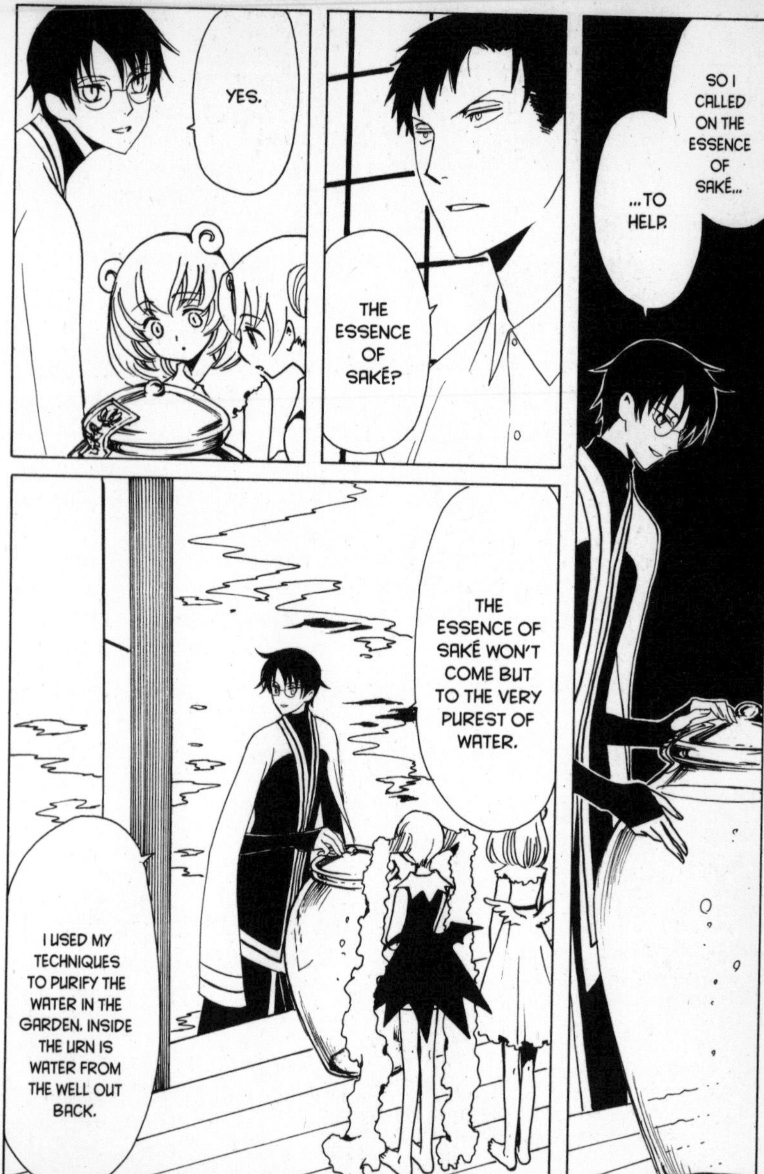
SO I CALLED ON THE ESSENCE OF SAKÉ...
...TO HELP.
THE ESSENCE OF SAKÉ?
YES.
THE ESSENCE OF SAKÉ WON'T COME BUT TO THE VERY PUREST OF WATER.
I USED MY TECHNIQUES TO PURIFY THE WATER IN THE GARDEN. INSIDE THE URN IS WATER FROM THE WELL OUT BACK.

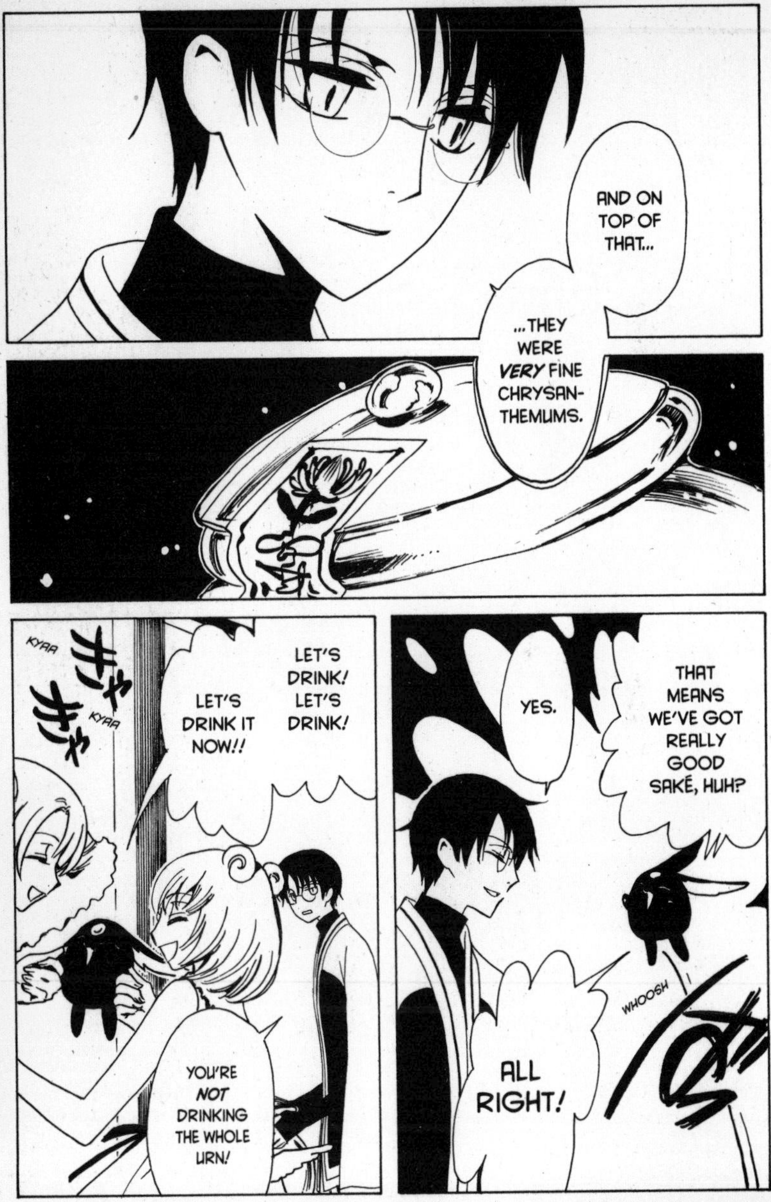
AND ON TOP OF THAT...
...THEY WERE *VERY* FINE CHRYSANTHEMUMS.
THAT MEANS WE'VE GOT REALLY GOOD SAKÉ, HUH?
YES.
WHOOSH
ALL RIGHT!
LET'S DRINK! LET'S DRINK!
LET'S DRINK IT NOW!!
KYAA
KYAA
YOU'RE *NOT* DRINKING THE WHOLE URN!

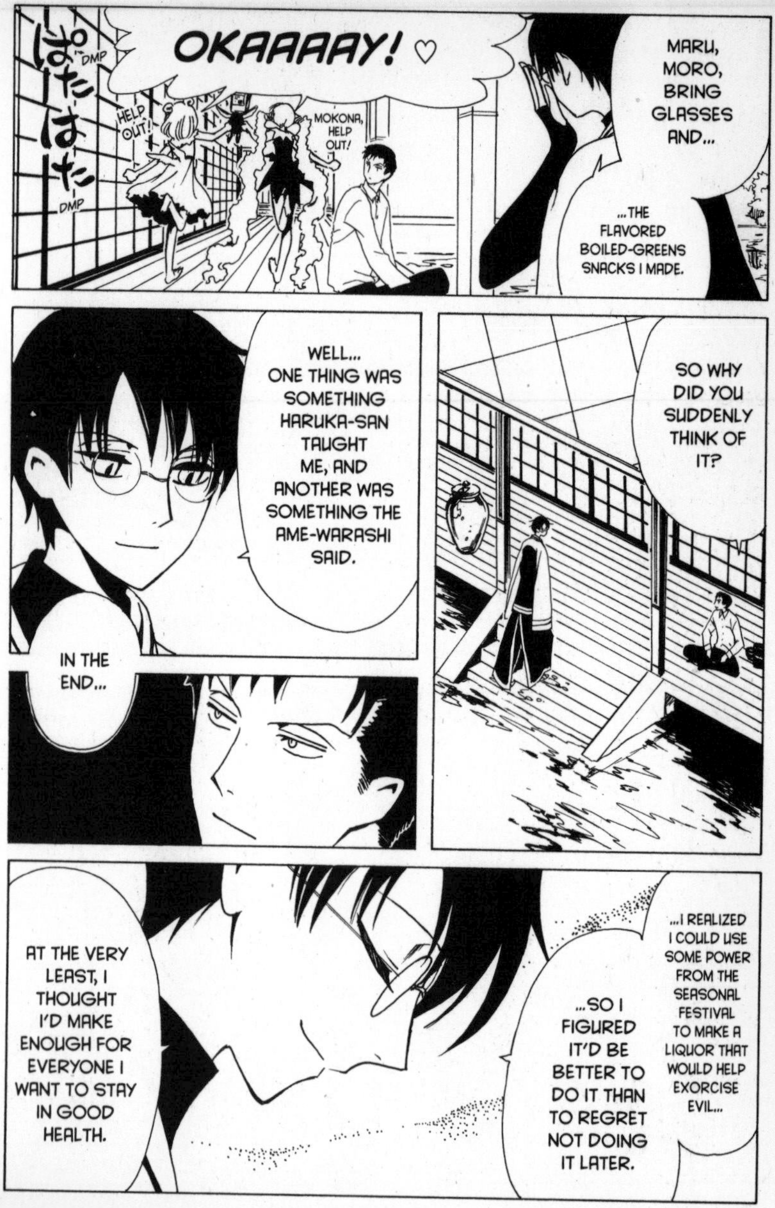
MARU, MORO, BRING GLASSES AND...
...THE FLAVORED BOILED-GREENS SNACKS I MADE.
OKAAAAY! ♡
MOKONA, HELP OUT!
HELP OUT!
ぱたぱた
DMP
DMP
SO WHY DID YOU SUDDENLY THINK OF IT?
WELL... ONE THING WAS SOMETHING HARUKA-SAN TAUGHT ME, AND ANOTHER WAS SOMETHING THE AME-WARASHI SAID.
IN THE END...
...I REALIZED I COULD USE SOME POWER FROM THE SEASONAL FESTIVAL TO MAKE A LIQUOR THAT WOULD HELP EXORCISE EVIL...
...SO I FIGURED IT'D BE BETTER TO DO IT THAN TO REGRET NOT DOING IT LATER.
AT THE VERY LEAST, I THOUGHT I'D MAKE ENOUGH FOR EVERYONE I WANT TO STAY IN GOOD HEALTH.

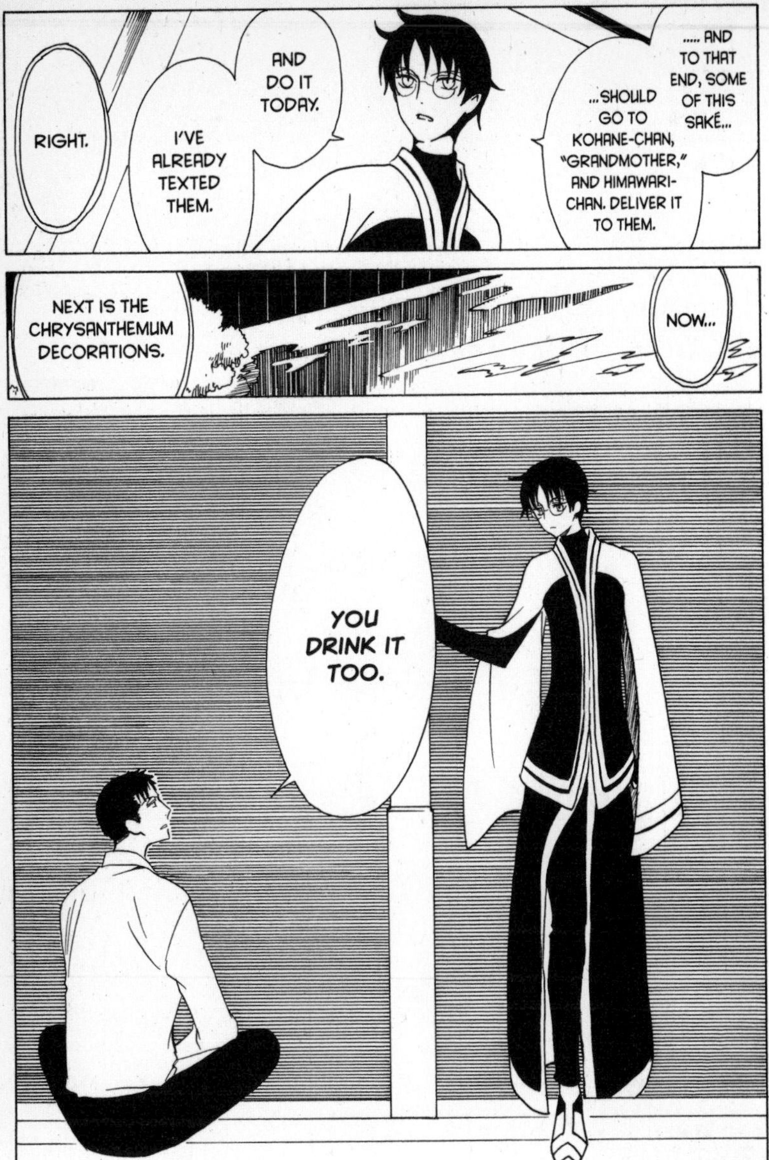
..... AND TO THAT END, SOME OF THIS SAKÉ...
...SHOULD GO TO KOHANE-CHAN, "GRANDMOTHER," AND HIMAWARI-CHAN. DELIVER IT TO THEM.
AND DO IT TODAY.
I'VE ALREADY TEXTED THEM.
RIGHT.
NOW...
NEXT IS THE CHRYSANTHEMUM DECORATIONS.
YOU DRINK IT TOO.

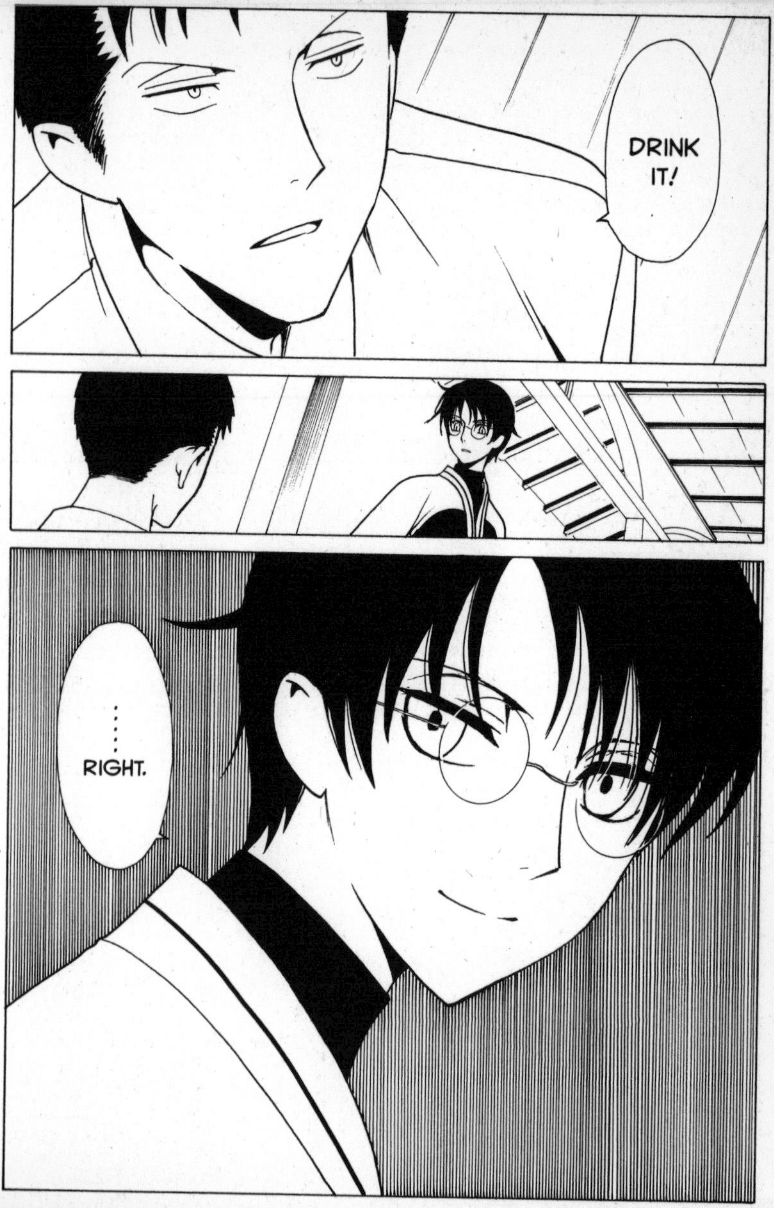
DRINK IT!
......
RIGHT.

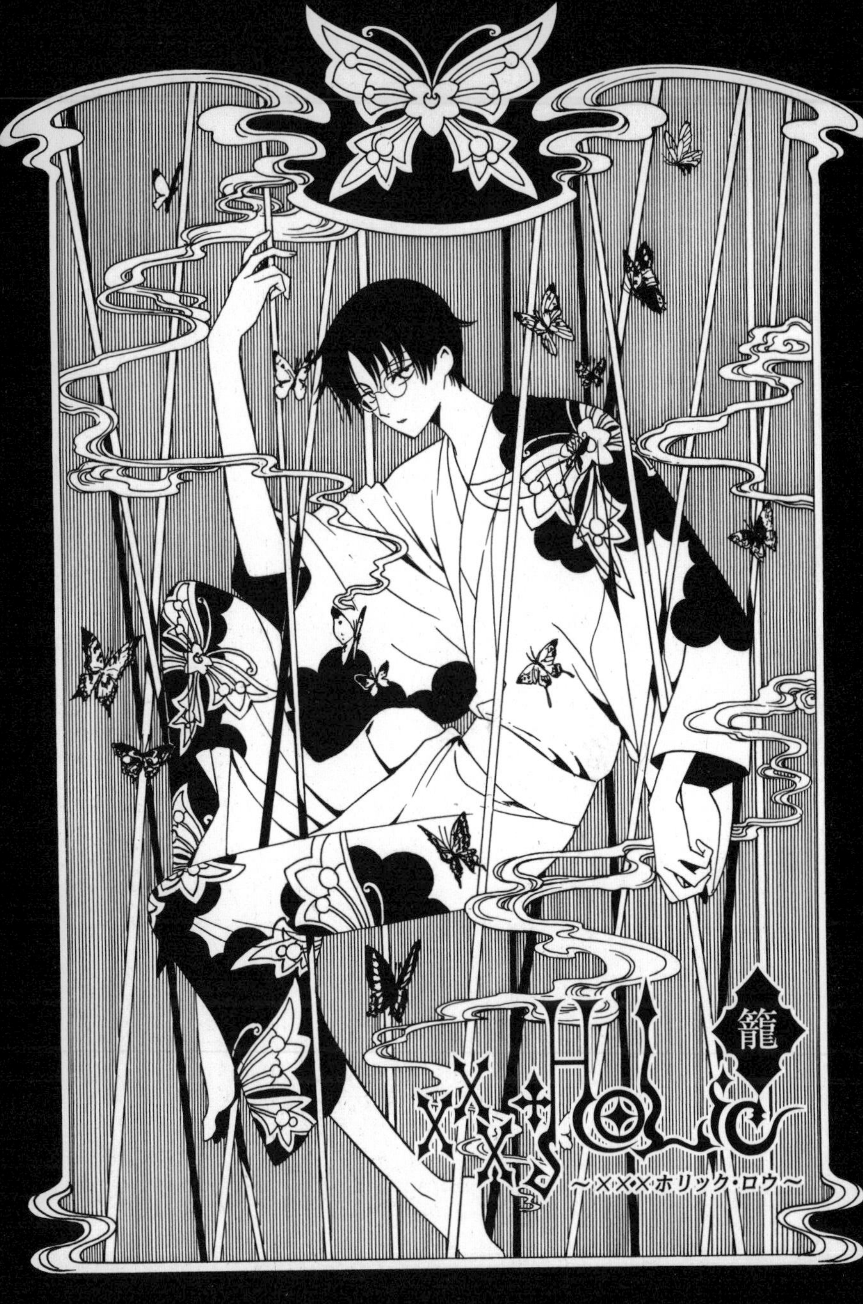

籠
xxxHOLiC
〜×××ホリック・ロウ〜

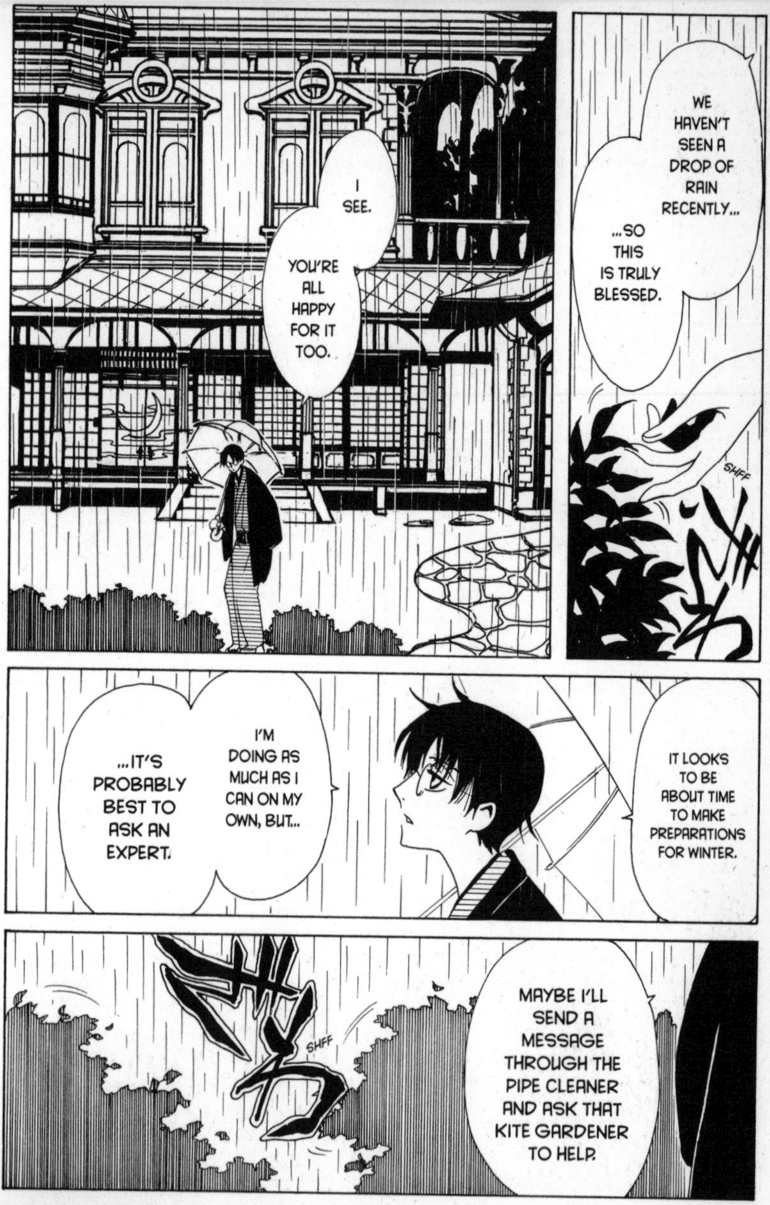
WE HAVEN'T SEEN A DROP OF RAIN RECENTLY...
...SO THIS IS TRULY BLESSED.
SHFF
I SEE.
YOU'RE ALL HAPPY FOR IT TOO.
IT LOOKS TO BE ABOUT TIME TO MAKE PREPARATIONS FOR WINTER.
I'M DOING AS MUCH AS I CAN ON MY OWN, BUT...
...IT'S PROBABLY BEST TO ASK AN EXPERT.
MAYBE I'LL SEND A MESSAGE THROUGH THE PIPE CLEANER AND ASK THAT KITE GARDENER TO HELP.
SHFF

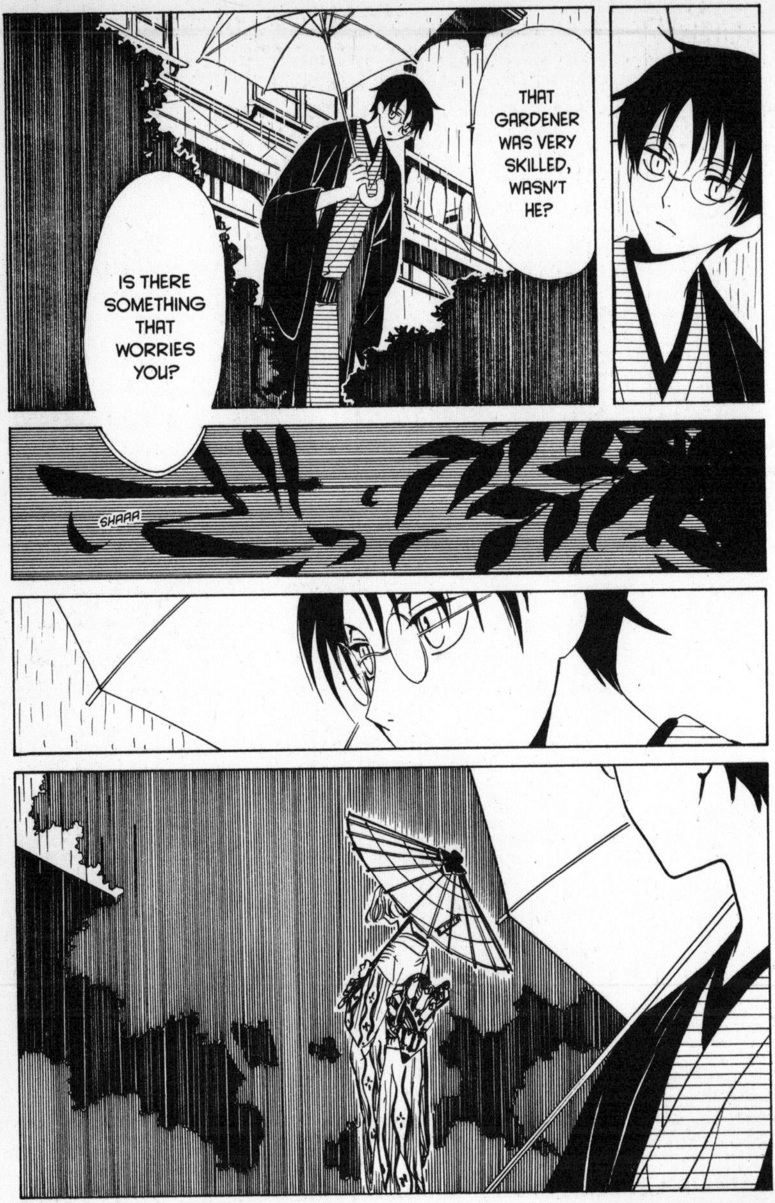
THAT GARDENER WAS VERY SKILLED, WASN'T HE?
IS THERE SOMETHING THAT WORRIES YOU?
SHAAA

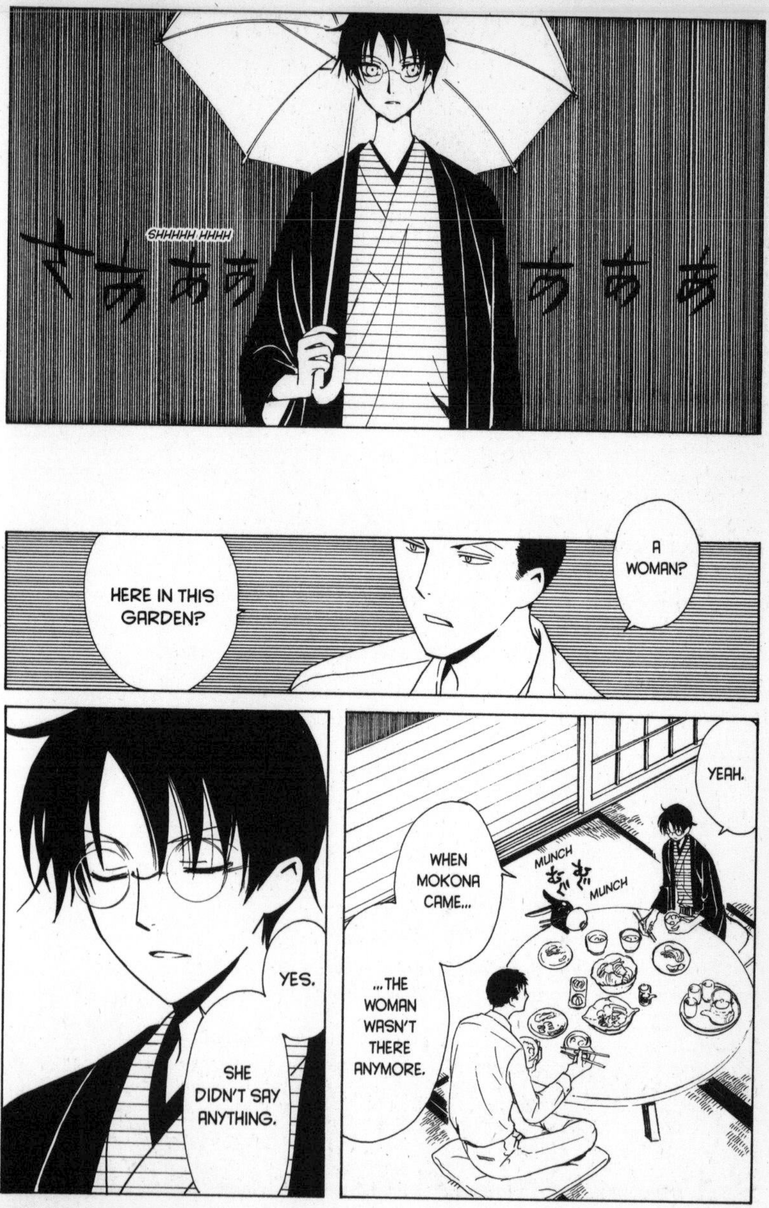
SHHHHH HHHH
さあああ
あああ
A WOMAN?
HERE IN THIS GARDEN?
YEAH.
MUNCH
むぐむぐ
MUNCH
WHEN MOKONA CAME...
...THE WOMAN WASN'T THERE ANYMORE.
YES.
SHE DIDN'T SAY ANYTHING.

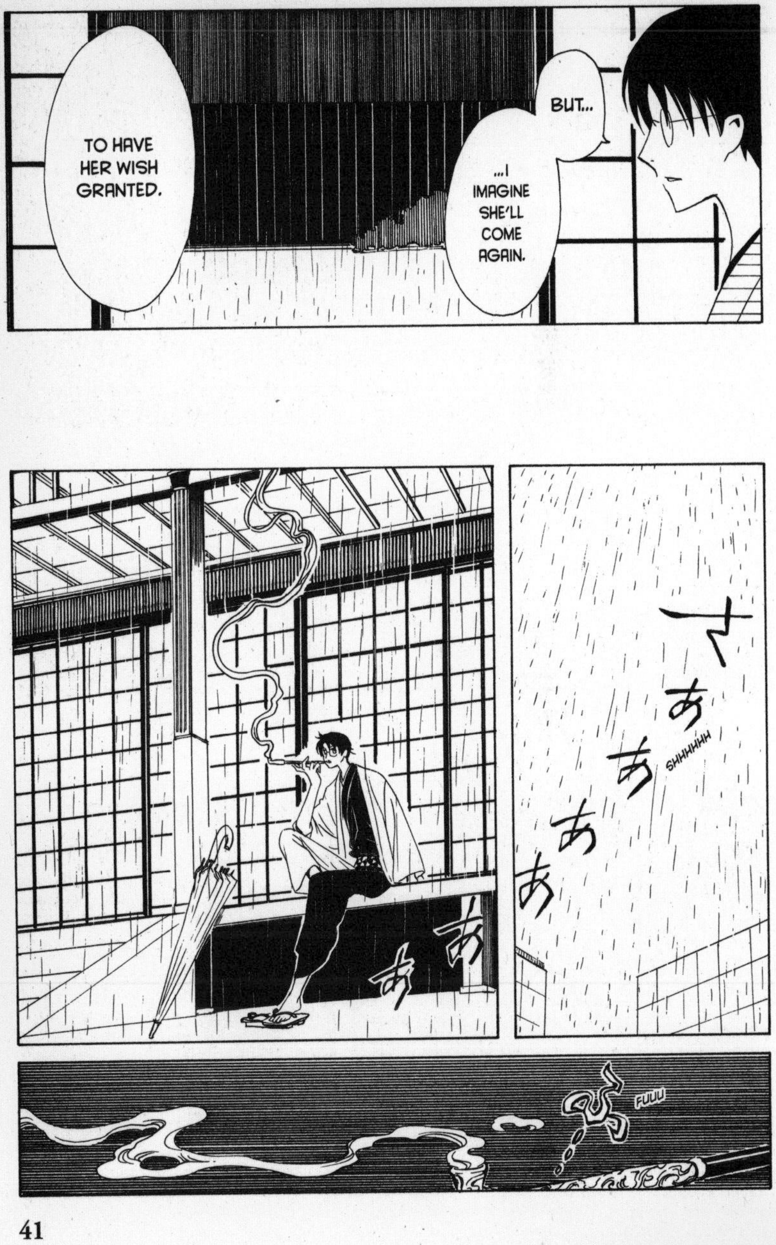
BUT...
...I IMAGINE SHE'LL COME AGAIN.
TO HAVE HER WISH GRANTED.
さああああ
SHHHHHH
ああ
FUUU

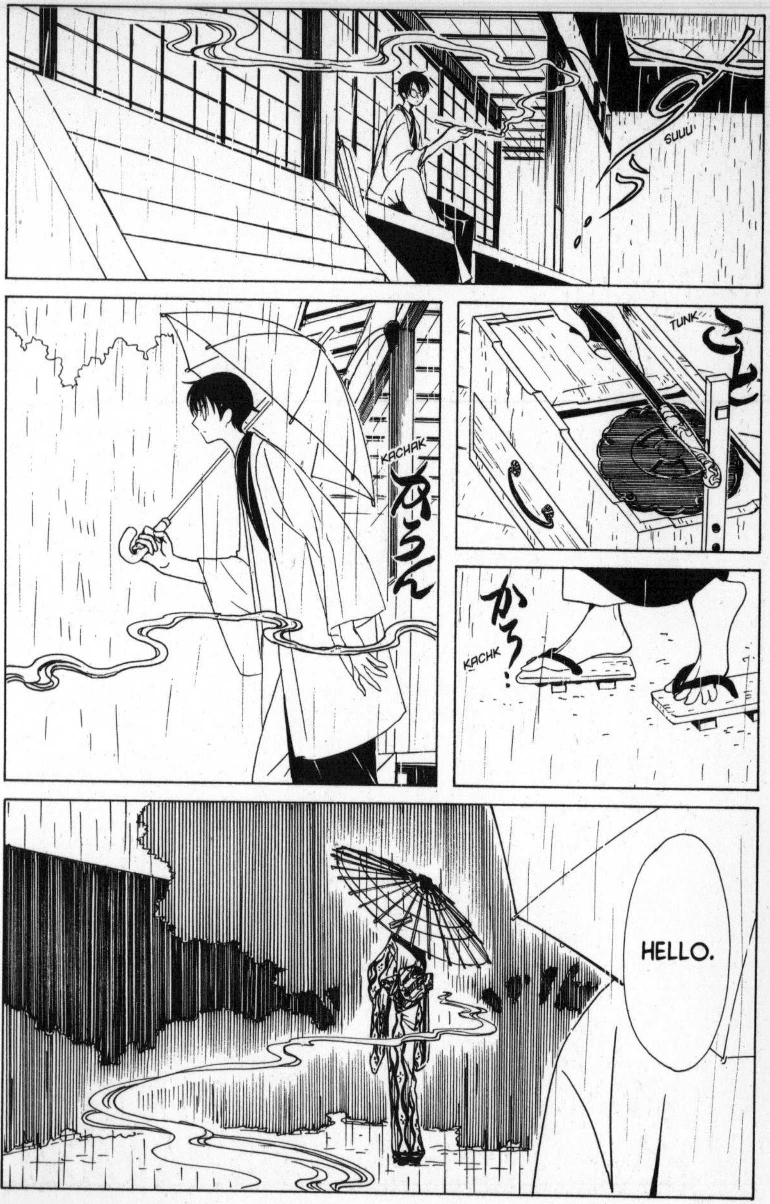
SUUU
TUNK
KACHK
KACHAK
HELLO.

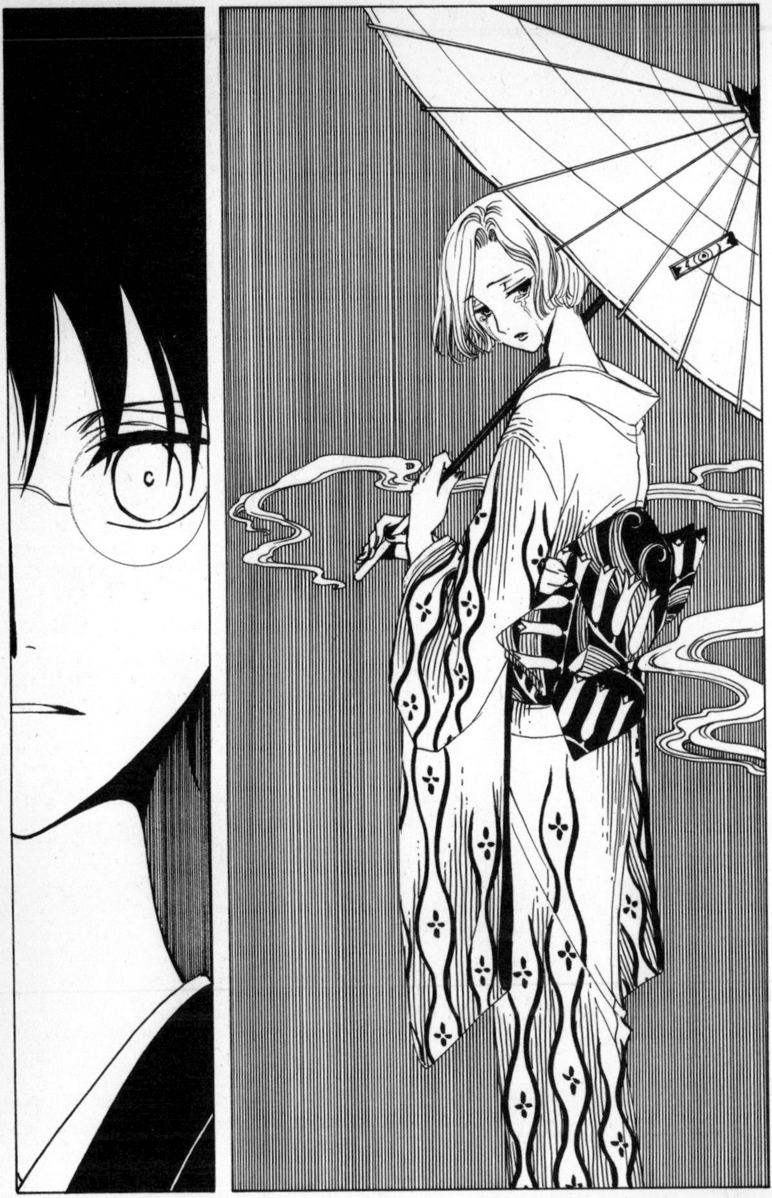

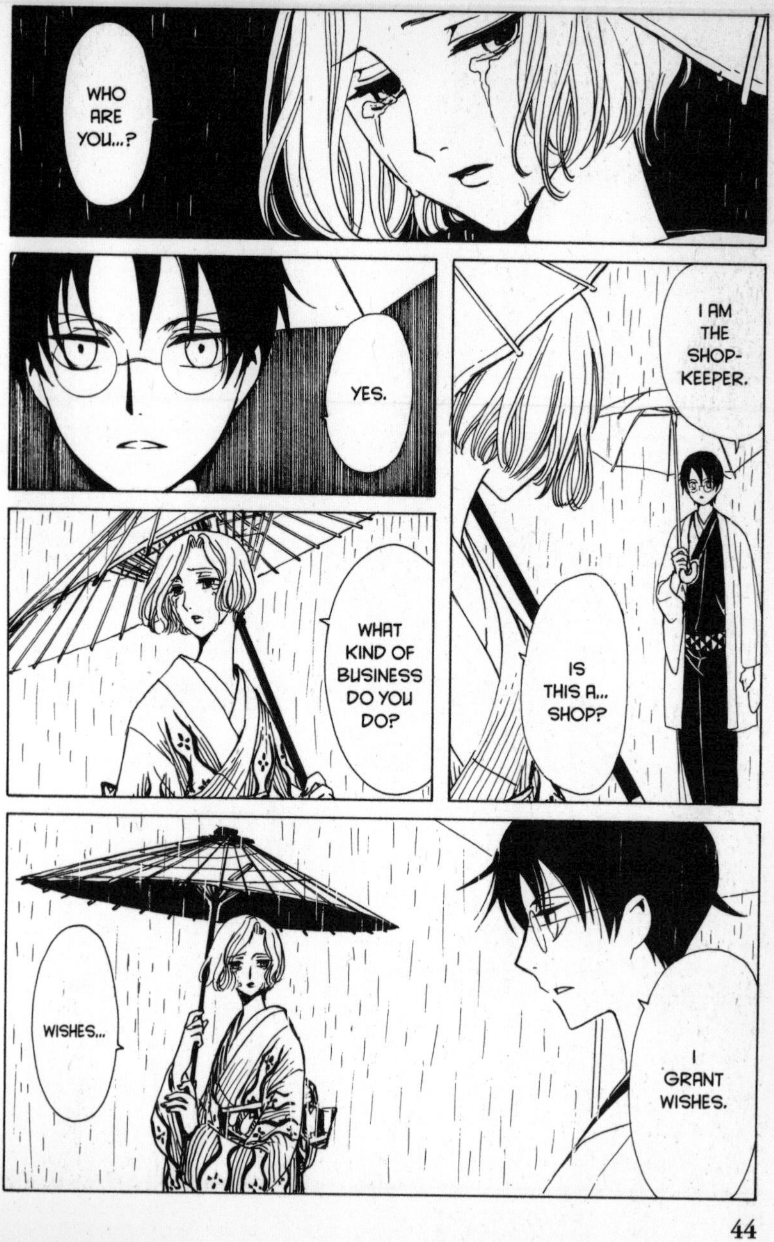
WHO ARE YOU...?
I AM THE SHOP-KEEPER.
IS THIS A... SHOP?
YES.
WHAT KIND OF BUSINESS DO YOU DO?
I GRANT WISHES.
WISHES...

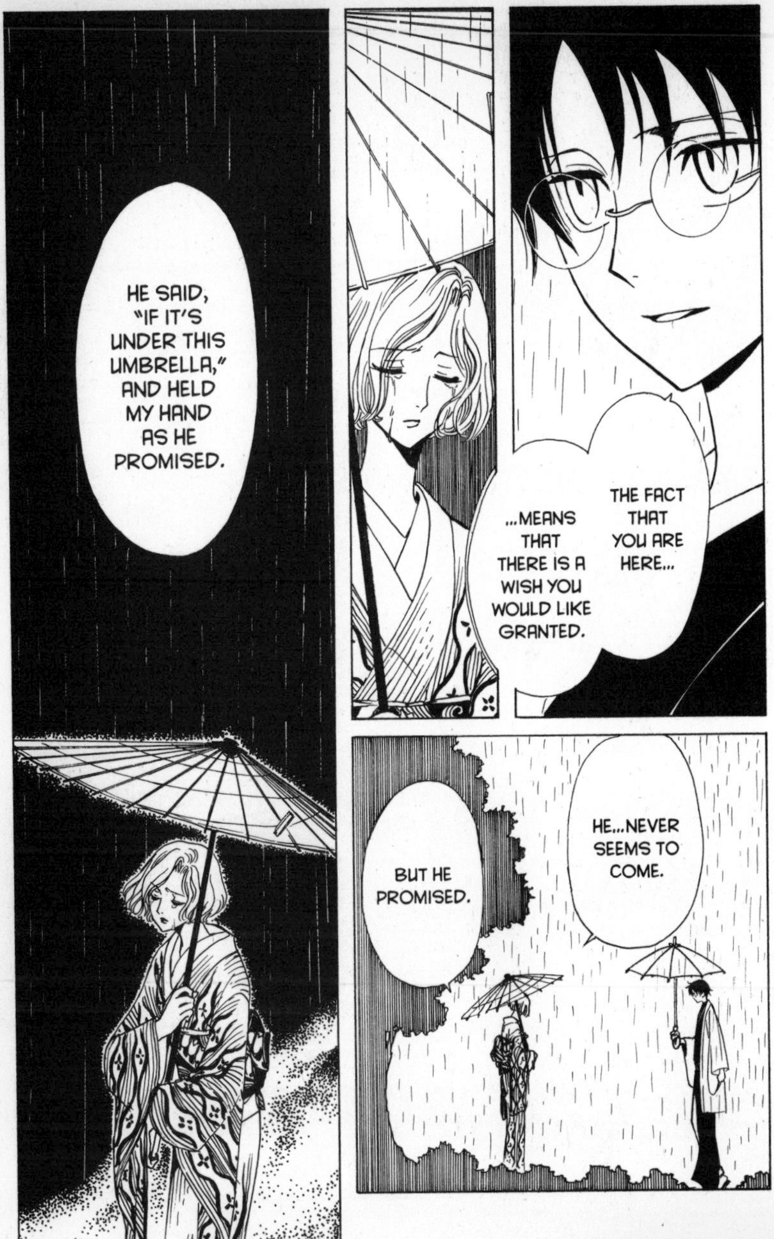
THE FACT THAT YOU ARE HERE...
...MEANS THAT THERE IS A WISH YOU WOULD LIKE GRANTED.
HE...NEVER SEEMS TO COME.
BUT HE PROMISED.
HE SAID, "IF IT'S UNDER THIS UMBRELLA," AND HELD MY HAND AS HE PROMISED.

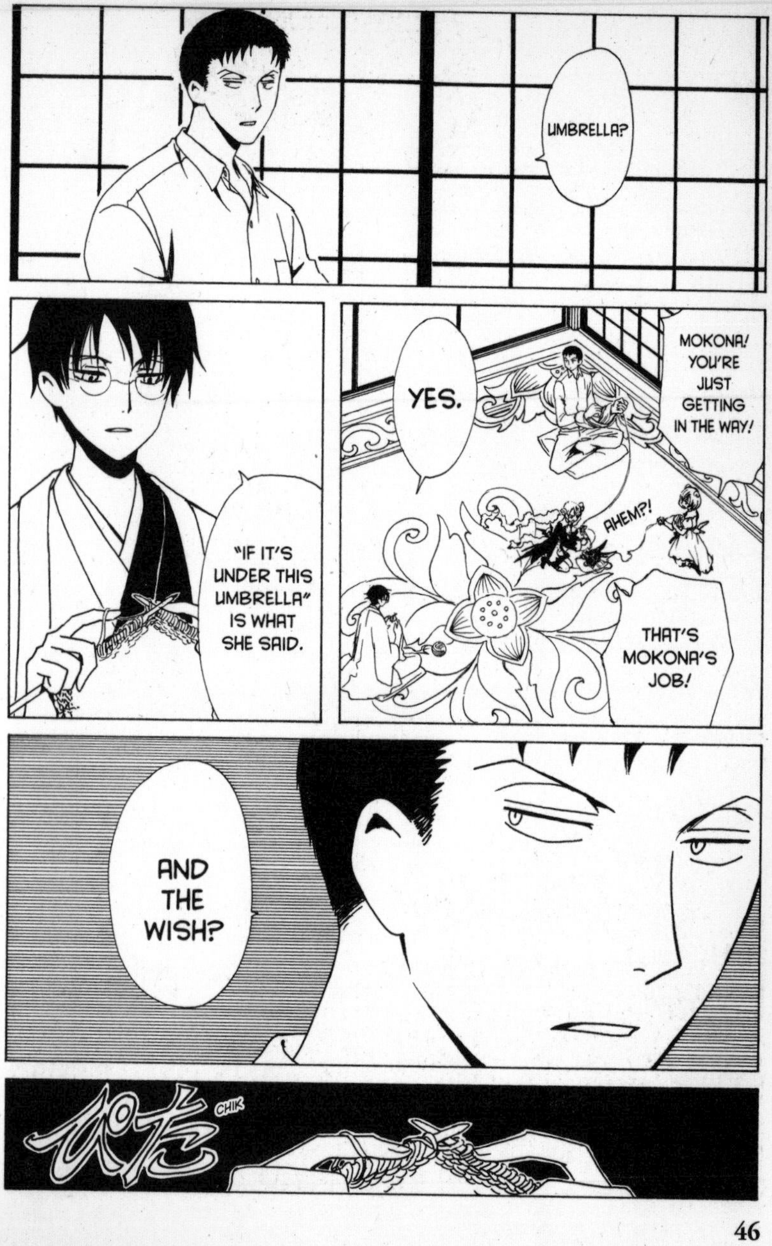
UMBRELLA?
MOKONA! YOU'RE JUST GETTING IN THE WAY!
YES.
AHEM?!
THAT'S MOKONA'S JOB!
"IF IT'S UNDER THIS UMBRELLA" IS WHAT SHE SAID.
AND THE WISH?
CHIK
ぴた

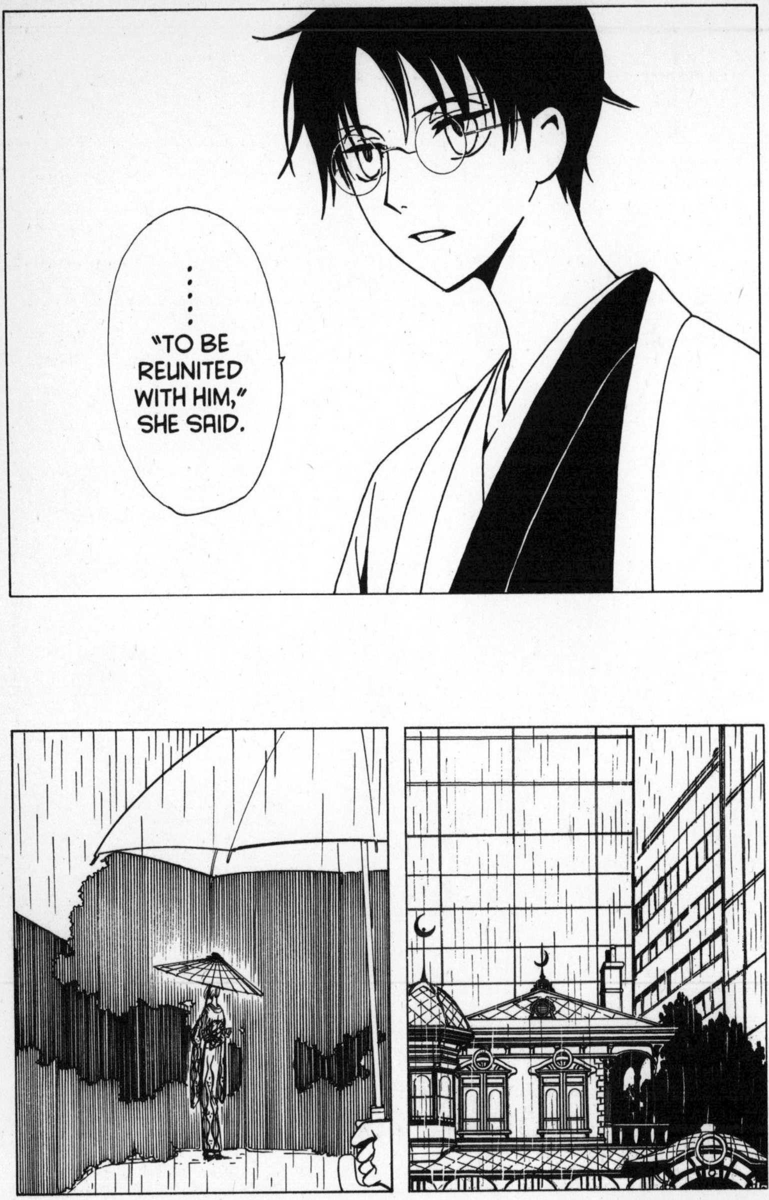
……"TO BE REUNITED WITH HIM," SHE SAID.

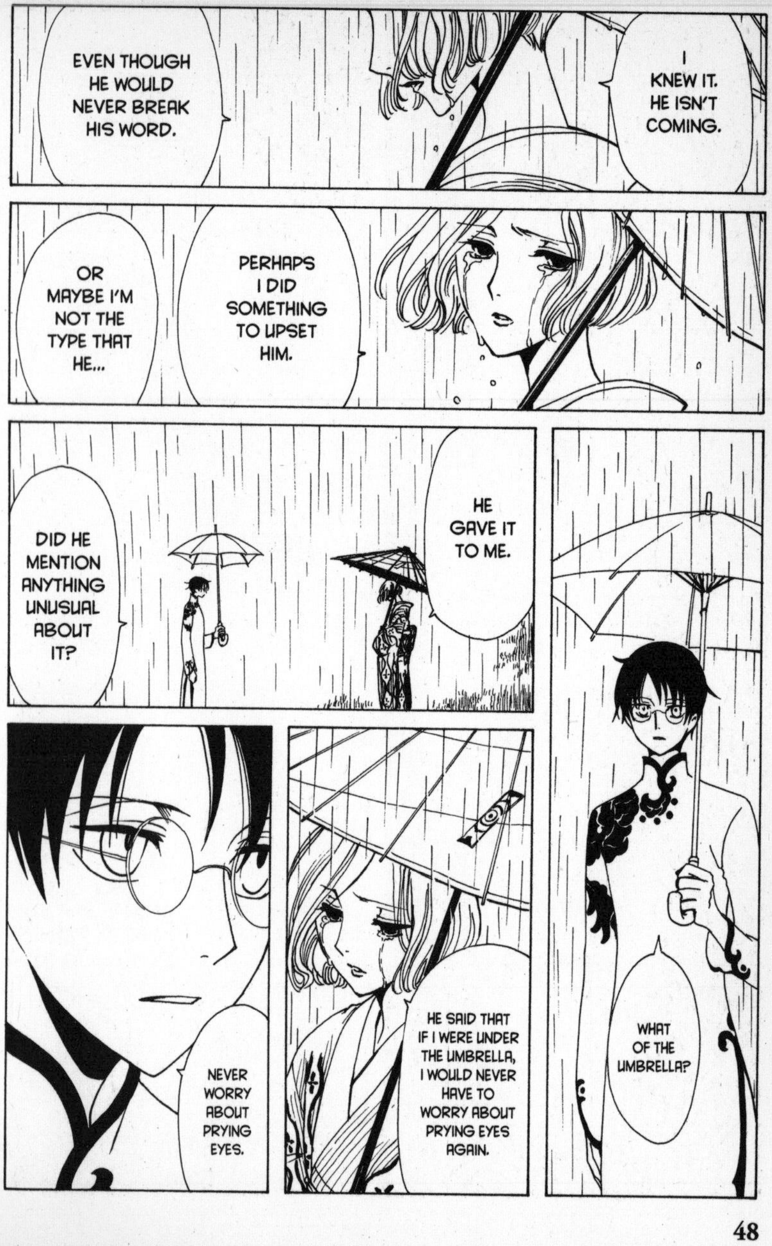
I KNEW IT. HE ISN'T COMING.
EVEN THOUGH HE WOULD NEVER BREAK HIS WORD.
PERHAPS I DID SOMETHING TO UPSET HIM.
OR MAYBE I'M NOT THE TYPE THAT HE...
WHAT OF THE UMBRELLA?
HE GAVE IT TO ME.
DID HE MENTION ANYTHING UNUSUAL ABOUT IT?
HE SAID THAT IF I WERE UNDER THE UMBRELLA, I WOULD NEVER HAVE TO WORRY ABOUT PRYING EYES AGAIN.
NEVER WORRY ABOUT PRYING EYES.

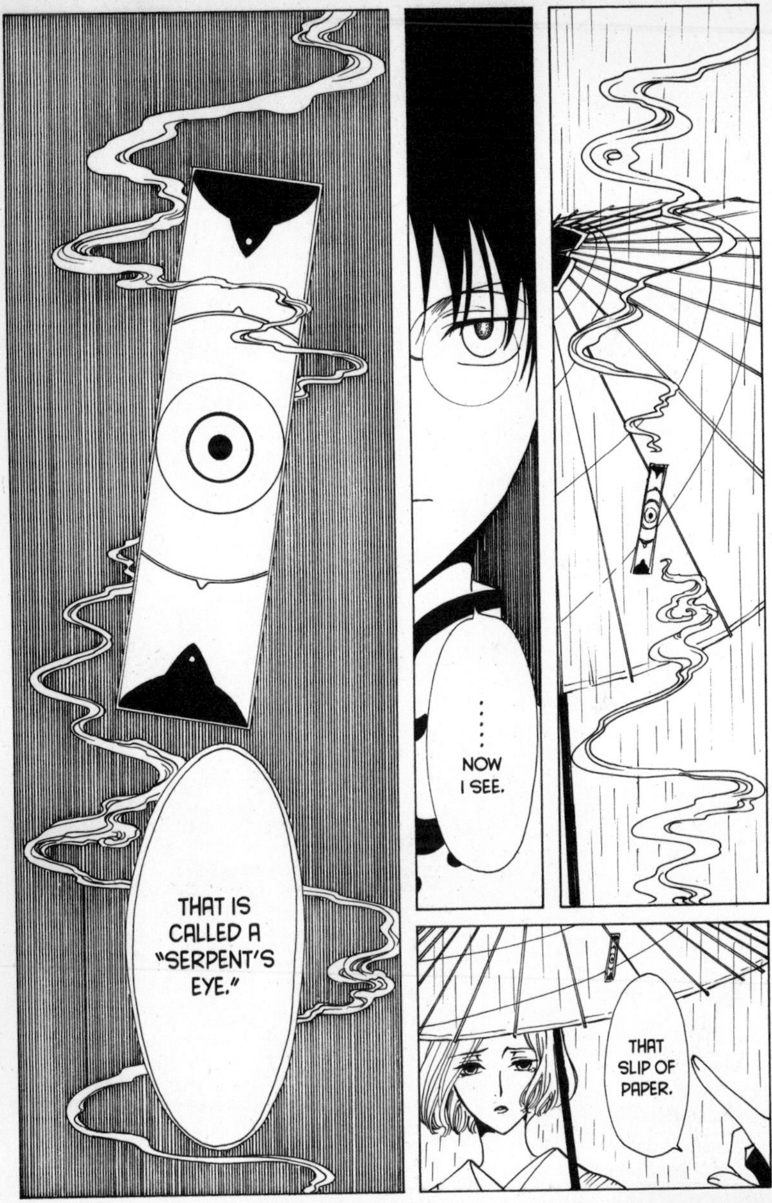
......
NOW I SEE.
THAT SLIP OF PAPER.
THAT IS CALLED A "SERPENT'S EYE."

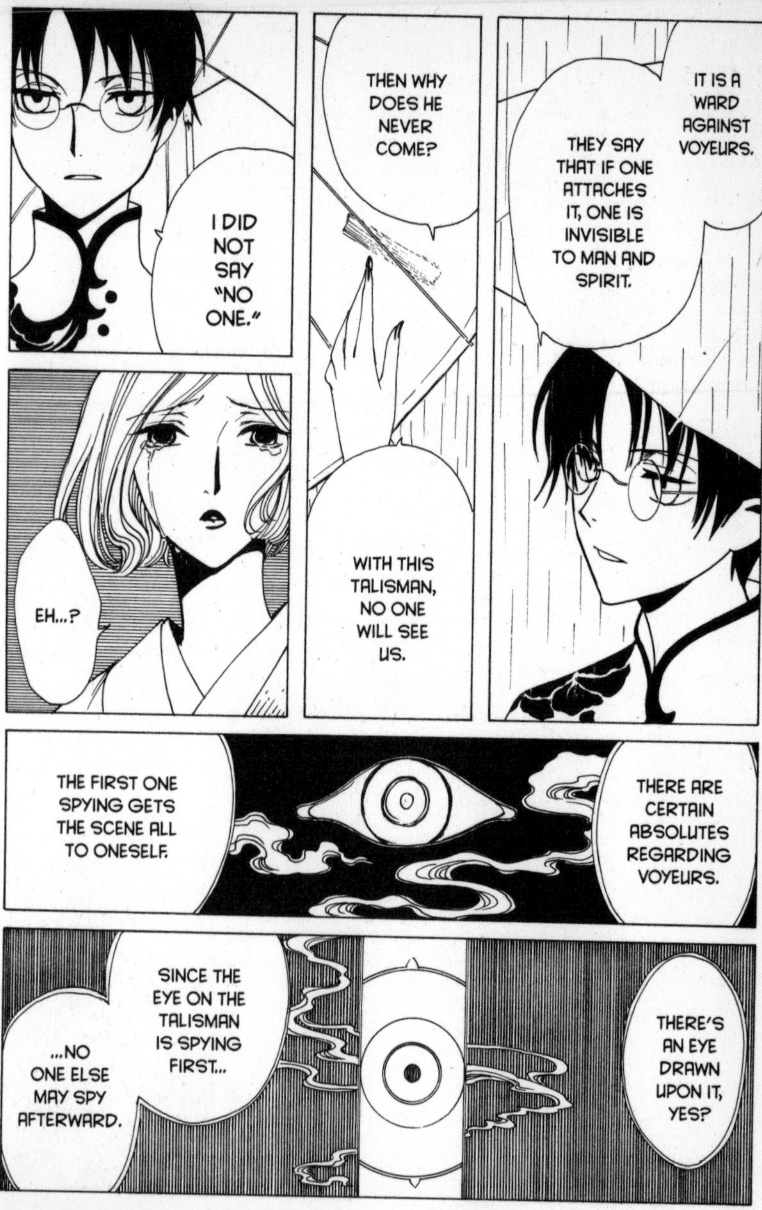
IT IS A WARD AGAINST VOYEURS.
THEY SAY THAT IF ONE ATTACHES IT, ONE IS INVISIBLE TO MAN AND SPIRIT.
THEN WHY DOES HE NEVER COME?
WITH THIS TALISMAN, NO ONE WILL SEE US.
I DID NOT SAY "NO ONE."
EH...?
THERE ARE CERTAIN ABSOLUTES REGARDING VOYEURS.
THE FIRST ONE SPYING GETS THE SCENE ALL TO ONESELF.
THERE'S AN EYE DRAWN UPON IT, YES?
SINCE THE EYE ON THE TALISMAN IS SPYING FIRST...
...NO ONE ELSE MAY SPY AFTERWARD.

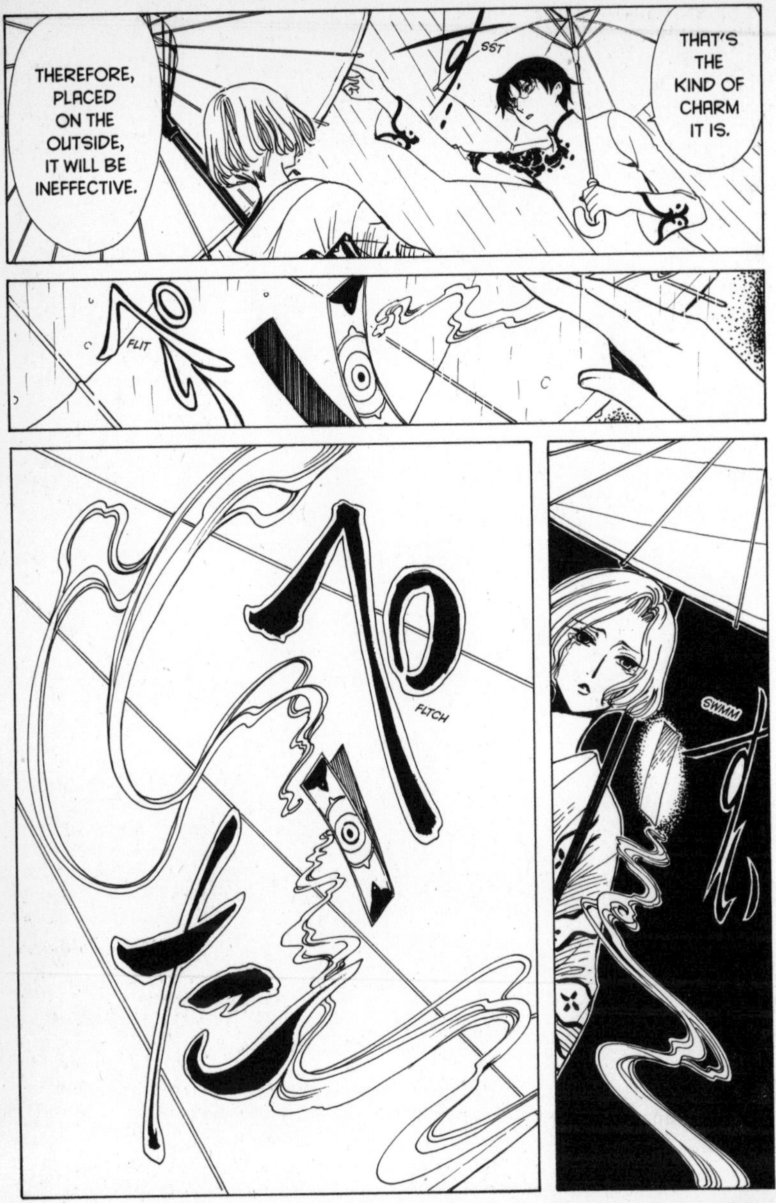
THAT'S THE KIND OF CHARM IT IS.
SST
THEREFORE, PLACED ON THE OUTSIDE, IT WILL BE INEFFECTIVE.
FLIT
SWMM
FLTCH

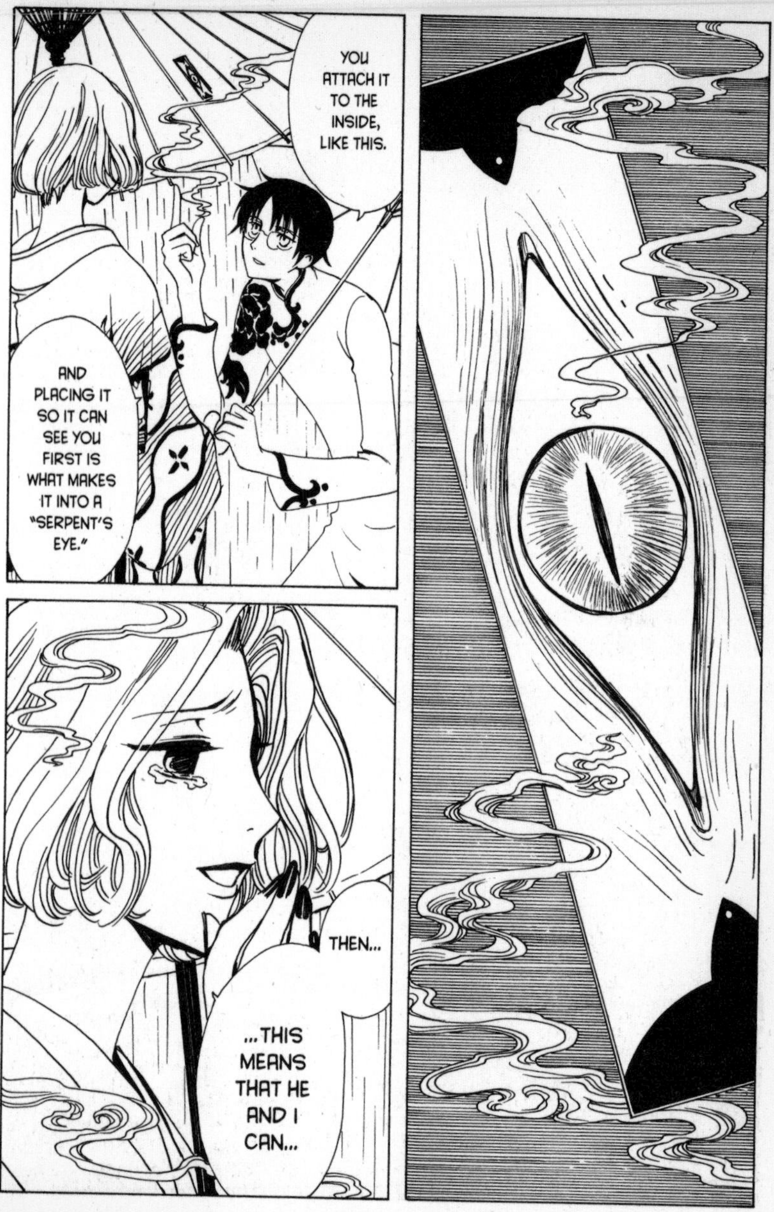
YOU ATTACH IT TO THE INSIDE, LIKE THIS.
AND PLACING IT SO IT CAN SEE YOU FIRST IS WHAT MAKES IT INTO A "SERPENT'S EYE."
THEN...
...THIS MEANS THAT HE AND I CAN...

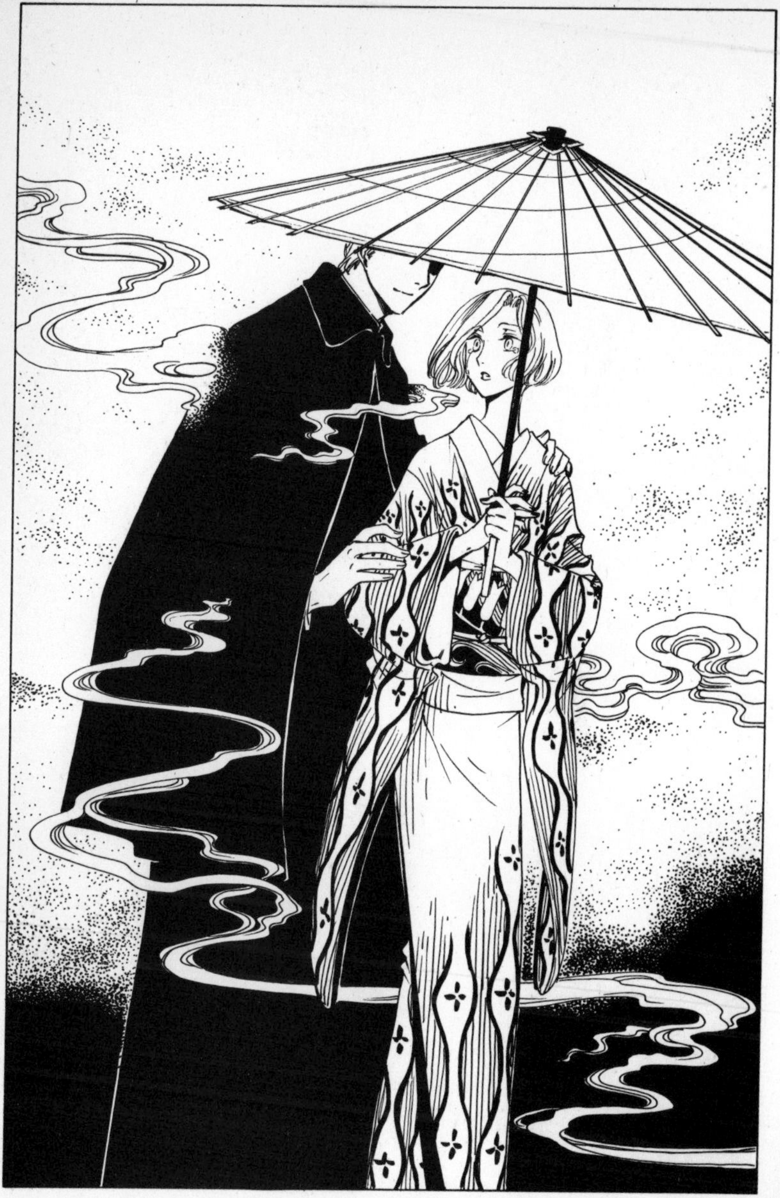

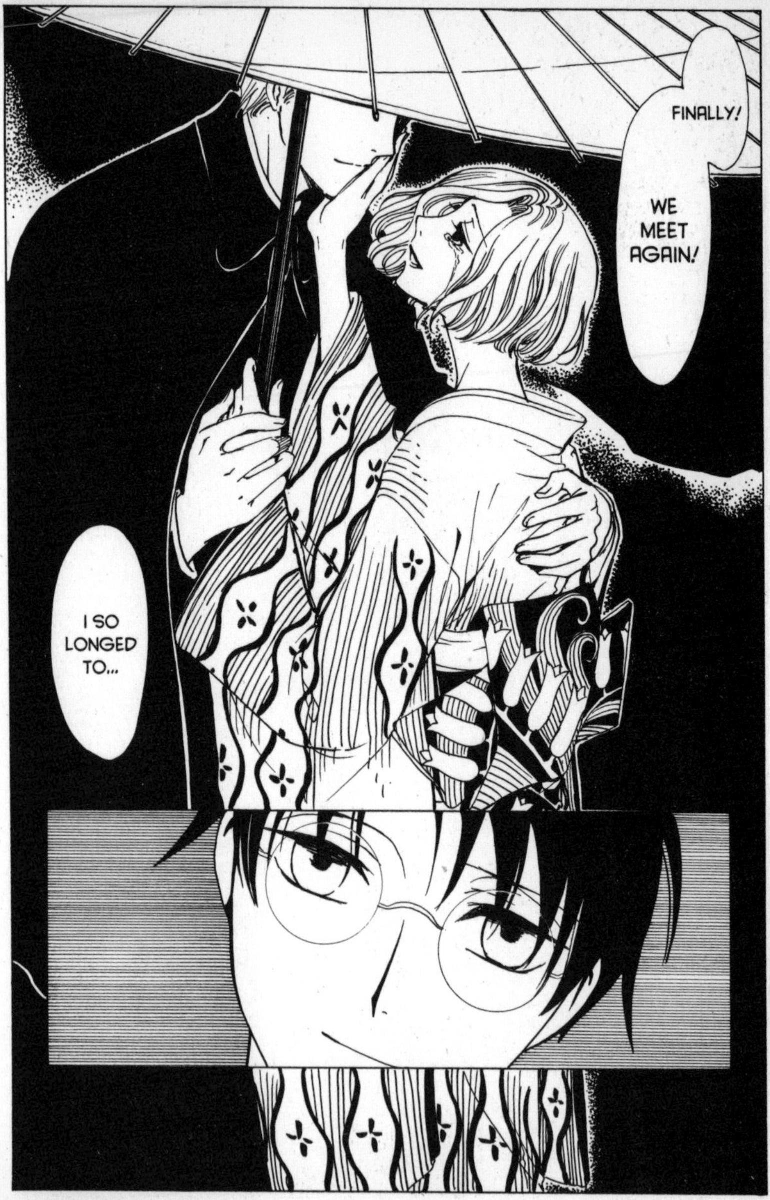
FINALLY! WE MEET AGAIN!
I SO LONGED TO...

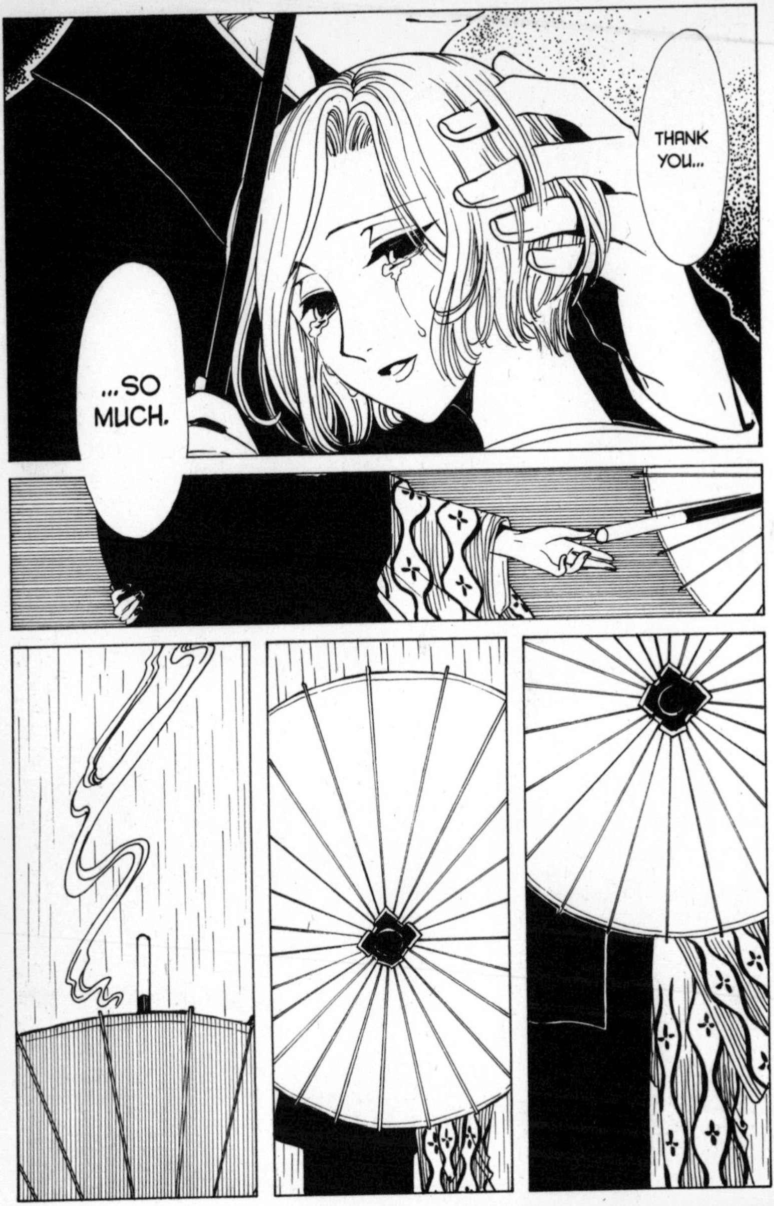
THANK YOU...
...SO MUCH.

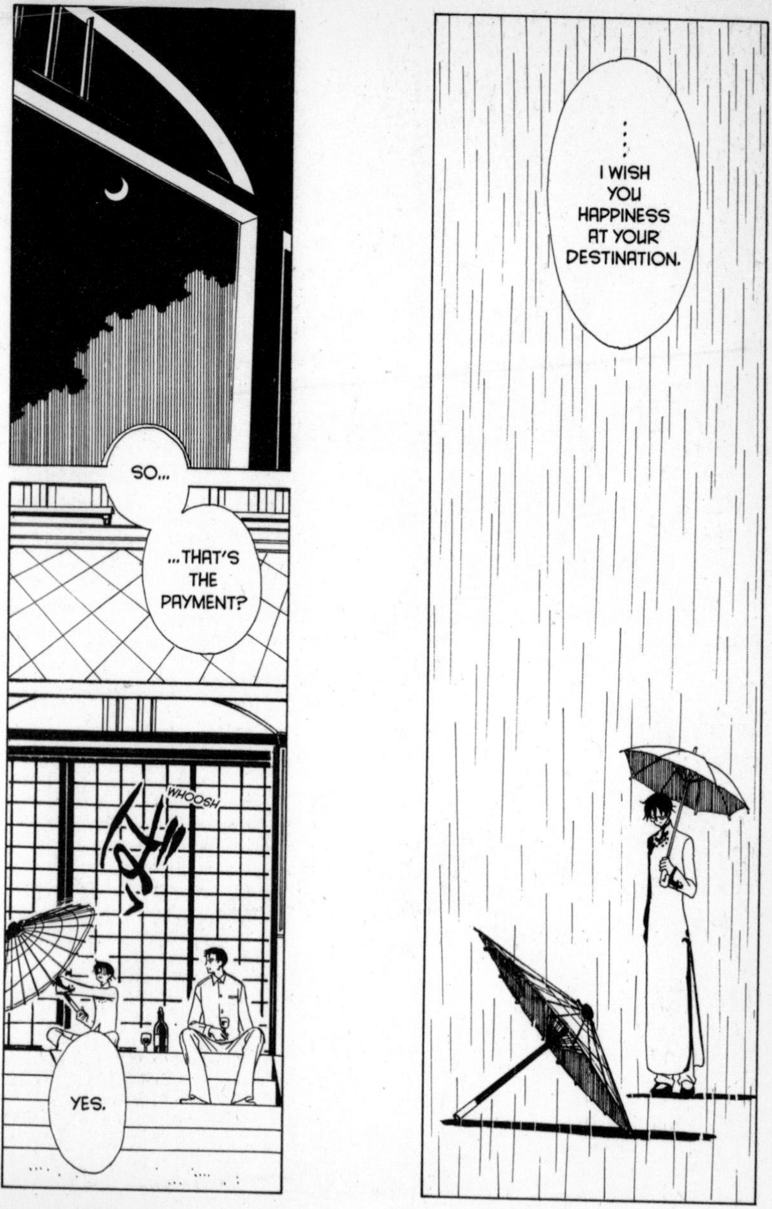
......
I WISH YOU HAPPINESS AT YOUR DESTINATION.
SO...
...THAT'S THE PAYMENT?
WHOOSH
YES.

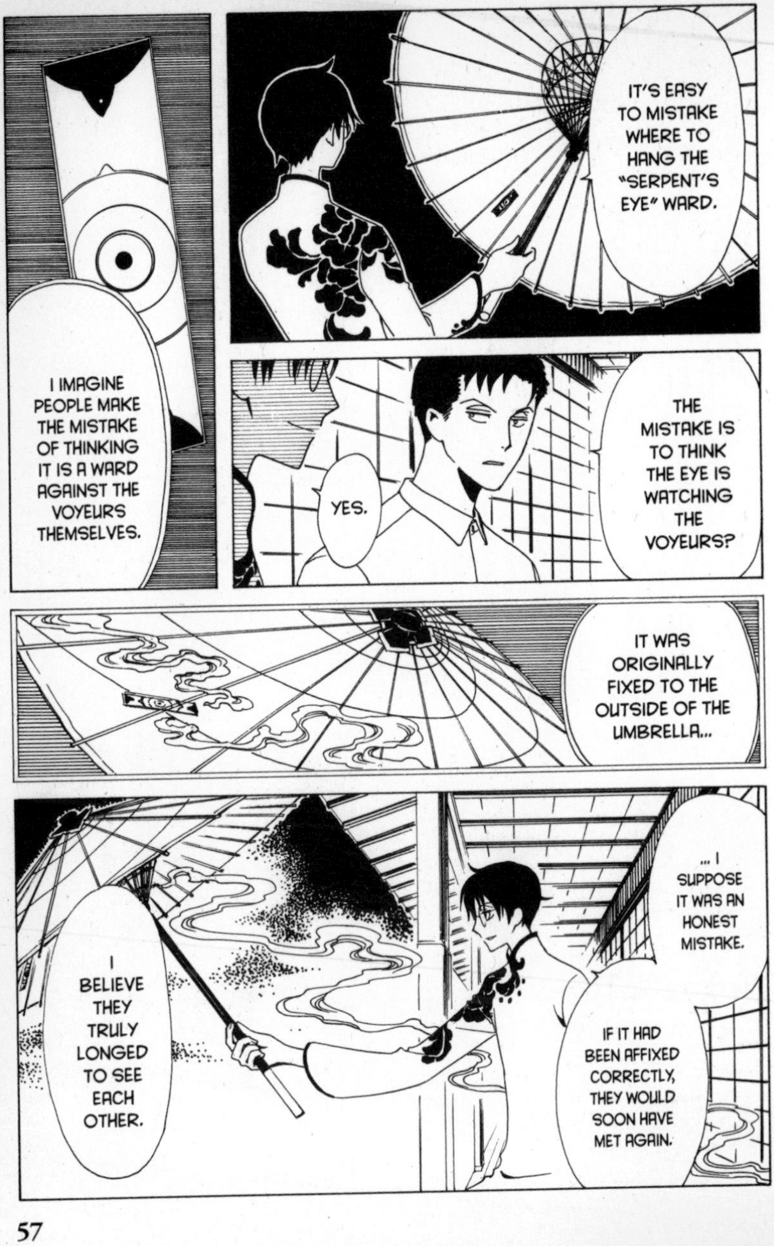
IT'S EASY TO MISTAKE WHERE TO HANG THE "SERPENT'S EYE" WARD.
THE MISTAKE IS TO THINK THE EYE IS WATCHING THE VOYEURS?
YES.
I IMAGINE PEOPLE MAKE THE MISTAKE OF THINKING IT IS A WARD AGAINST THE VOYEURS THEMSELVES.
IT WAS ORIGINALLY FIXED TO THE OUTSIDE OF THE UMBRELLA...
...I SUPPOSE IT WAS AN HONEST MISTAKE.
IF IT HAD BEEN AFFIXED CORRECTLY, THEY WOULD SOON HAVE MET AGAIN.
I BELIEVE THEY TRULY LONGED TO SEE EACH OTHER.

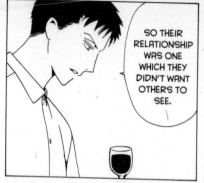

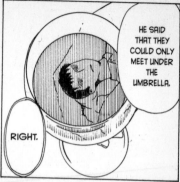

HE SAID THAT THEY COULD ONLY MEET UNDER THE UMBRELLA.
RIGHT.
SO THEIR RELATIONSHIP WAS ONE WHICH THEY DIDN'T WANT OTHERS TO SEE.
PROB-ABLY.
BUT...
...THEY SAY, "AT NIGHT, FROM A DISTANCE, OR UNDER AN UMBRELLA."
I'VE HEARD OF THAT. UNDER THOSE CONDITIONS, WOMEN LOOK MORE BEAUTIFUL.

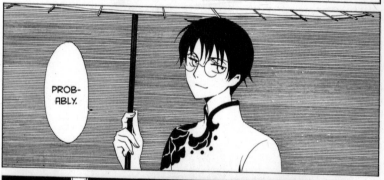

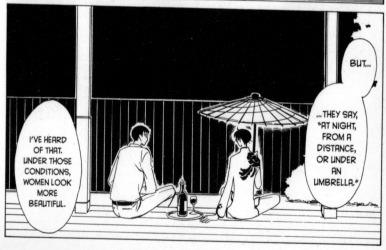

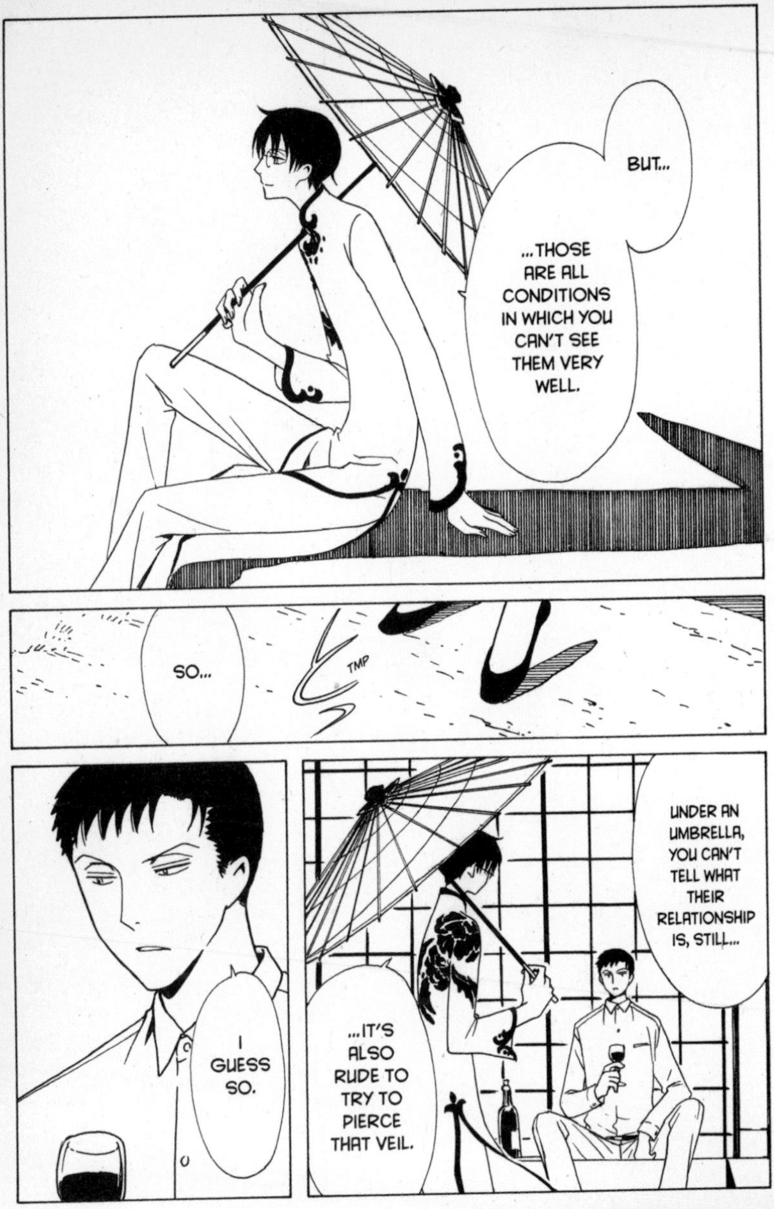
BUT...
...THOSE ARE ALL CONDITIONS IN WHICH YOU CAN'T SEE THEM VERY WELL.
TMP
SO...
UNDER AN UMBRELLA, YOU CAN'T TELL WHAT THEIR RELATIONSHIP IS, STILL...
...IT'S ALSO RUDE TO TRY TO PIERCE THAT VEIL.
I GUESS SO.

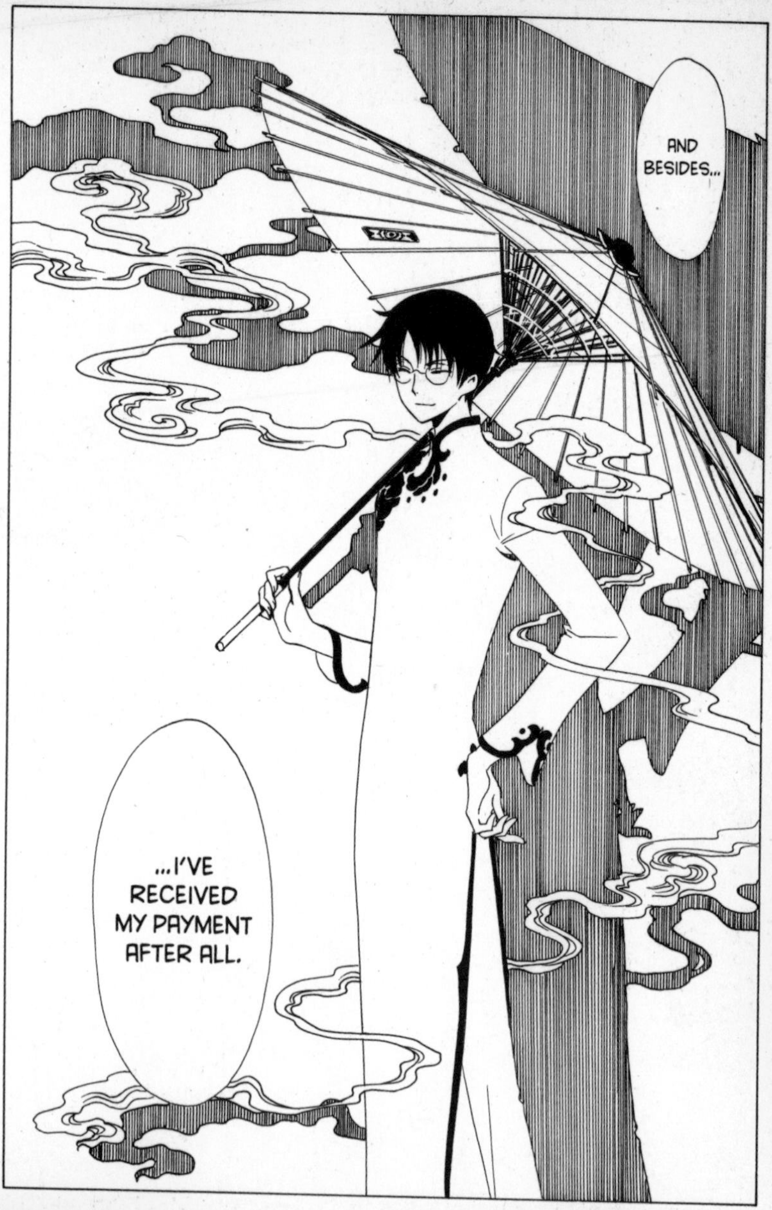
AND BESIDES...
...I'VE RECEIVED MY PAYMENT AFTER ALL.

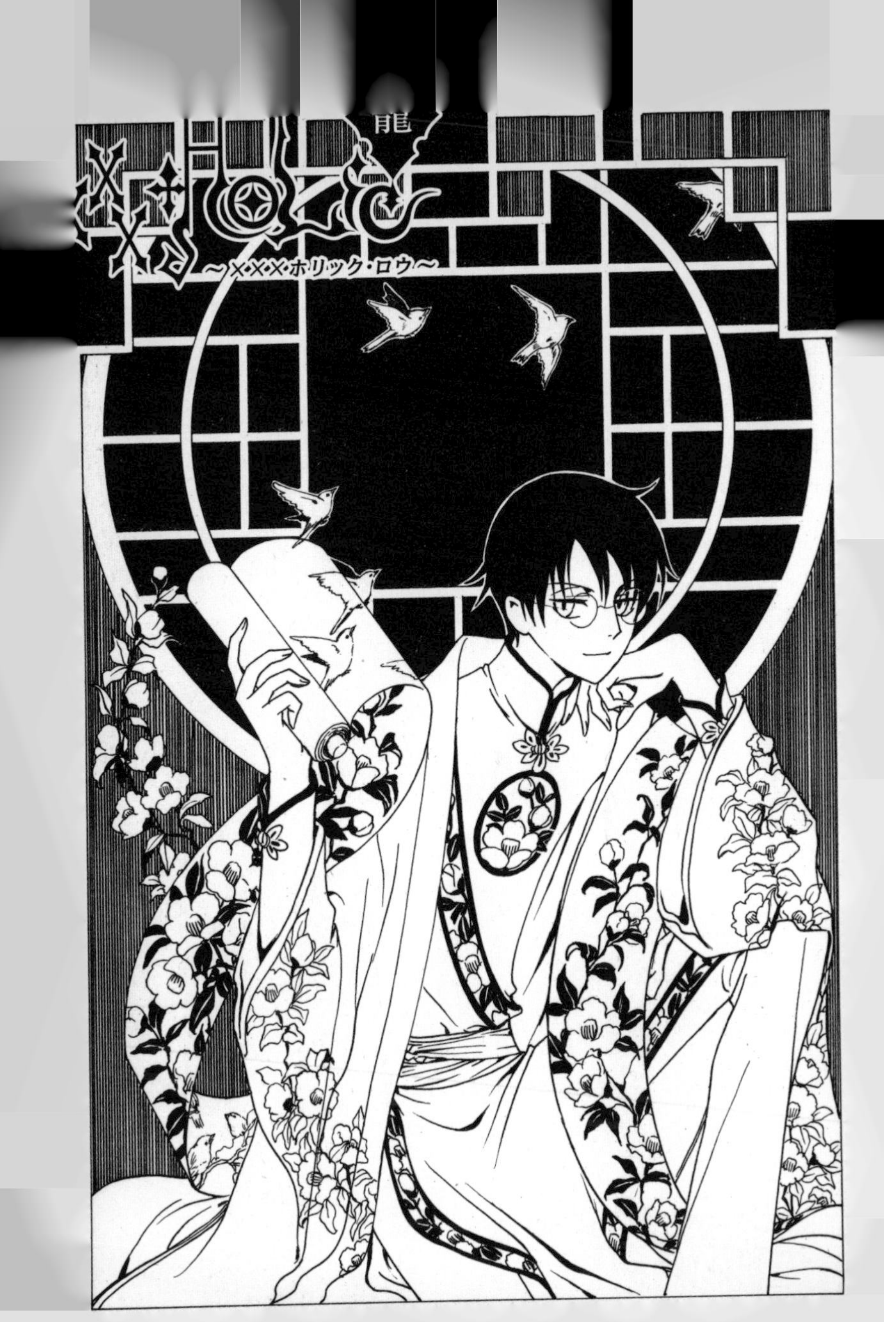
龍
～×××ホリック・ロウ～

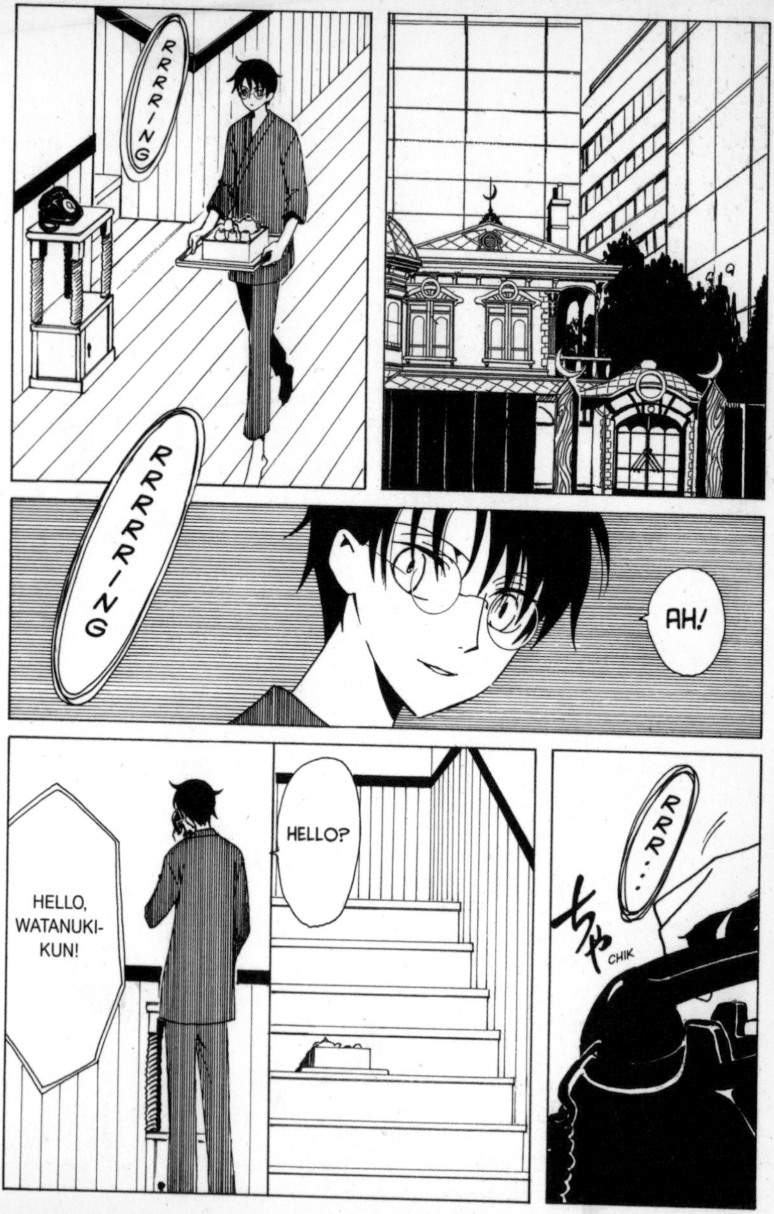
RRRRING
RRRRRING
AH!
RRR...
ちゃ
CHIK
HELLO?
HELLO, WATANUKI-KUN!

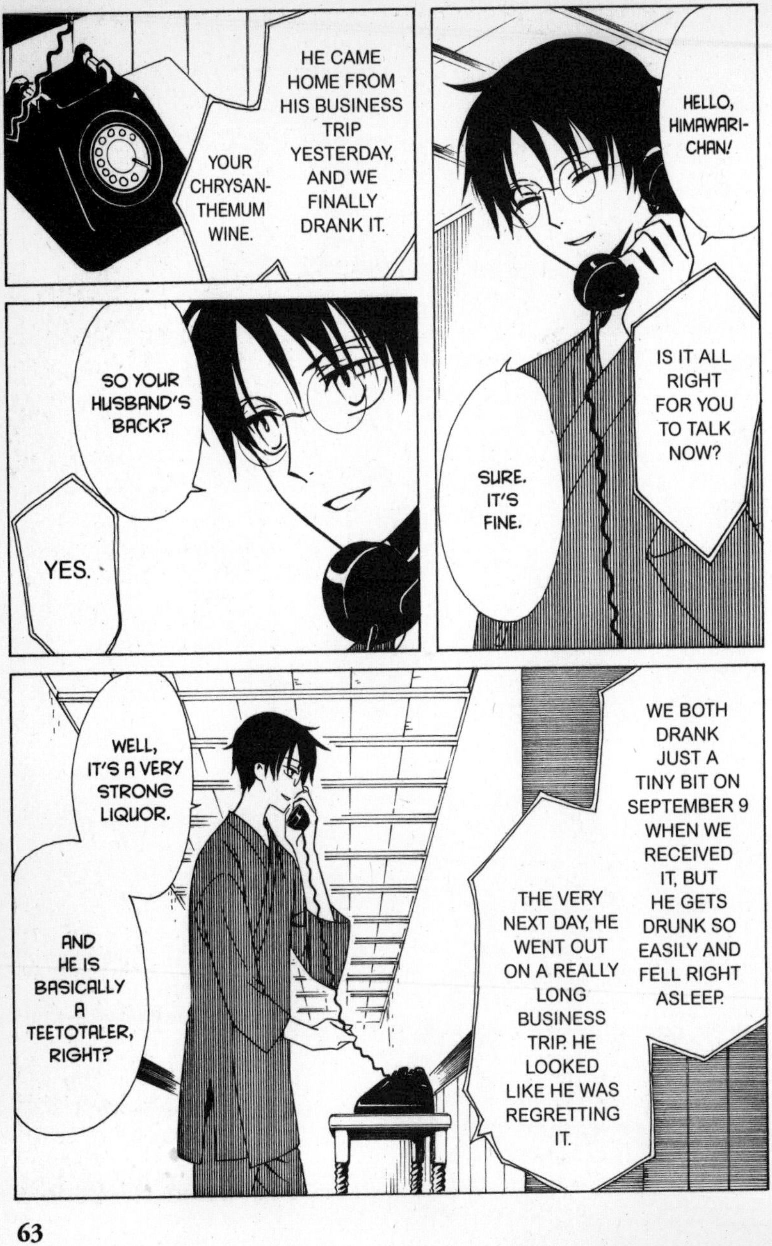
HELLO, HIMAWARI-CHAN!
IS IT ALL RIGHT FOR YOU TO TALK NOW?
SURE. IT'S FINE.
HE CAME HOME FROM HIS BUSINESS TRIP YESTERDAY, AND WE FINALLY DRANK IT.
YOUR CHRYSANTHEMUM WINE.
SO YOUR HUSBAND'S BACK?
YES.
WE BOTH DRANK JUST A TINY BIT ON SEPTEMBER 9 WHEN WE RECEIVED IT, BUT HE GETS DRUNK SO EASILY AND FELL RIGHT ASLEEP.
THE VERY NEXT DAY, HE WENT OUT ON A REALLY LONG BUSINESS TRIP. HE LOOKED LIKE HE WAS REGRETTING IT.
WELL, IT'S A VERY STRONG LIQUOR.
AND HE IS BASICALLY A TEETOTALER, RIGHT?

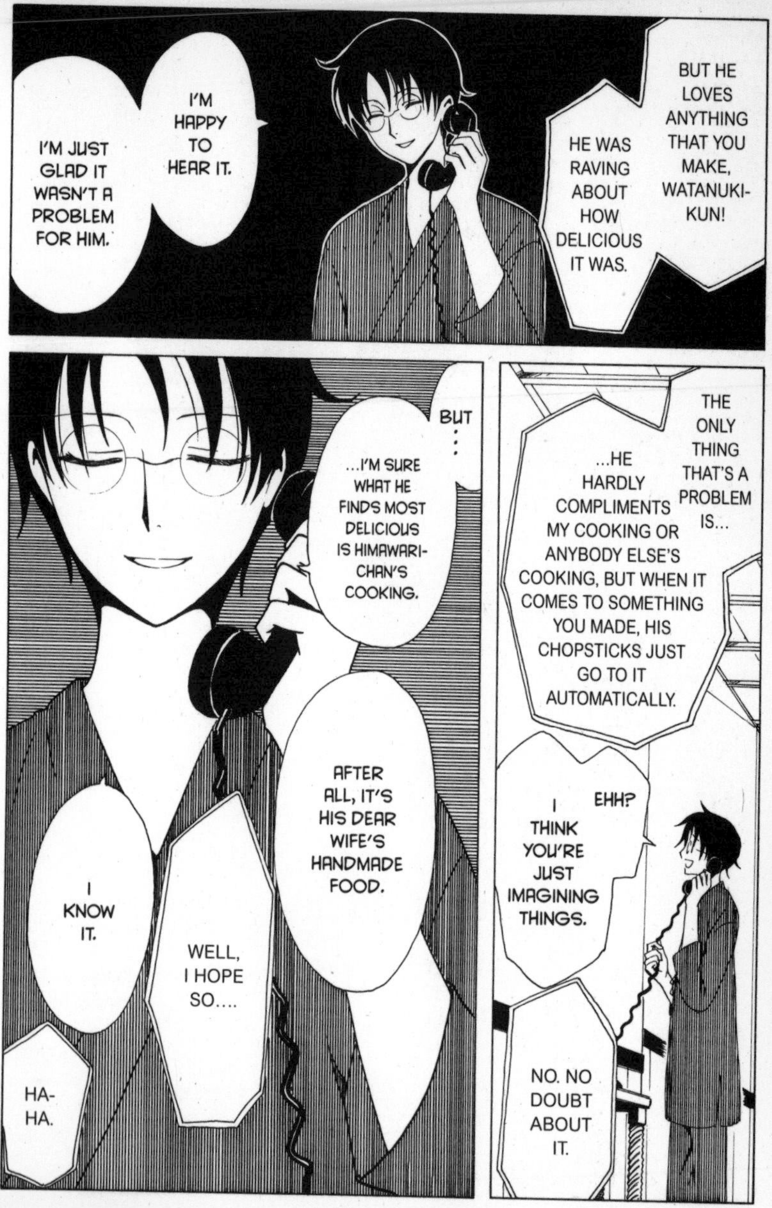
BUT HE LOVES ANYTHING THAT YOU MAKE, WATANUKI-KUN! HE WAS RAVING ABOUT HOW DELICIOUS IT WAS.
I'M HAPPY TO HEAR IT. I'M JUST GLAD IT WASN'T A PROBLEM FOR HIM.
THE ONLY THING THAT'S A PROBLEM IS... ...HE HARDLY COMPLIMENTS MY COOKING OR ANYBODY ELSE'S COOKING, BUT WHEN IT COMES TO SOMETHING YOU MADE, HIS CHOPSTICKS JUST GO TO IT AUTOMATICALLY.
EHH? I THINK YOU'RE JUST IMAGINING THINGS.
NO. NO DOUBT ABOUT IT.
BUT... ...I'M SURE WHAT HE FINDS MOST DELICIOUS IS HIMAWARI-CHAN'S COOKING.
AFTER ALL, IT'S HIS DEAR WIFE'S HANDMADE FOOD.
WELL, I HOPE SO....
I KNOW IT.
HA-HA.

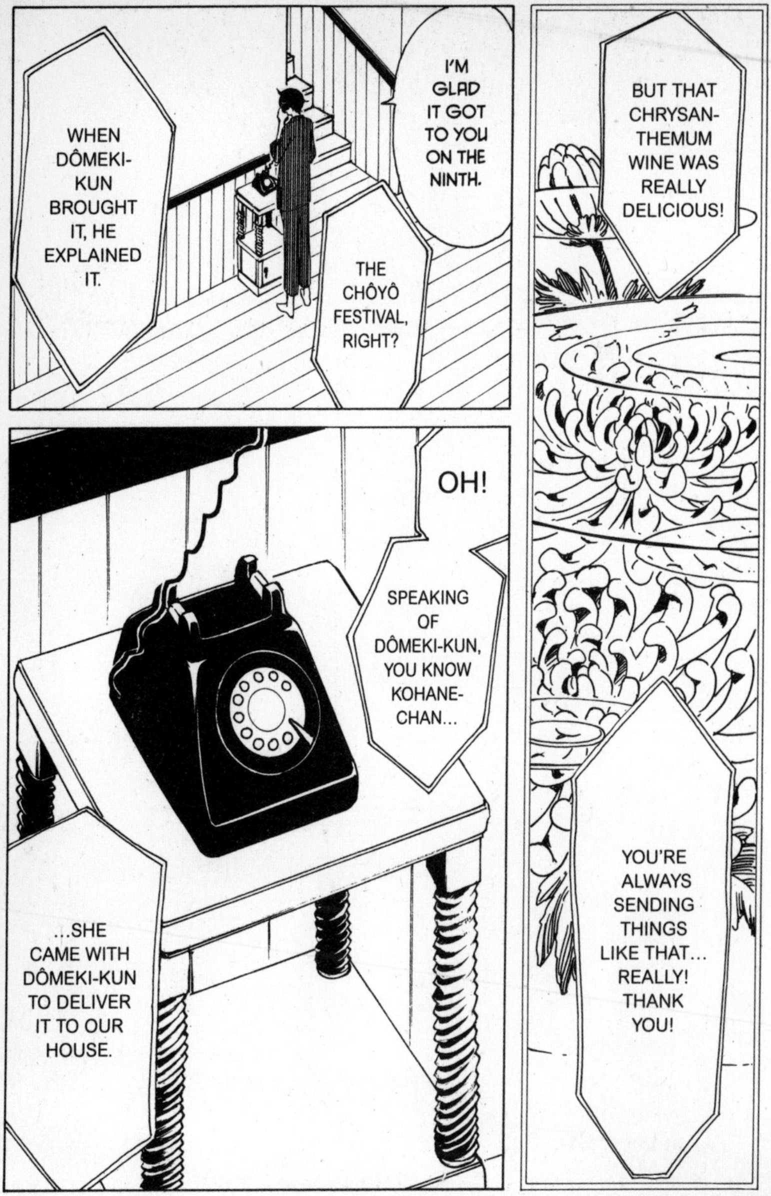
BUT THAT CHRYSANTHEMUM WINE WAS REALLY DELICIOUS!
YOU'RE ALWAYS SENDING THINGS LIKE THAT... REALLY! THANK YOU!
I'M GLAD IT GOT TO YOU ON THE NINTH.
THE CHÔYÔ FESTIVAL, RIGHT?
WHEN DÔMEKI-KUN BROUGHT IT, HE EXPLAINED IT.
OH!
SPEAKING OF DÔMEKI-KUN, YOU KNOW KOHANE-CHAN...
...SHE CAME WITH DÔMEKI-KUN TO DELIVER IT TO OUR HOUSE.

I ALWAYS THOUGHT SHE WAS PRETTY, BUT RECENTLY SHE'S JUST GETTING MORE AND MORE BEAUTIFUL.

YEAH...

.....SHE SURE IS.

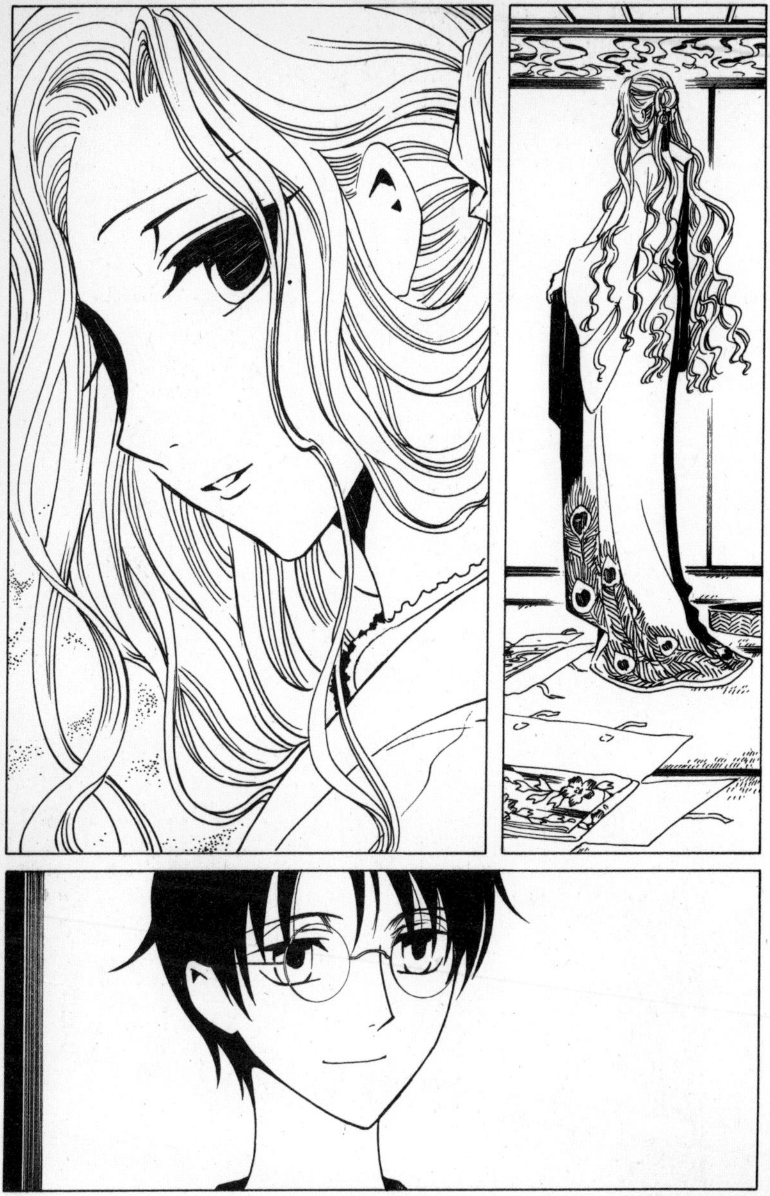

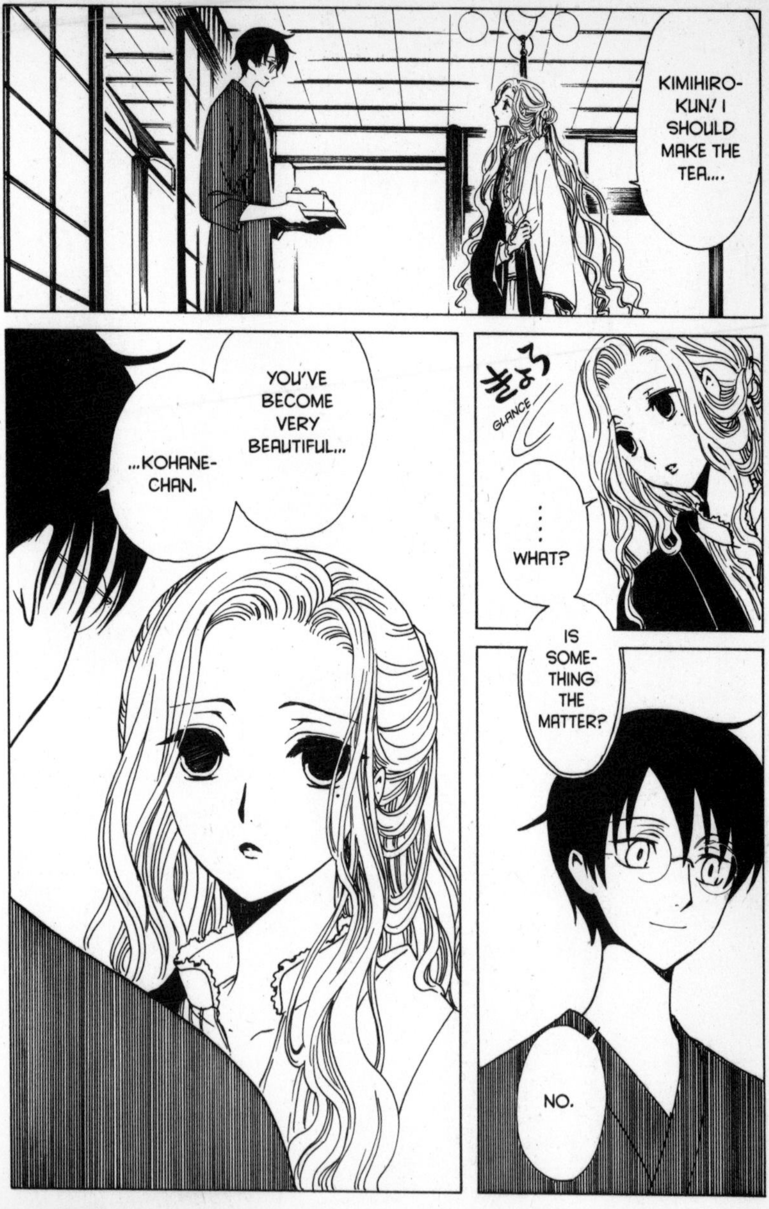
KIMIHIRO-KUN! I SHOULD MAKE THE TEA....
きょろ
GLANCE
... WHAT?
IS SOME-THING THE MATTER?
NO.
YOU'VE BECOME VERY BEAUTIFUL...
...KOHANE-CHAN.

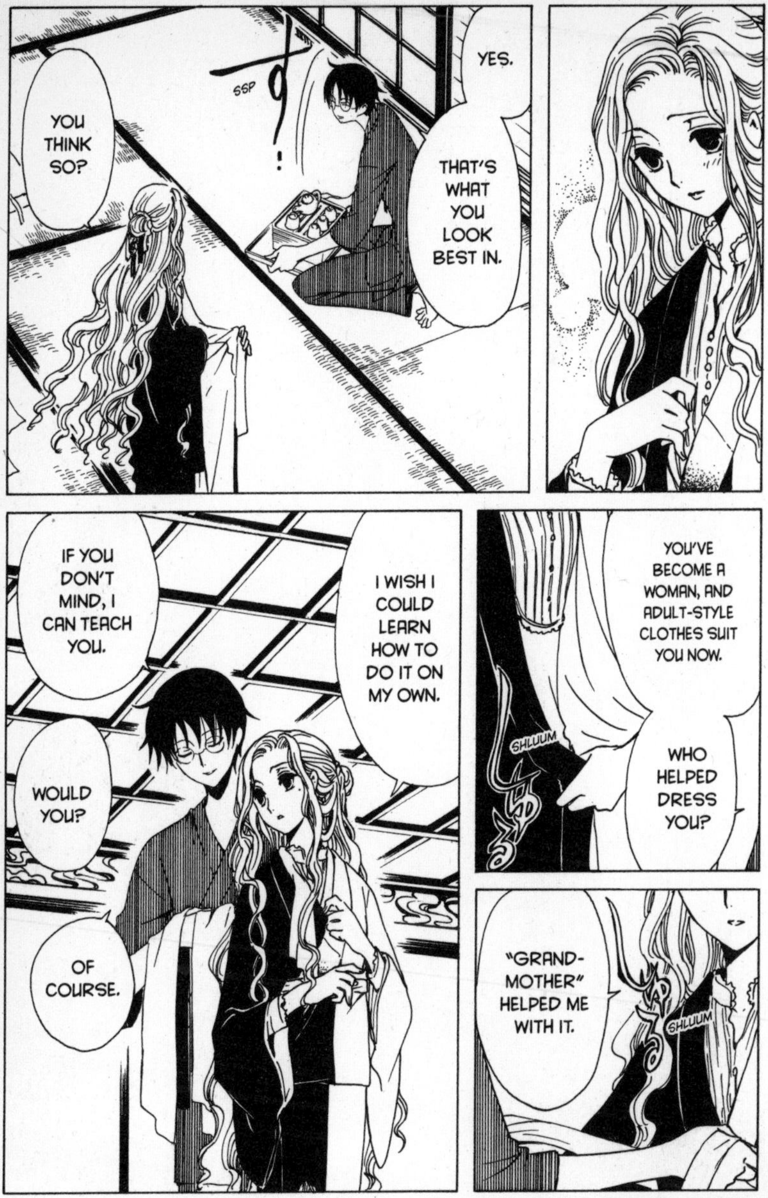
YES.
THAT'S WHAT YOU LOOK BEST IN.
SSP
!
YOU THINK SO?
YOU'VE BECOME A WOMAN, AND ADULT-STYLE CLOTHES SUIT YOU NOW.
SHLUUM
WHO HELPED DRESS YOU?
"GRAND-MOTHER" HELPED ME WITH IT.
SHLUUM
I WISH I COULD LEARN HOW TO DO IT ON MY OWN.
IF YOU DON'T MIND, I CAN TEACH YOU.
WOULD YOU?
OF COURSE.

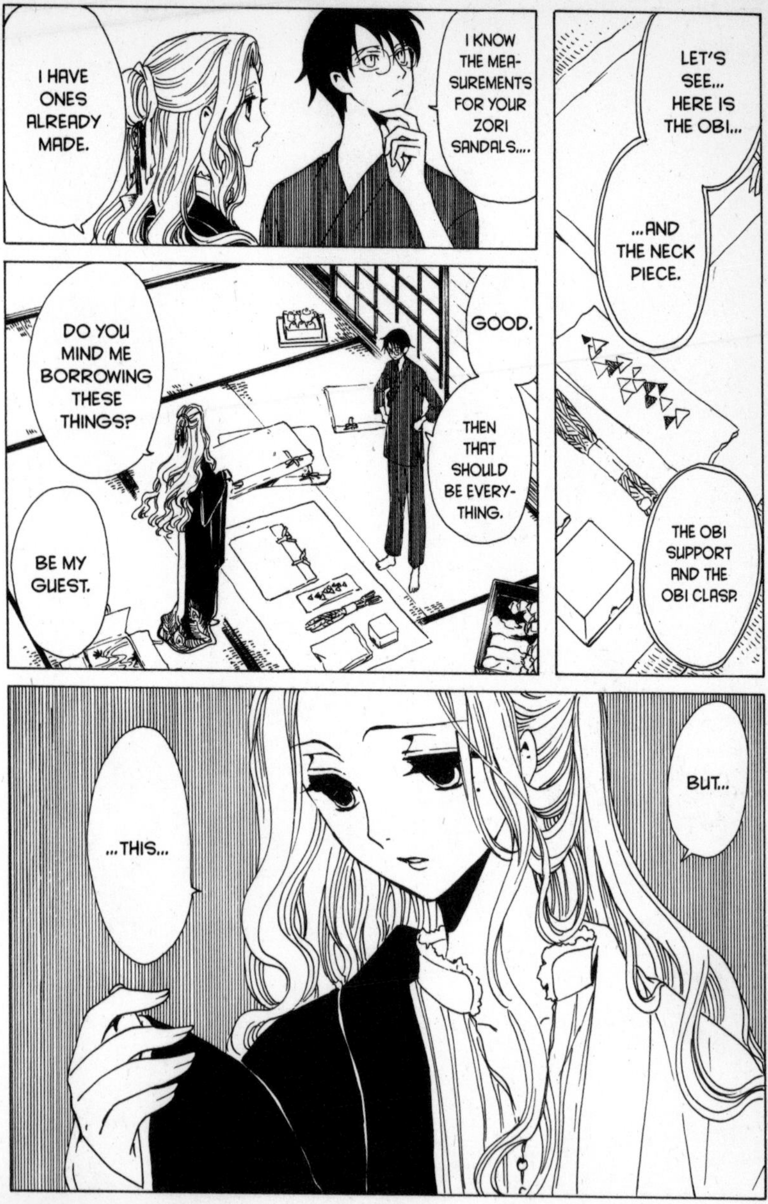
LET'S SEE... HERE IS THE OBI...
...AND THE NECK PIECE.
THE OBI SUPPORT AND THE OBI CLASP.
I KNOW THE MEA-SUREMENTS FOR YOUR ZORI SANDALS....
I HAVE ONES ALREADY MADE.
GOOD.
THEN THAT SHOULD BE EVERY-THING.
DO YOU MIND ME BORROWING THESE THINGS?
BE MY GUEST.
BUT...
...THIS...

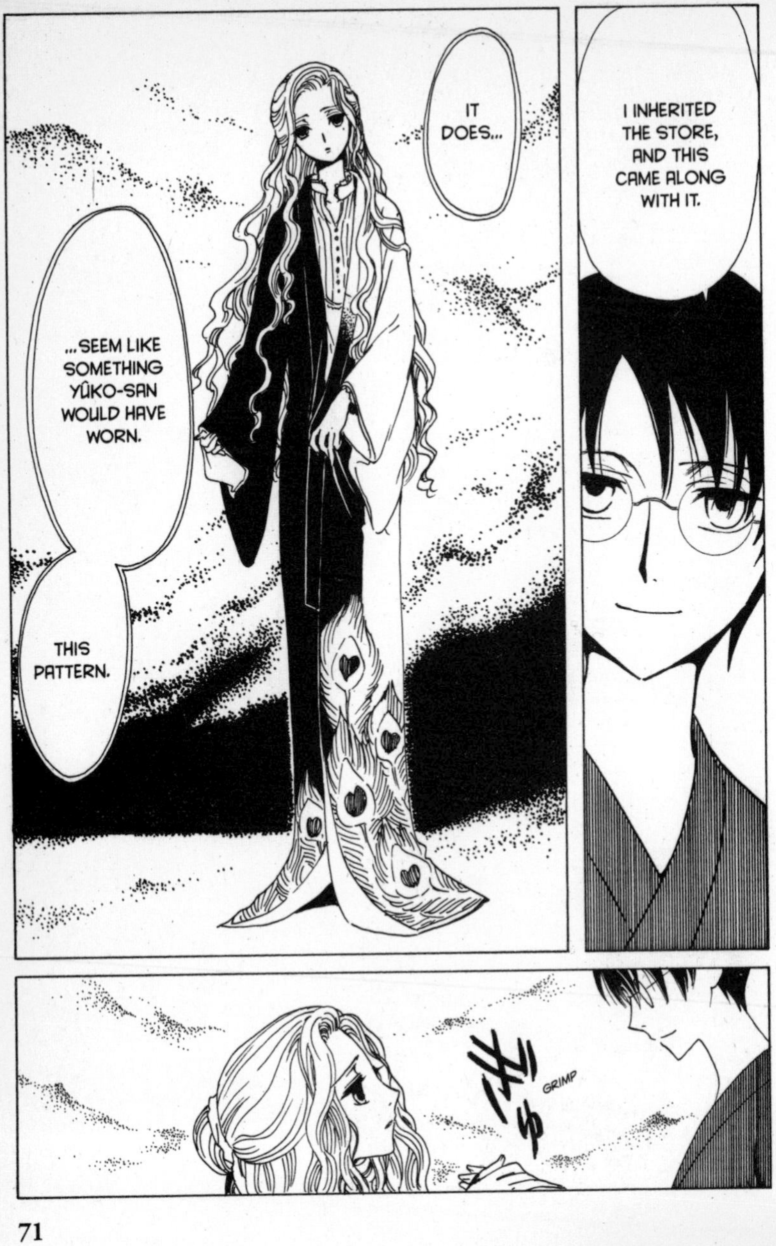
I INHERITED THE STORE, AND THIS CAME ALONG WITH IT.
IT DOES...
...SEEM LIKE SOMETHING YÛKO-SAN WOULD HAVE WORN.
THIS PATTERN.
GRIMP

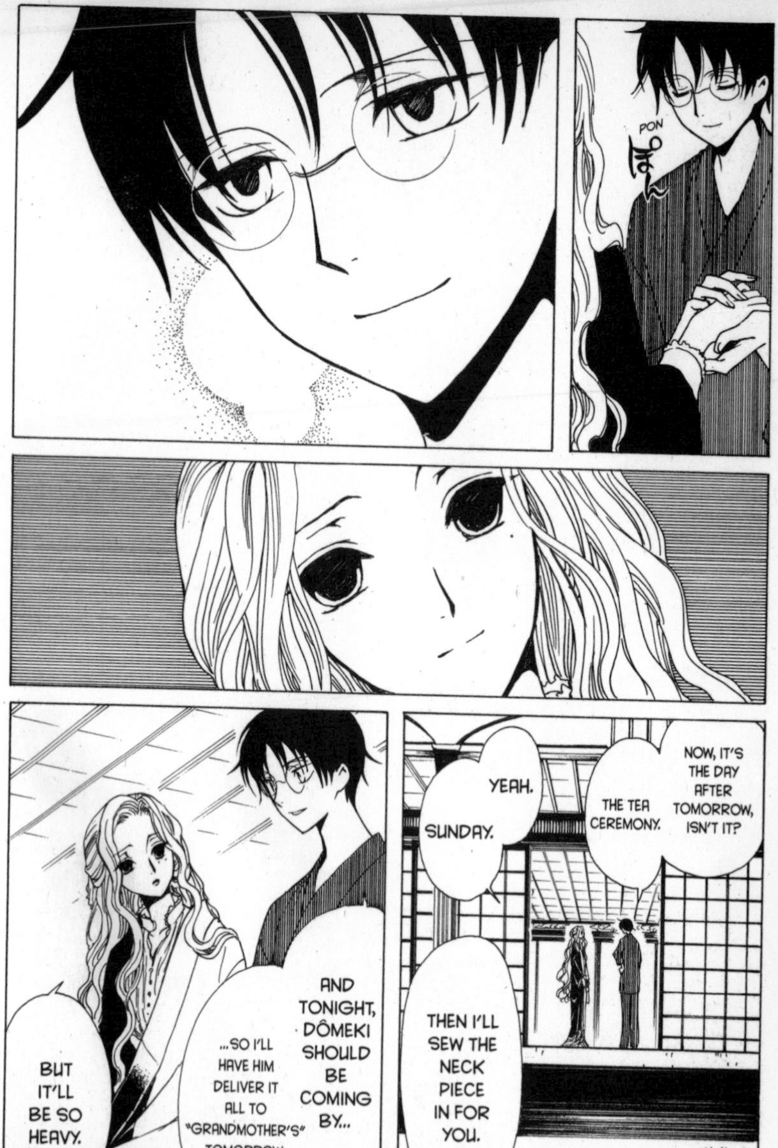
PON
ぽん
NOW, IT'S THE DAY AFTER TOMORROW, ISN'T IT?
THE TEA CEREMONY.
YEAH.
SUNDAY.
THEN I'LL SEW THE NECK PIECE IN FOR YOU.
AND TONIGHT, DÔMEKI SHOULD BE COMING BY...
...SO I'LL HAVE HIM DELIVER IT ALL TO "GRANDMOTHER'S" TOMORROW.
BUT IT'LL BE SO HEAVY.

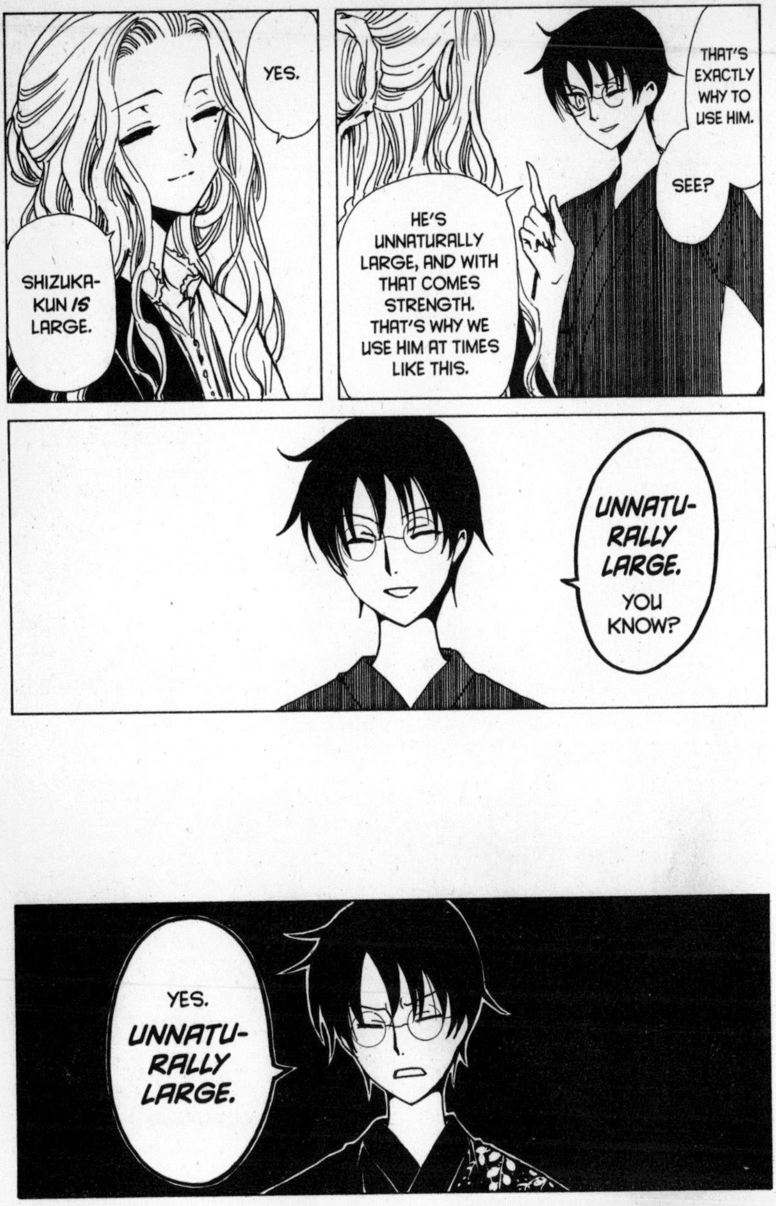
THAT'S EXACTLY WHY TO USE HIM.
SEE?
HE'S UNNATURALLY LARGE, AND WITH THAT COMES STRENGTH. THAT'S WHY WE USE HIM AT TIMES LIKE THIS.
YES.
SHIZUKA-KUN *IS* LARGE.
UNNATU-RALLY LARGE. YOU KNOW?
YES. *UNNATU-RALLY LARGE.*

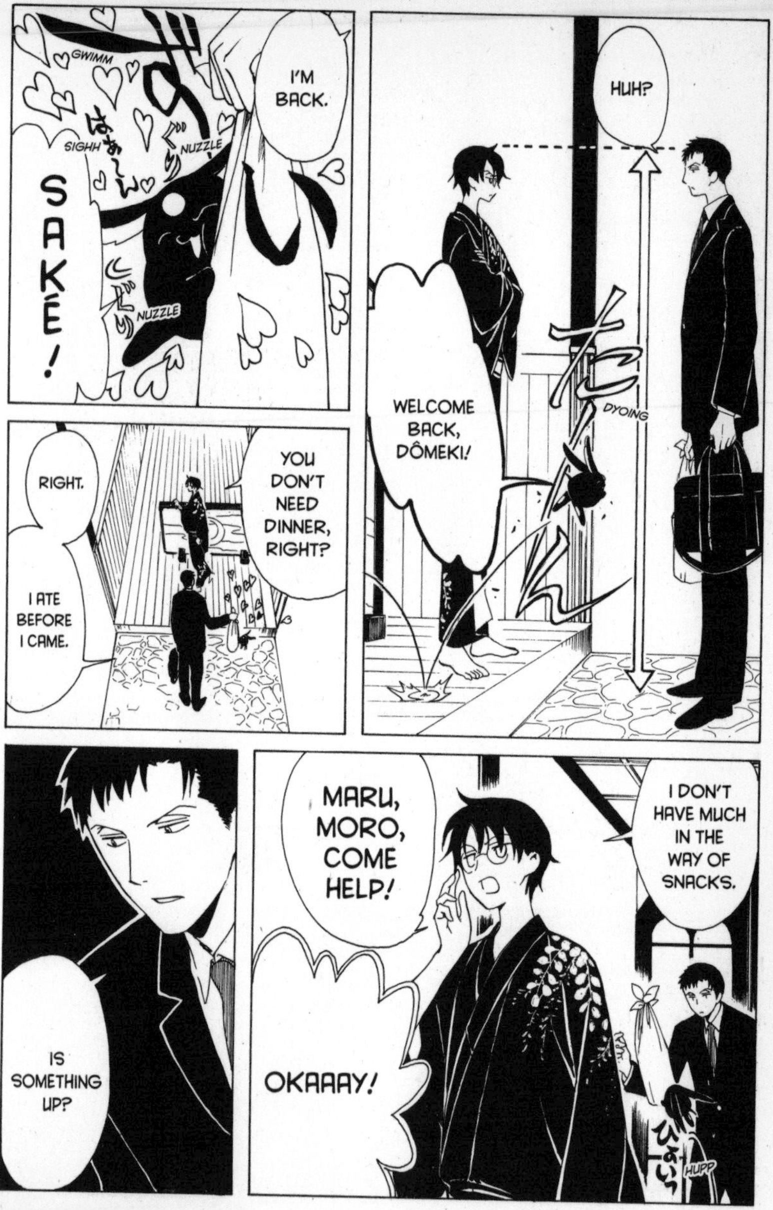
HUH?
DYOING
WELCOME BACK, DÔMEKI!
I'M BACK.
GWIMM
NUZZLE
SIGHH
SAKÉ!
NUZZLE
YOU DON'T NEED DINNER, RIGHT?
RIGHT.
I ATE BEFORE I CAME.
I DON'T HAVE MUCH IN THE WAY OF SNACKS.
MARU, MORO, COME HELP!
OKAAAY!
HUPP
IS SOMETHING UP?

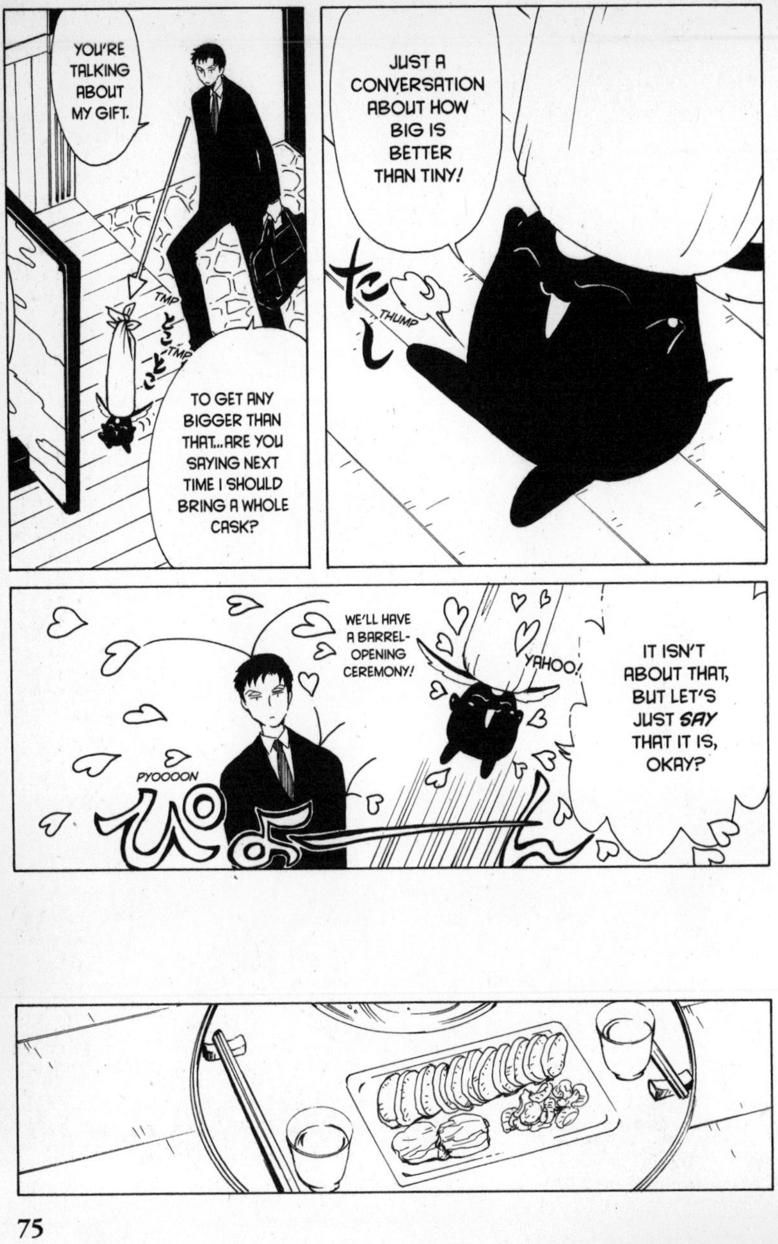
JUST A CONVERSATION ABOUT HOW BIG IS BETTER THAN TINY!
たし
THUMP
YOU'RE TALKING ABOUT MY GIFT.
TMP
とことこ
TMP
TO GET ANY BIGGER THAN THAT...ARE YOU SAYING NEXT TIME I SHOULD BRING A WHOLE CASK?
IT ISN'T ABOUT THAT, BUT LET'S JUST *SAY* THAT IT IS, OKAY?
YAHOO!
WE'LL HAVE A BARREL-OPENING CEREMONY!
PYOOOON
ぴょーん

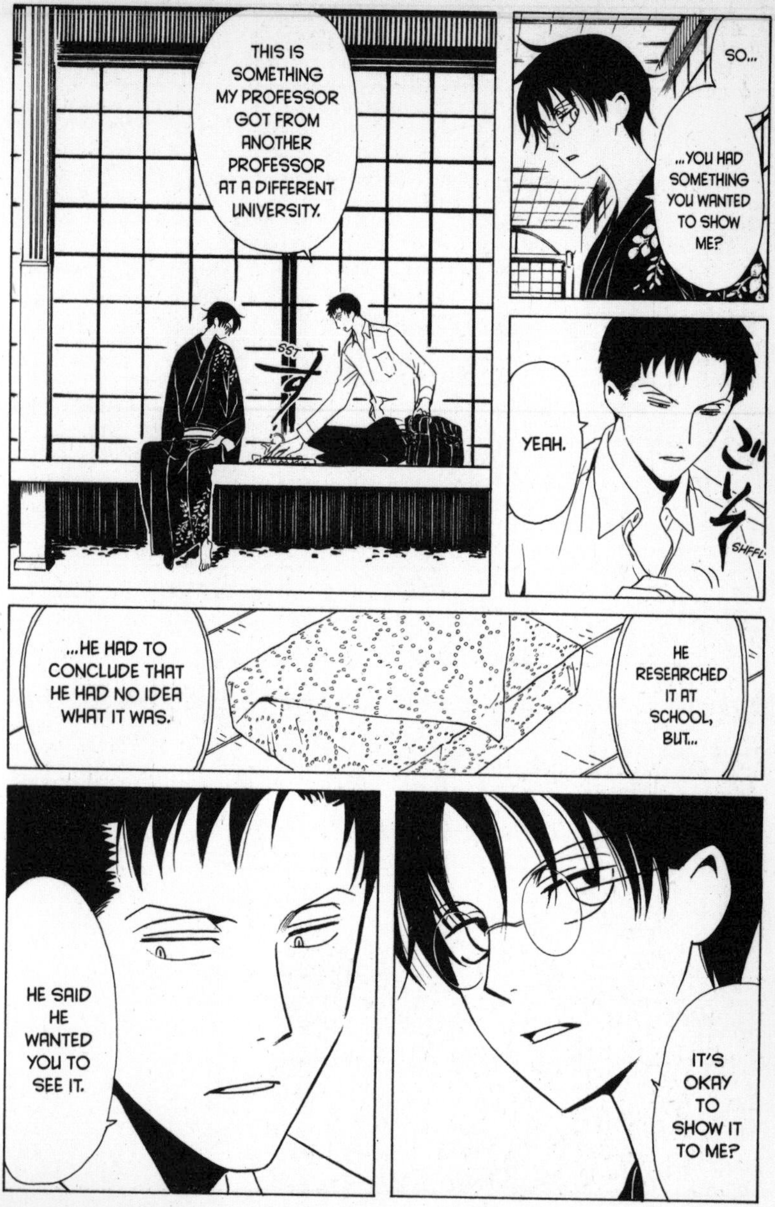
SO...
...YOU HAD SOMETHING YOU WANTED TO SHOW ME?
YEAH.
SHFFL
THIS IS SOMETHING MY PROFESSOR GOT FROM ANOTHER PROFESSOR AT A DIFFERENT UNIVERSITY.
SST
HE RESEARCHED IT AT SCHOOL, BUT...
...HE HAD TO CONCLUDE THAT HE HAD NO IDEA WHAT IT WAS.
IT'S OKAY TO SHOW IT TO ME?
HE SAID HE WANTED YOU TO SEE IT.

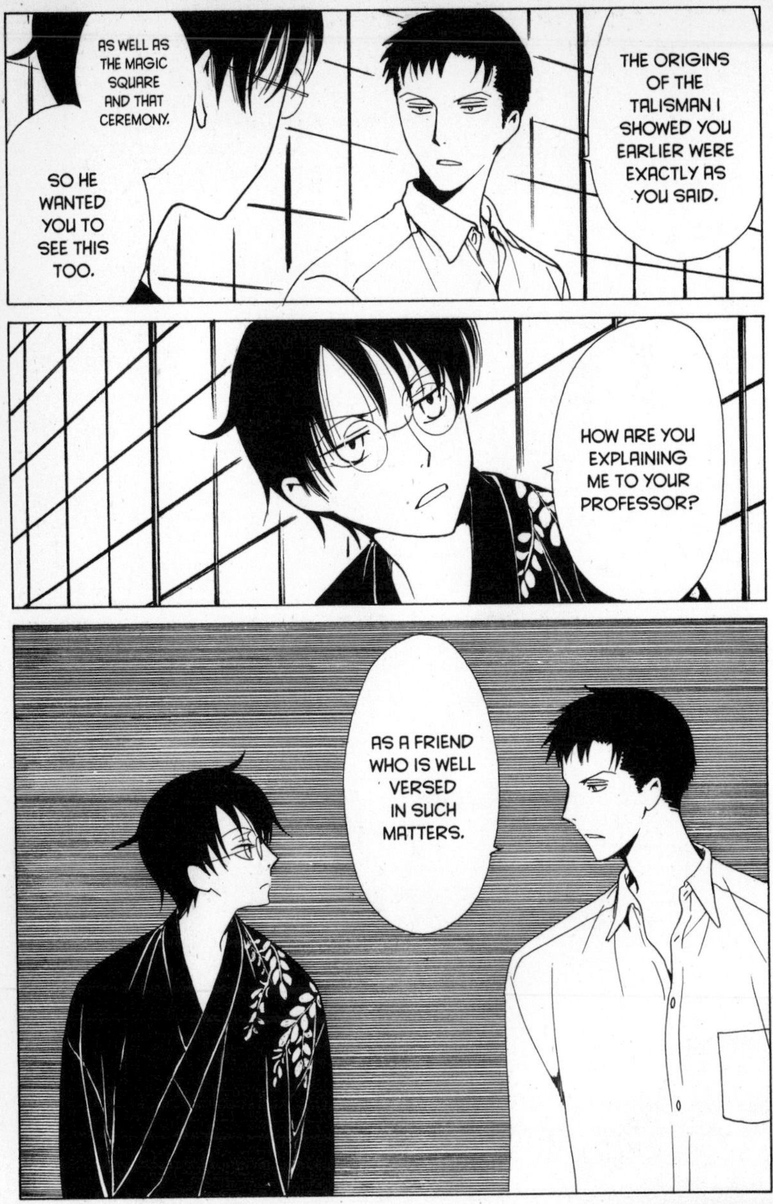
THE ORIGINS OF THE TALISMAN I SHOWED YOU EARLIER WERE EXACTLY AS YOU SAID.
AS WELL AS THE MAGIC SQUARE AND THAT CEREMONY.
SO HE WANTED YOU TO SEE THIS TOO.
HOW ARE YOU EXPLAINING ME TO YOUR PROFESSOR?
AS A FRIEND WHO IS WELL VERSED IN SUCH MATTERS.

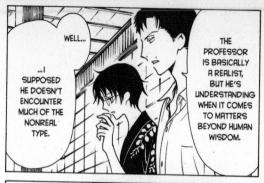

こと
TUNK
I GUESS THERE'S NO LIE IN THAT.
THE PROFESSOR IS BASICALLY A REALIST, BUT HE'S UNDERSTANDING WHEN IT COMES TO MATTERS BEYOND HUMAN WISDOM.
WELL...
...I SUPPOSED HE DOESN'T ENCOUNTER MUCH OF THE NONREAL TYPE.
I'VE ONLY SEEN HIM IN PHOTOS AND VIDEOS...
...BUT HE SEEMS LIKE A NICE GUY, YOUR PROFESSOR.
AND HE SENDS HIS PAYMENTS PROMPTLY AND POLITELY.
THIS TIME, TOO, I TOLD HIM TO BE AS PREPARED AS POSSIBLE.

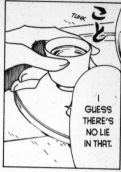

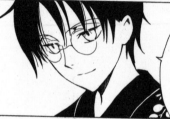

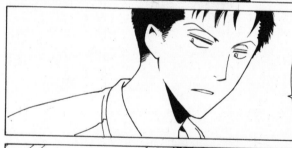

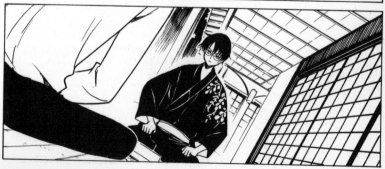

HIS WISH?

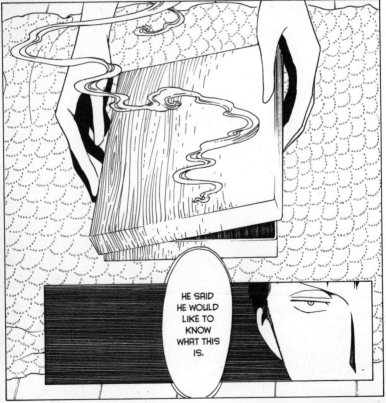

HE SAID HE WOULD LIKE TO KNOW WHAT THIS IS.

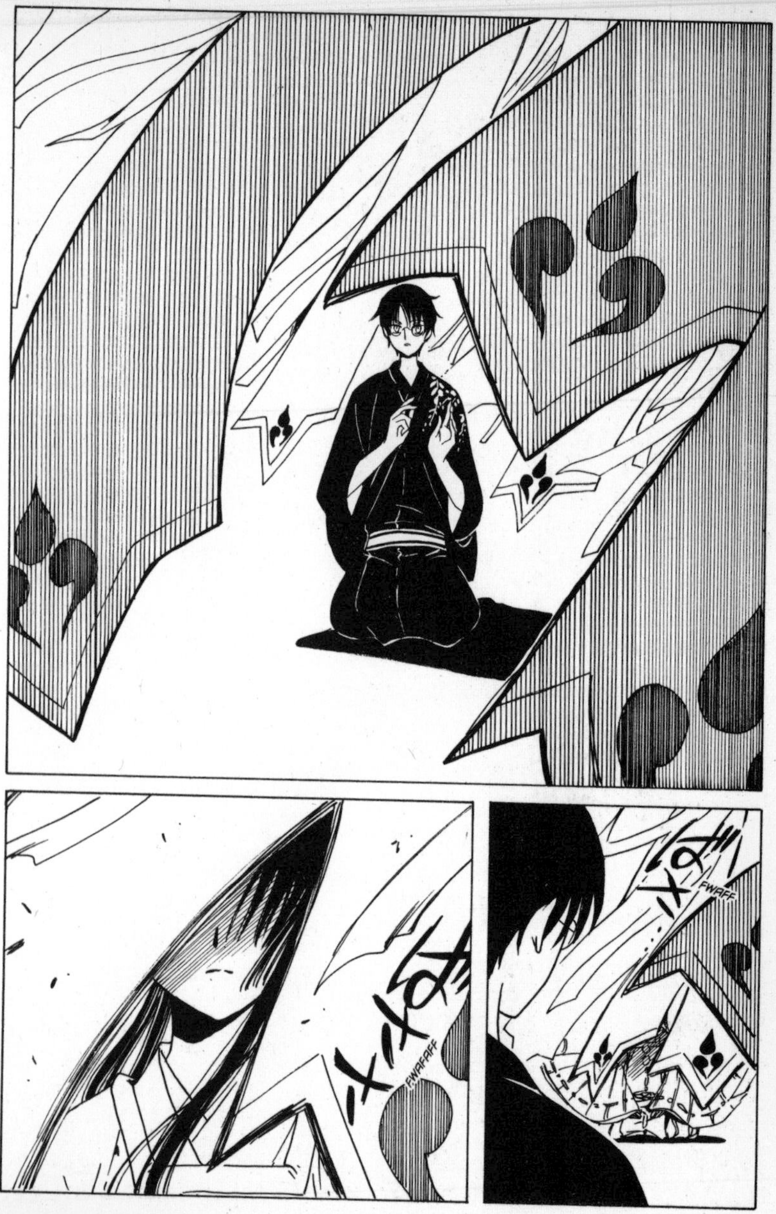
FWAFF
FWAFAFF

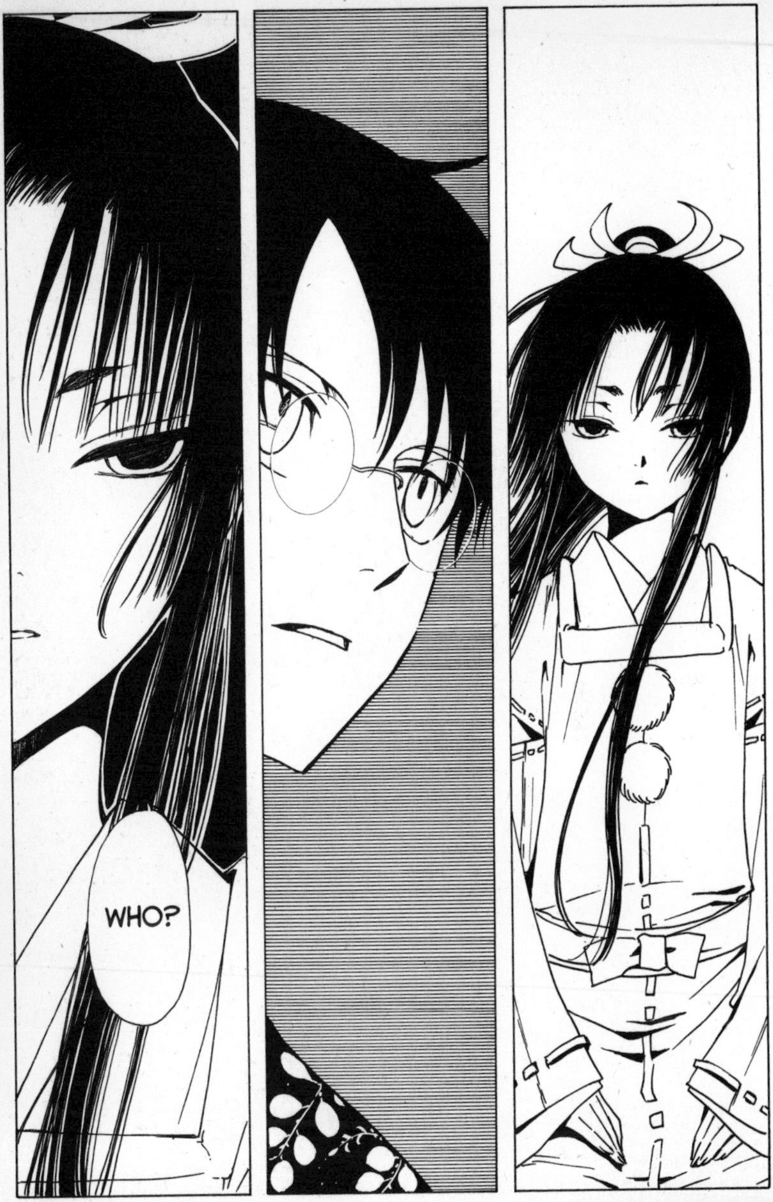
WHO?

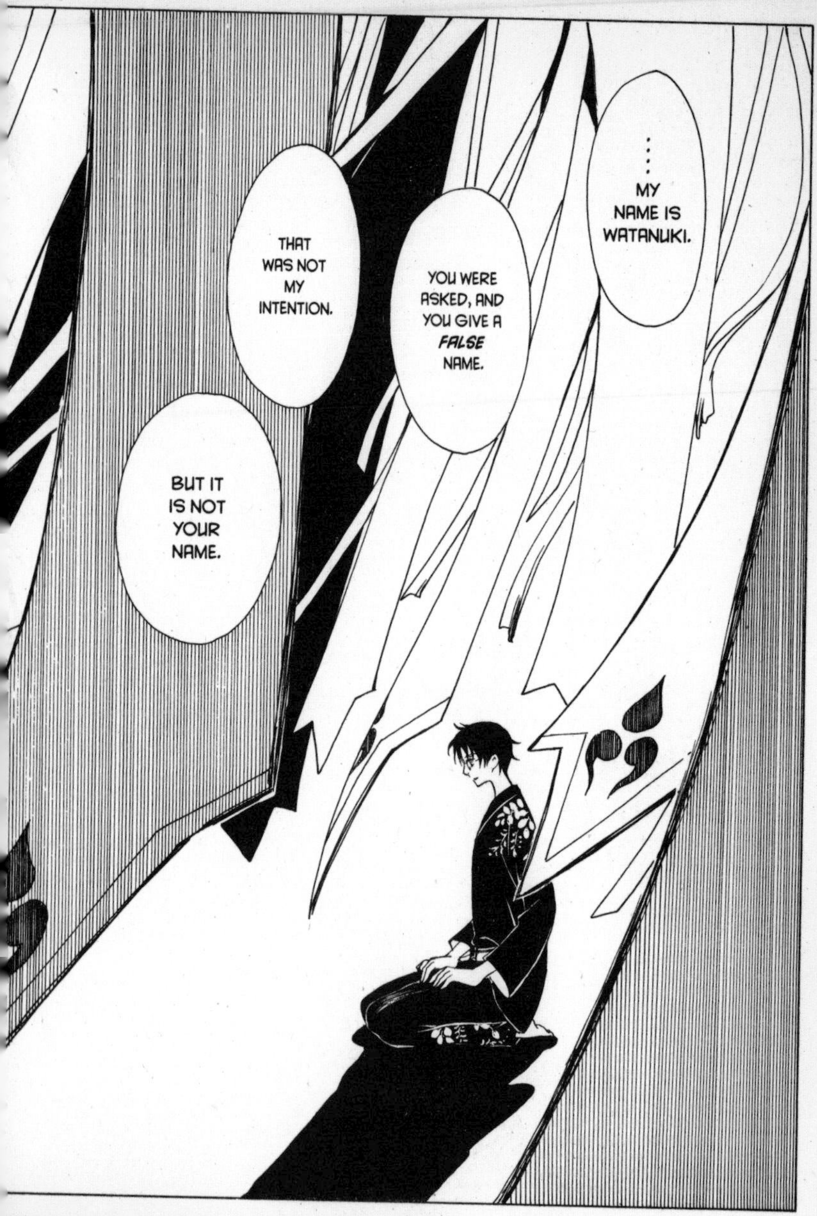

...
MY NAME IS WATANUKI.
YOU WERE ASKED, AND YOU GIVE A *FALSE* NAME.
THAT WAS NOT MY INTENTION.
BUT IT IS NOT YOUR NAME.

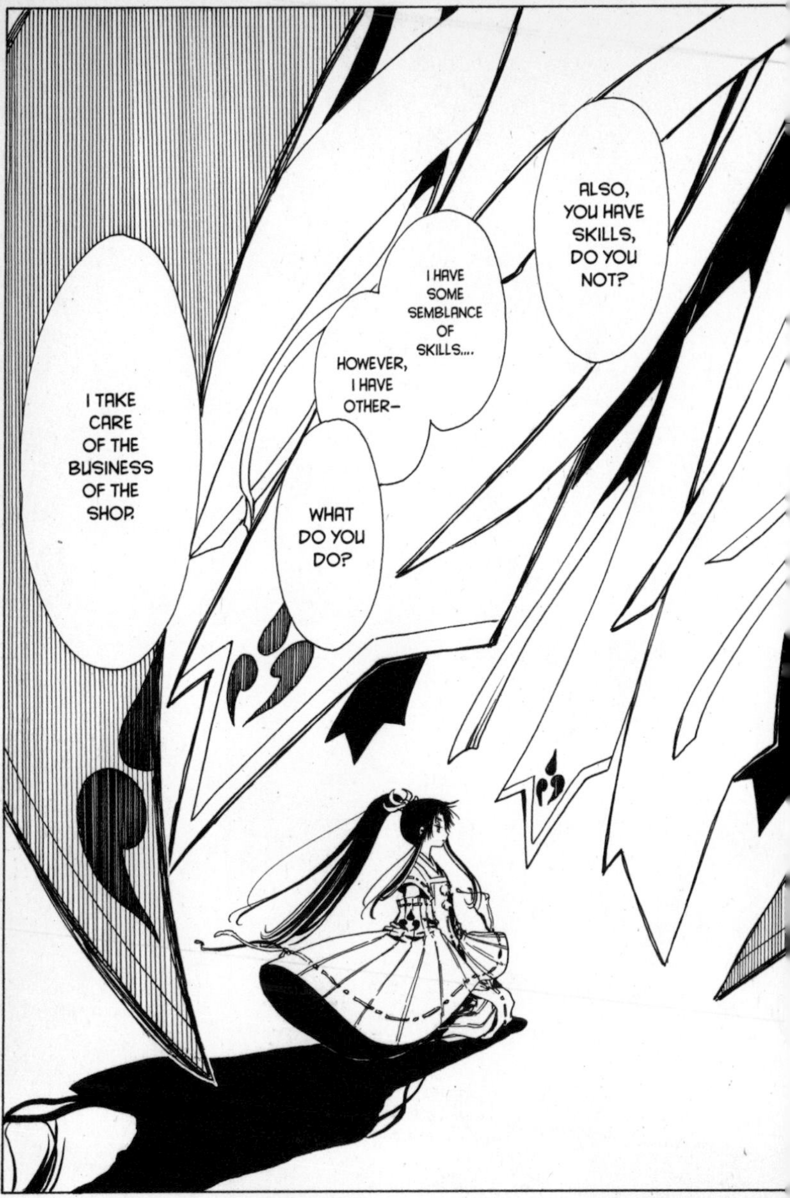
ALSO, YOU HAVE SKILLS, DO YOU NOT?
I HAVE SOME SEMBLANCE OF SKILLS....
HOWEVER, I HAVE OTHER–
WHAT DO YOU DO?
I TAKE CARE OF THE BUSINESS OF THE SHOP.

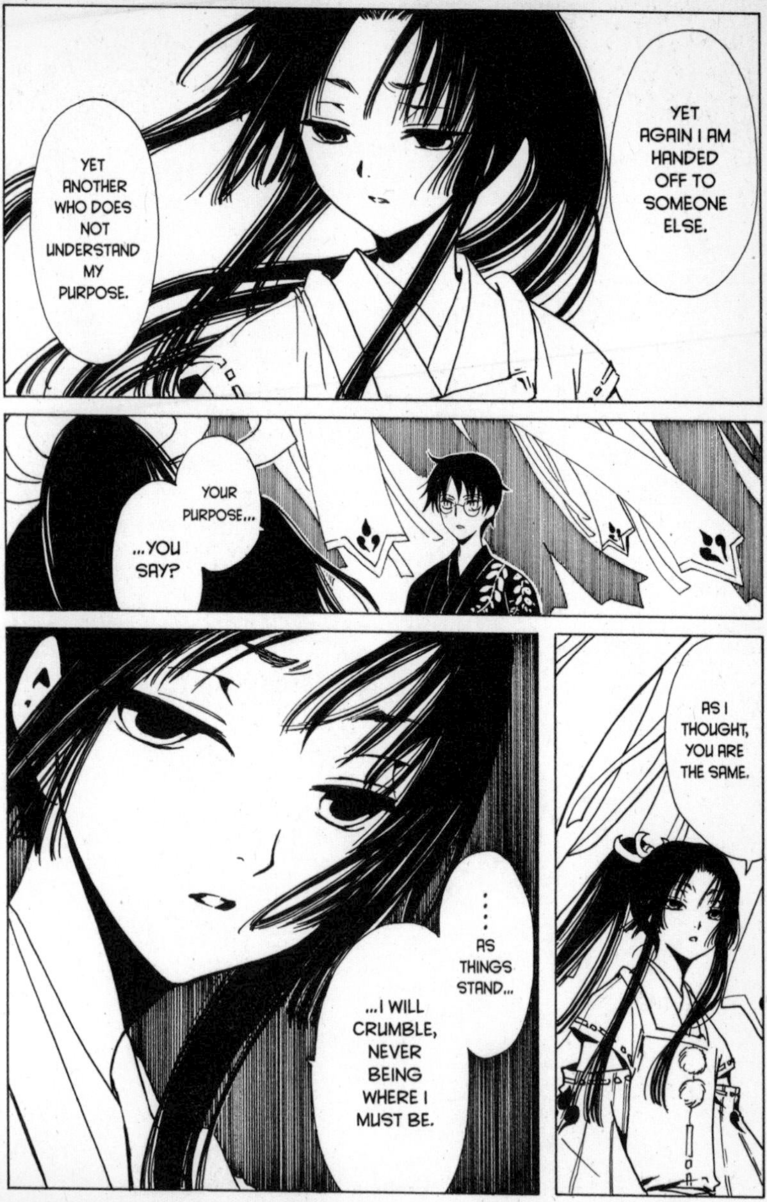
YET AGAIN I AM HANDED OFF TO SOMEONE ELSE.
YET ANOTHER WHO DOES NOT UNDERSTAND MY PURPOSE.
YOUR PURPOSE... ...YOU SAY?
AS I THOUGHT, YOU ARE THE SAME.
.... AS THINGS STAND...
...I WILL CRUMBLE, NEVER BEING WHERE I MUST BE.

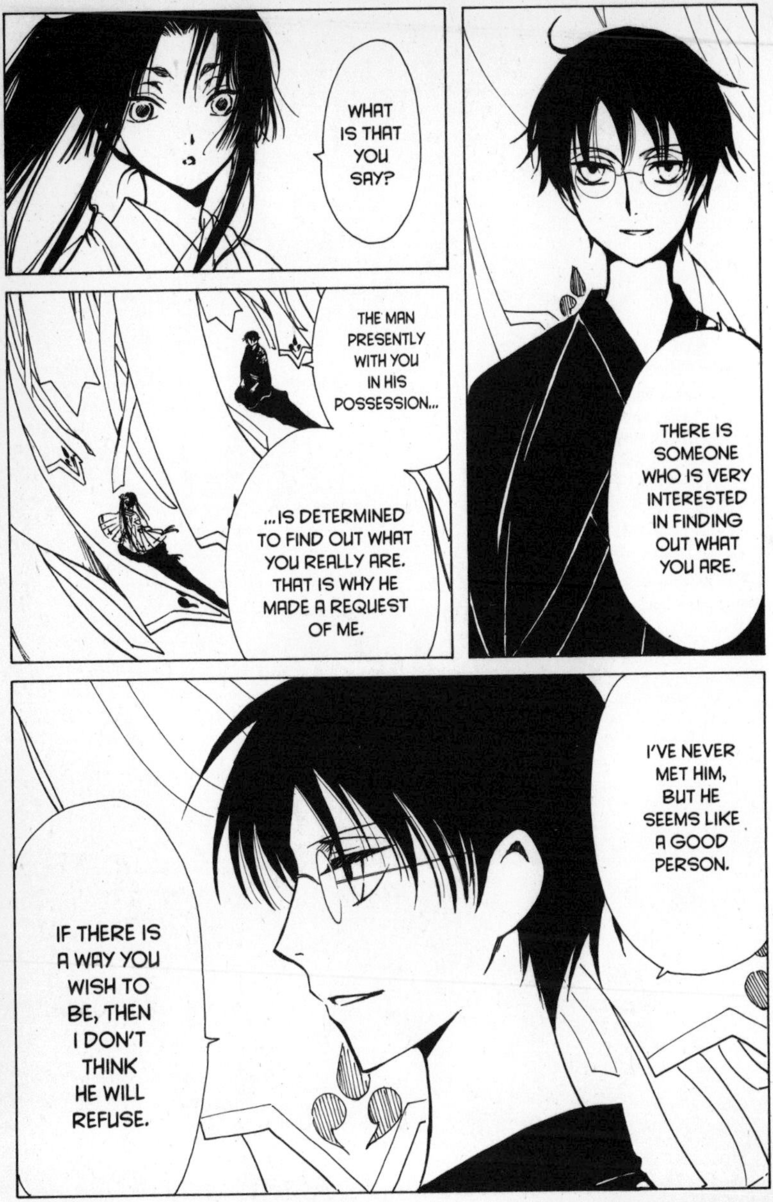
THERE IS SOMEONE WHO IS VERY INTERESTED IN FINDING OUT WHAT YOU ARE.
WHAT IS THAT YOU SAY?
THE MAN PRESENTLY WITH YOU IN HIS POSSESSION...
...IS DETERMINED TO FIND OUT WHAT YOU REALLY ARE. THAT IS WHY HE MADE A REQUEST OF ME.
I'VE NEVER MET HIM, BUT HE SEEMS LIKE A GOOD PERSON.
IF THERE IS A WAY YOU WISH TO BE, THEN I DON'T THINK HE WILL REFUSE.

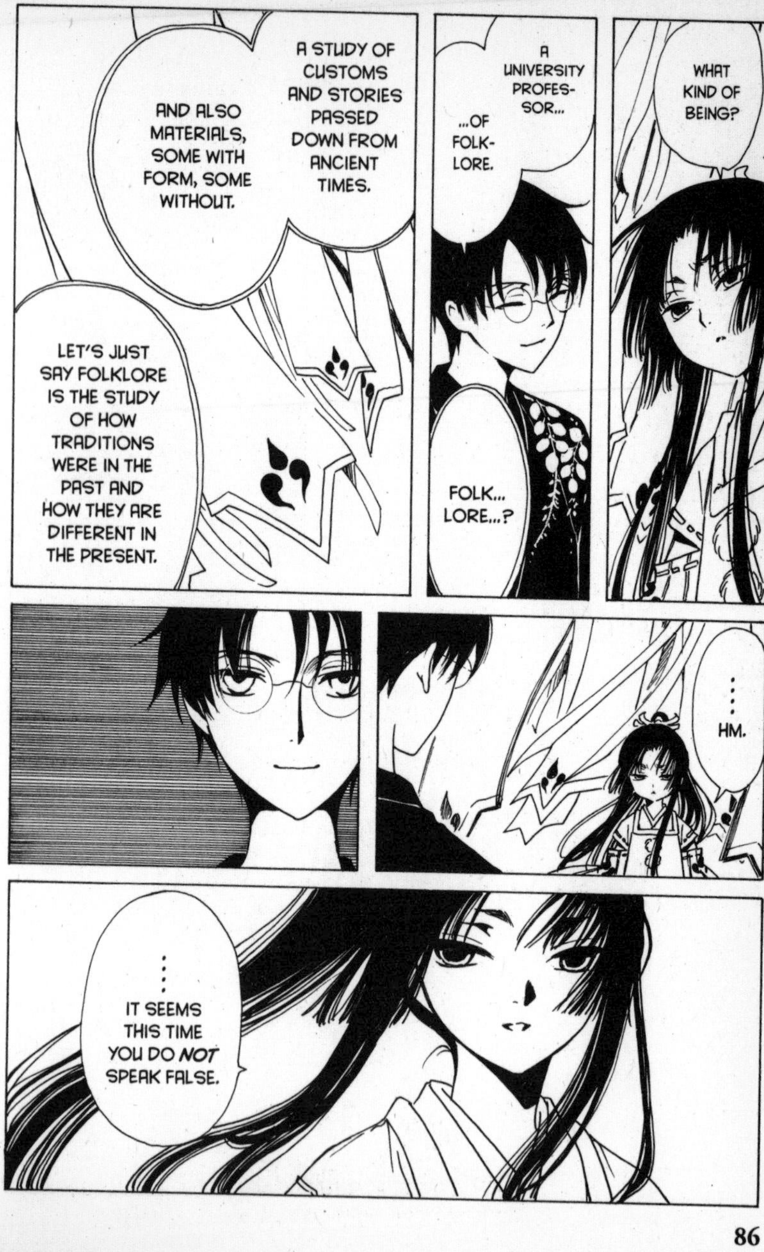
WHAT KIND OF BEING?
A UNIVERSITY PROFESSOR...
...OF FOLKLORE.
FOLK... LORE...?
A STUDY OF CUSTOMS AND STORIES PASSED DOWN FROM ANCIENT TIMES.
AND ALSO MATERIALS, SOME WITH FORM, SOME WITHOUT.
LET'S JUST SAY FOLKLORE IS THE STUDY OF HOW TRADITIONS WERE IN THE PAST AND HOW THEY ARE DIFFERENT IN THE PRESENT.
.... HM.
.... IT SEEMS THIS TIME YOU DO *NOT* SPEAK FALSE.

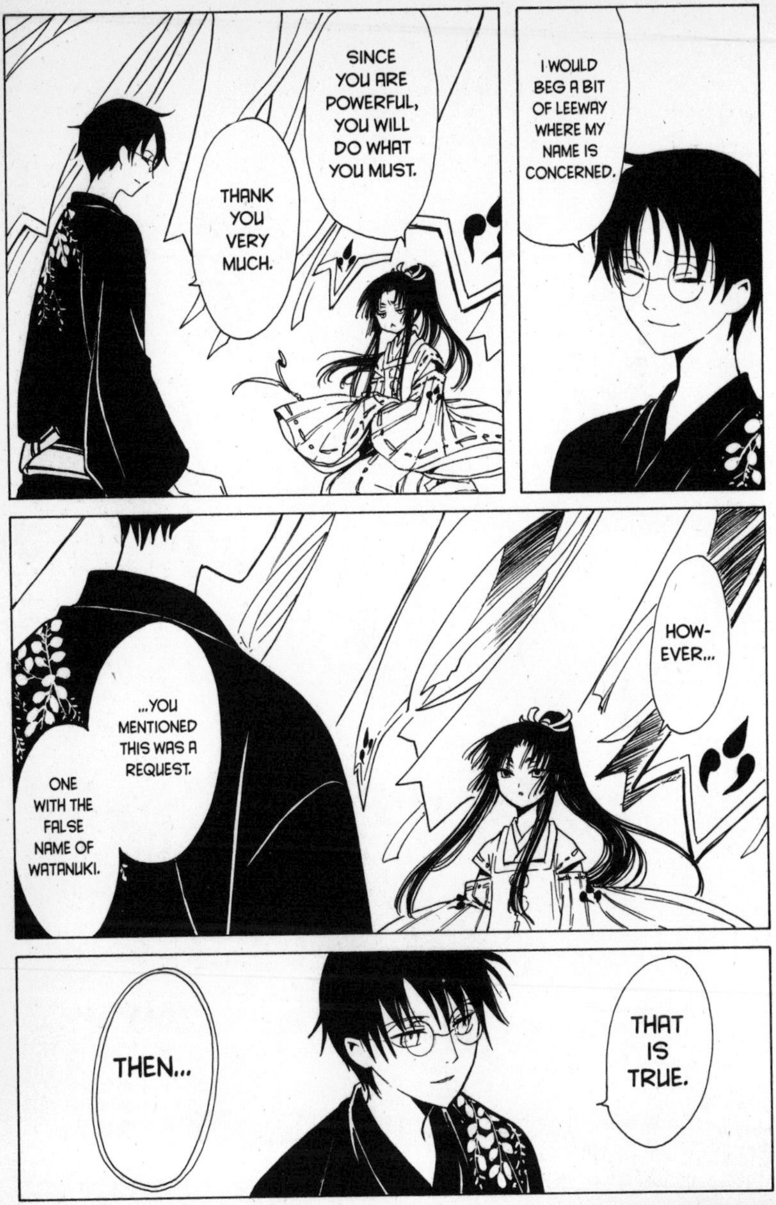
I WOULD BEG A BIT OF LEEWAY WHERE MY NAME IS CONCERNED.
SINCE YOU ARE POWERFUL, YOU WILL DO WHAT YOU MUST.
THANK YOU VERY MUCH.
HOW-EVER...
...YOU MENTIONED THIS WAS A REQUEST.
ONE WITH THE FALSE NAME OF WATANUKI.
THAT IS TRUE.
THEN...

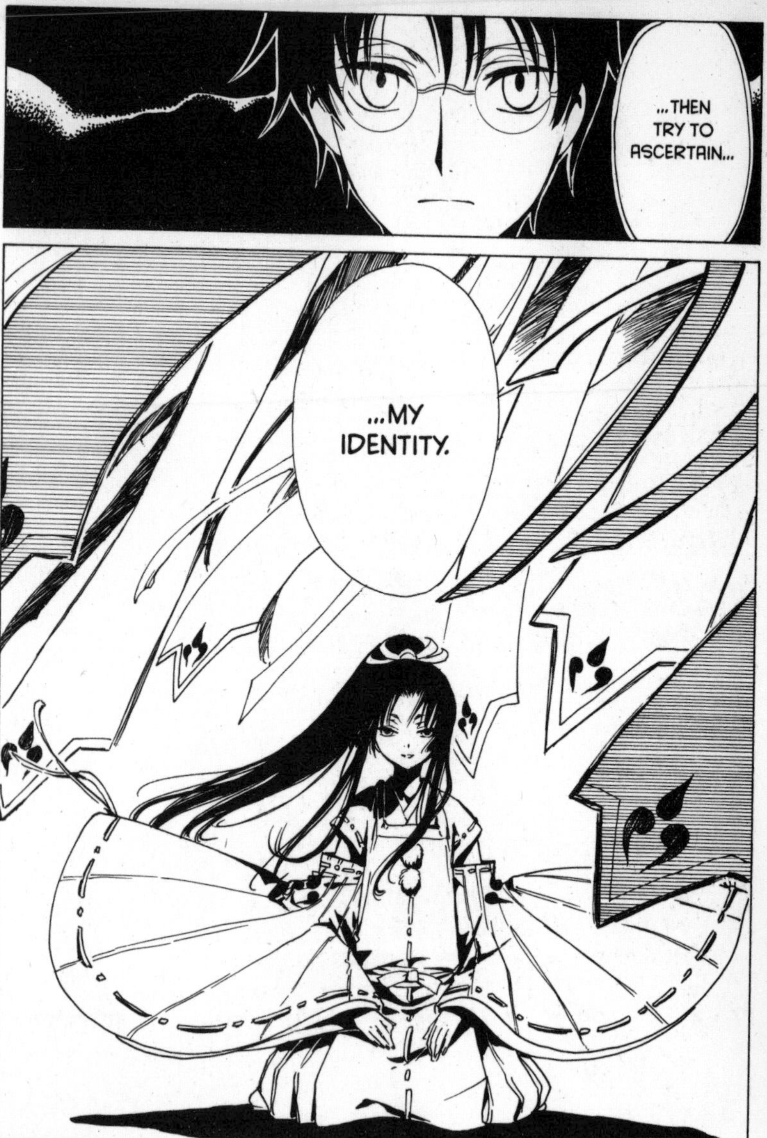
...THEN TRY TO ASCERTAIN...
...MY IDENTITY.

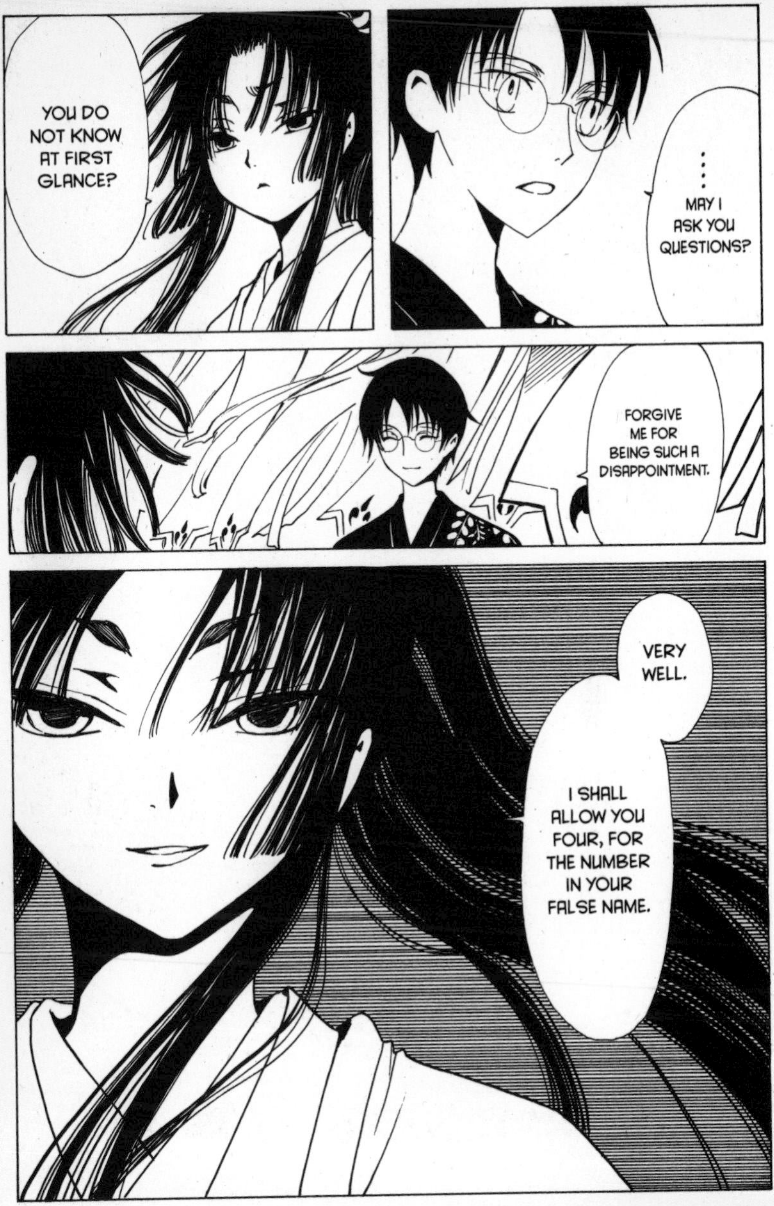

..... MAY I ASK YOU QUESTIONS?
YOU DO NOT KNOW AT FIRST GLANCE?
FORGIVE ME FOR BEING SUCH A DISAPPOINTMENT.
VERY WELL.
I SHALL ALLOW YOU FOUR, FOR THE NUMBER IN YOUR FALSE NAME.

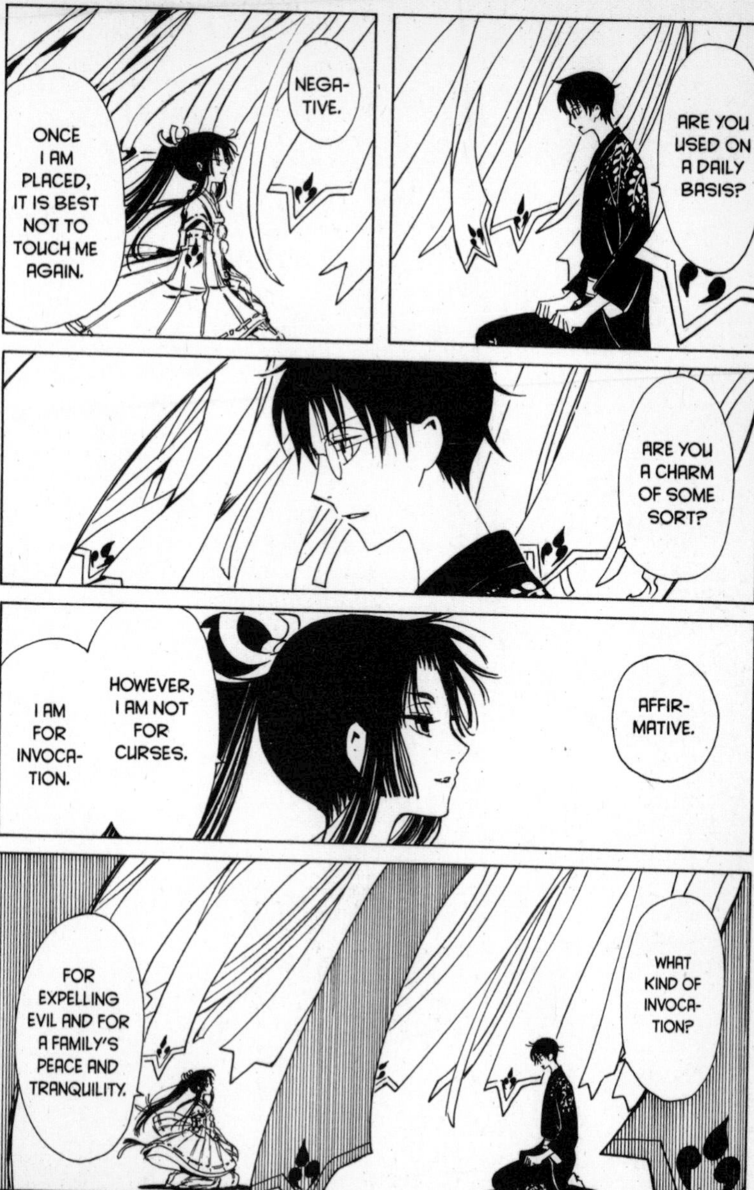
ARE YOU USED ON A DAILY BASIS?
NEGATIVE.
ONCE I AM PLACED, IT IS BEST NOT TO TOUCH ME AGAIN.
ARE YOU A CHARM OF SOME SORT?
AFFIRMATIVE.
HOWEVER, I AM NOT FOR CURSES.
I AM FOR INVOCATION.
WHAT KIND OF INVOCATION?
FOR EXPELLING EVIL AND FOR A FAMILY'S PEACE AND TRANQUILITY.

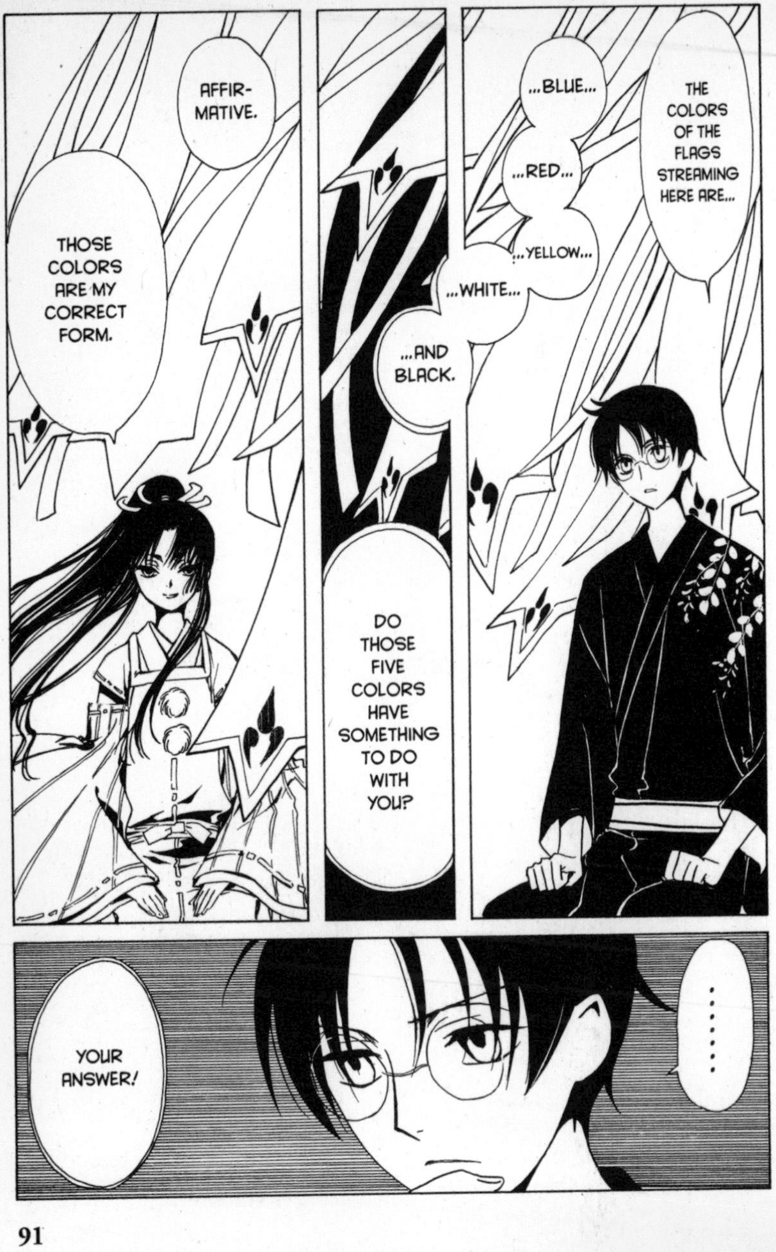
THE COLORS OF THE FLAGS STREAMING HERE ARE...
...BLUE...
...RED...
...YELLOW...
...WHITE...
...AND BLACK.
DO THOSE FIVE COLORS HAVE SOMETHING TO DO WITH YOU?
AFFIRMATIVE.
THOSE COLORS ARE MY CORRECT FORM.
......
YOUR ANSWER!

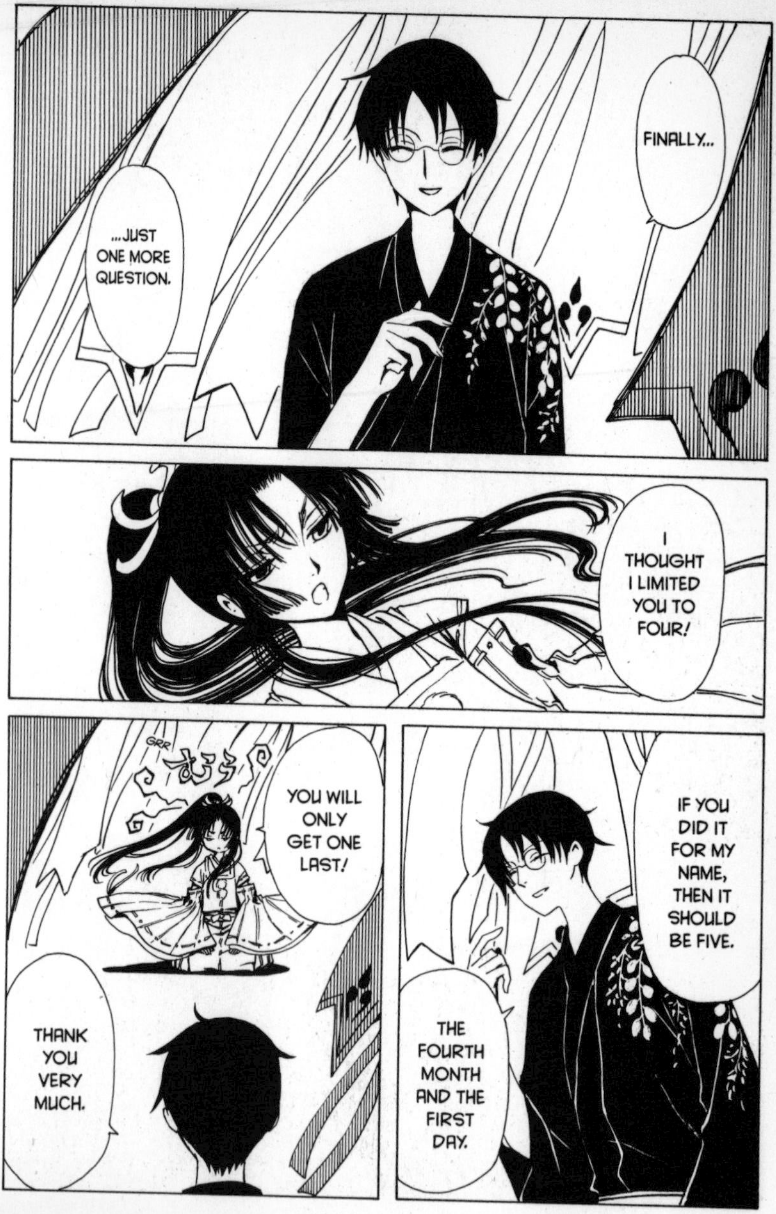
FINALLY...
...JUST ONE MORE QUESTION.
I THOUGHT I LIMITED YOU TO FOUR!
IF YOU DID IT FOR MY NAME, THEN IT SHOULD BE FIVE.
THE FOURTH MONTH AND THE FIRST DAY.
GRR
YOU WILL ONLY GET ONE LAST!
THANK YOU VERY MUCH.

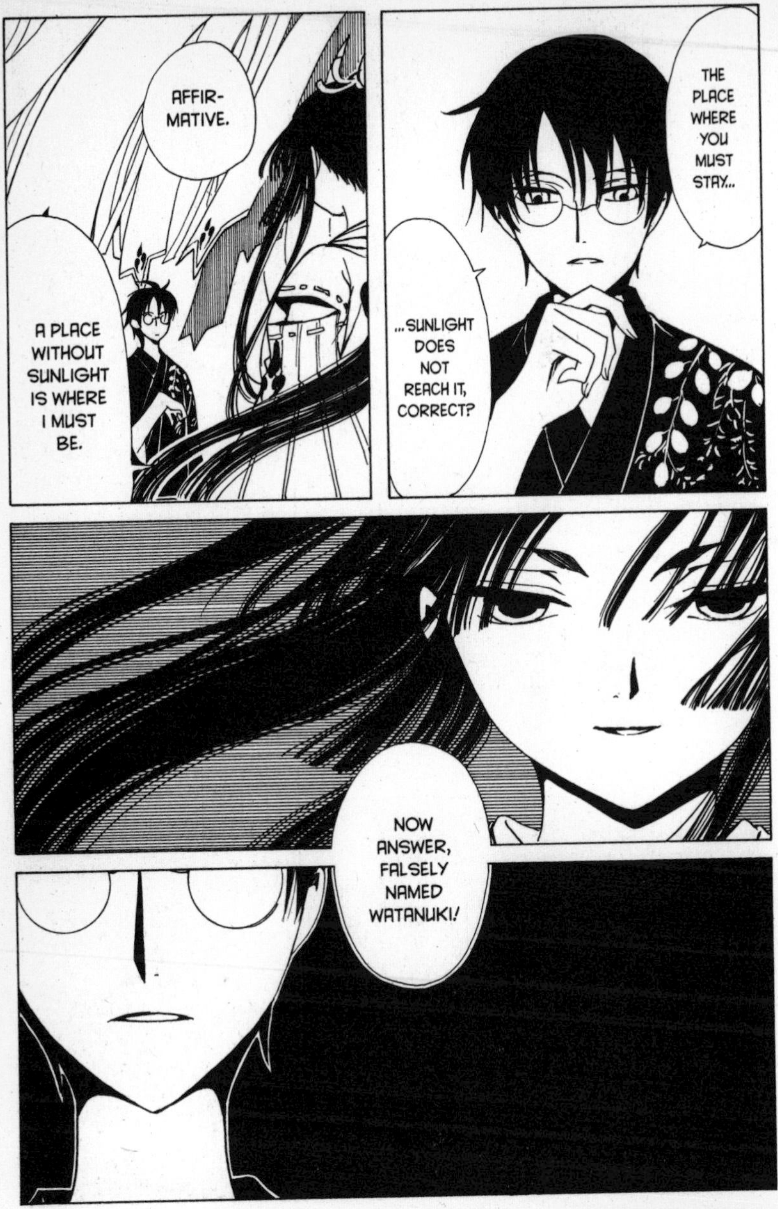
THE PLACE WHERE YOU MUST STAY...
...SUNLIGHT DOES NOT REACH IT, CORRECT?
AFFIRMATIVE.
A PLACE WITHOUT SUNLIGHT IS WHERE I MUST BE.
NOW ANSWER, FALSELY NAMED WATANUKI!

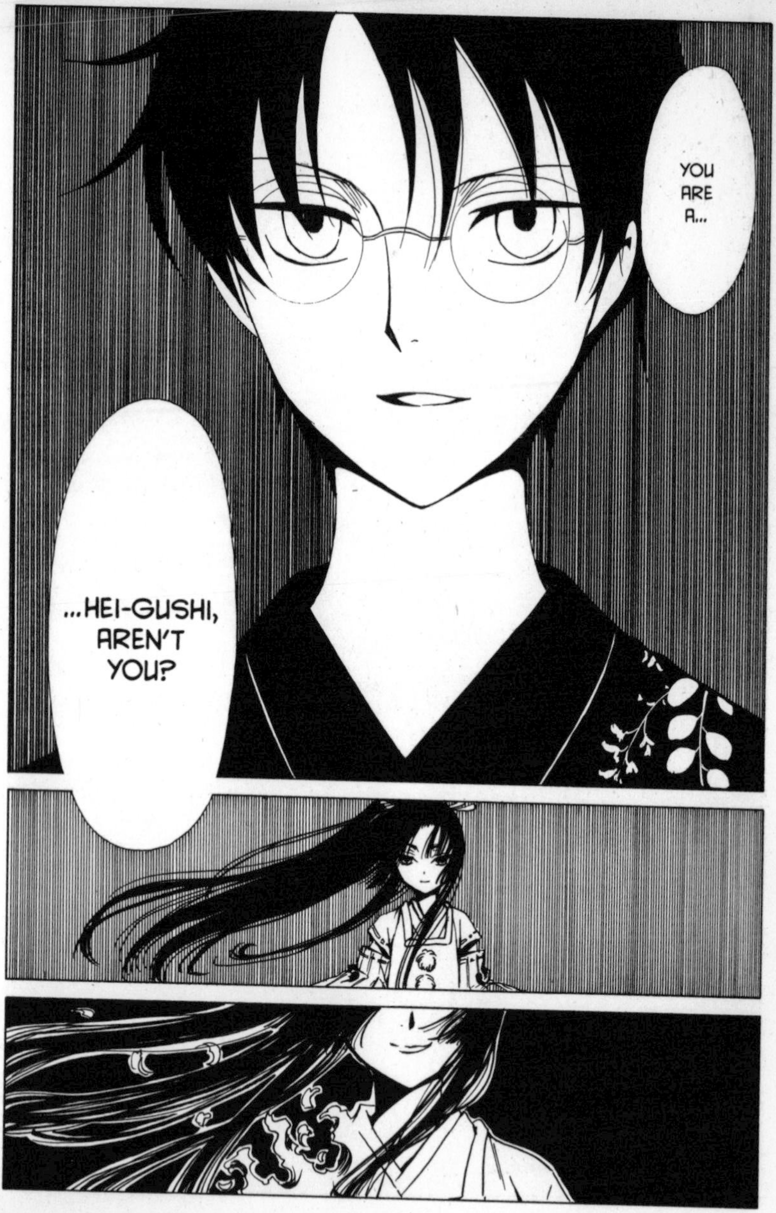
YOU ARE A...
...HEI-GUSHI, AREN'T YOU?

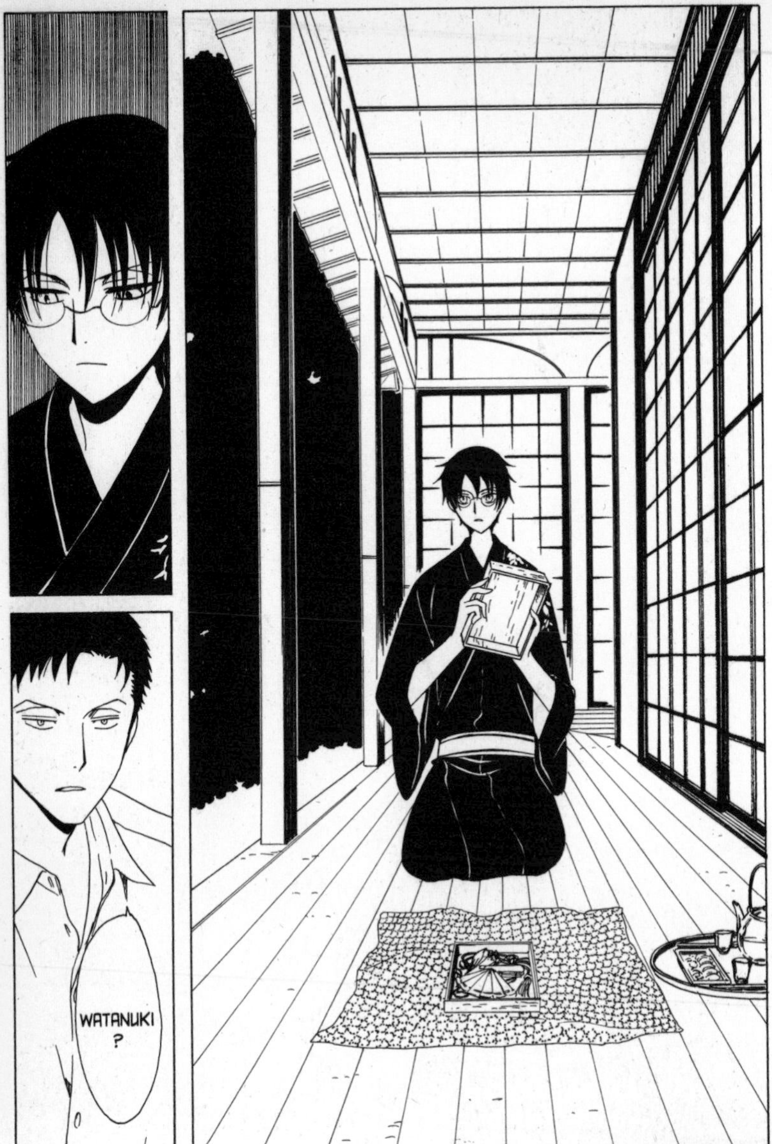
WATANUKI
?

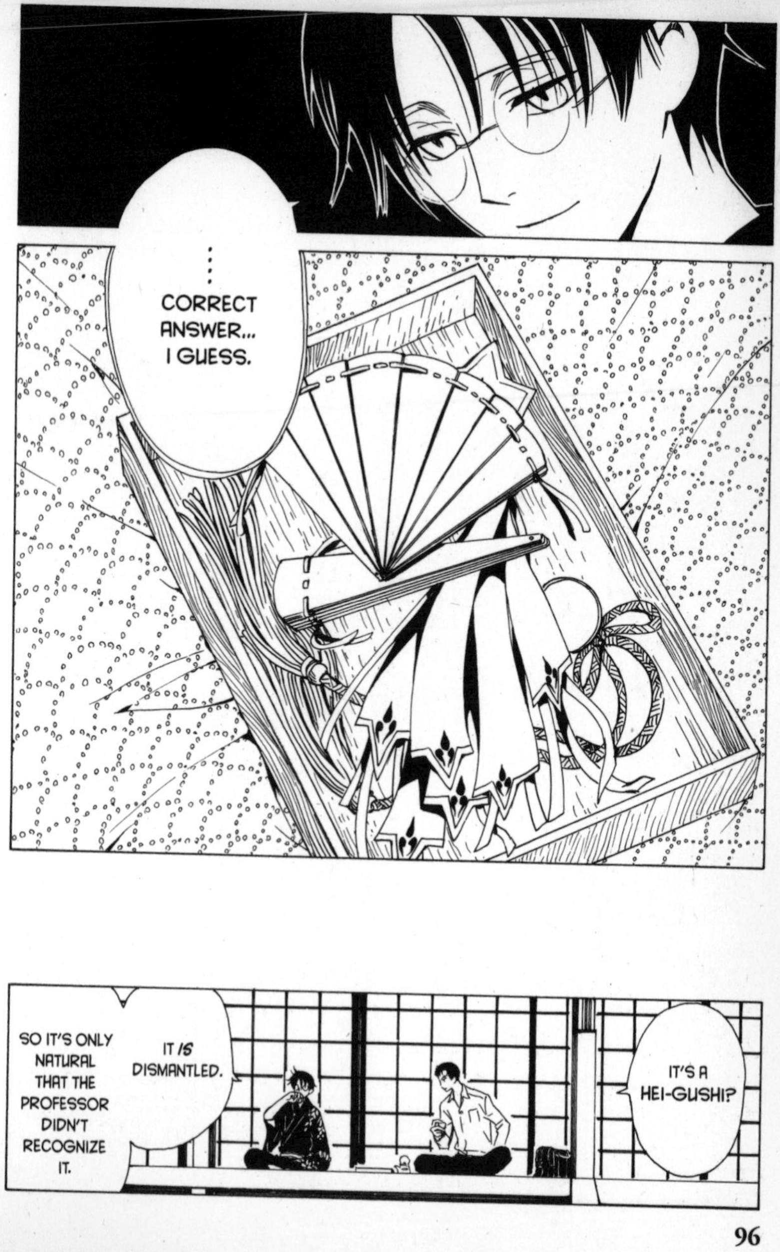
…CORRECT ANSWER… I GUESS.
IT'S A HEI-GUSHI?
IT *IS* DISMANTLED.
SO IT'S ONLY NATURAL THAT THE PROFESSOR DIDN'T RECOGNIZE IT.

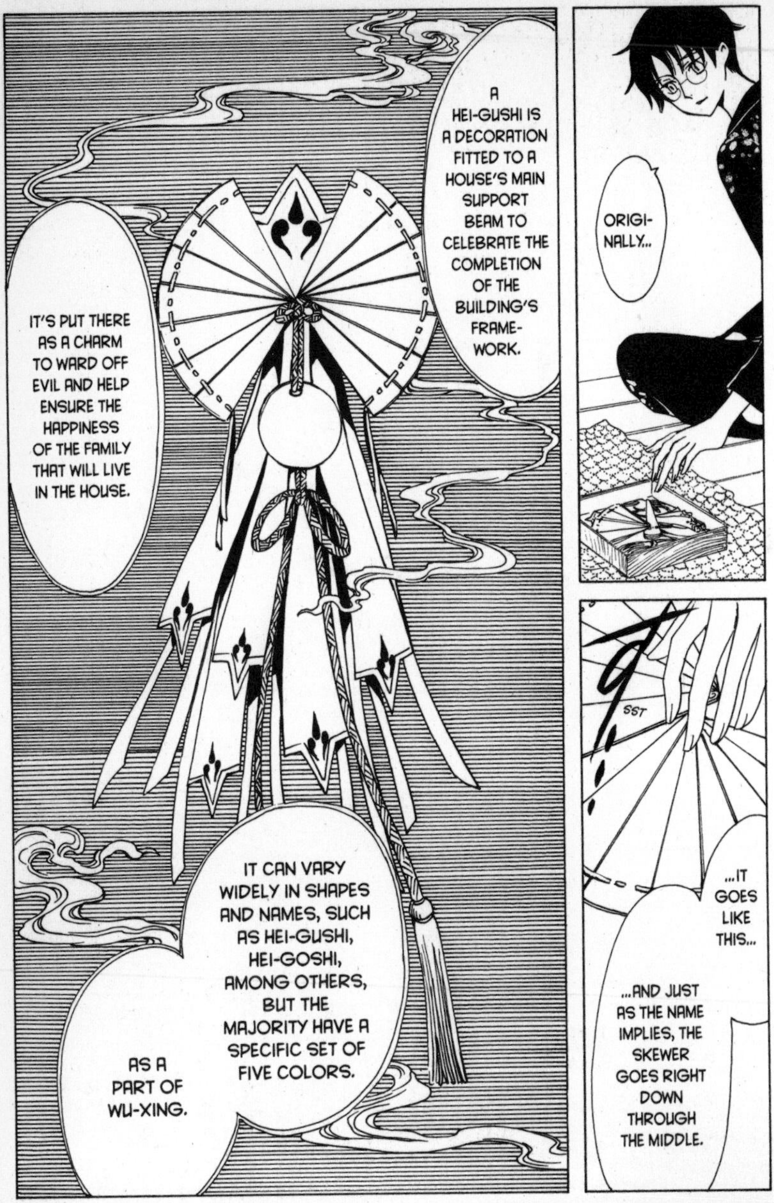
ORIGINALLY...
SST
...IT GOES LIKE THIS...
...AND JUST AS THE NAME IMPLIES, THE SKEWER GOES RIGHT DOWN THROUGH THE MIDDLE.
A HEI-GUSHI IS A DECORATION FITTED TO A HOUSE'S MAIN SUPPORT BEAM TO CELEBRATE THE COMPLETION OF THE BUILDING'S FRAMEWORK.
IT'S PUT THERE AS A CHARM TO WARD OFF EVIL AND HELP ENSURE THE HAPPINESS OF THE FAMILY THAT WILL LIVE IN THE HOUSE.
IT CAN VARY WIDELY IN SHAPES AND NAMES, SUCH AS HEI-GUSHI, HEI-GOSHI, AMONG OTHERS, BUT THE MAJORITY HAVE A SPECIFIC SET OF FIVE COLORS.
AS A PART OF WU-XING.

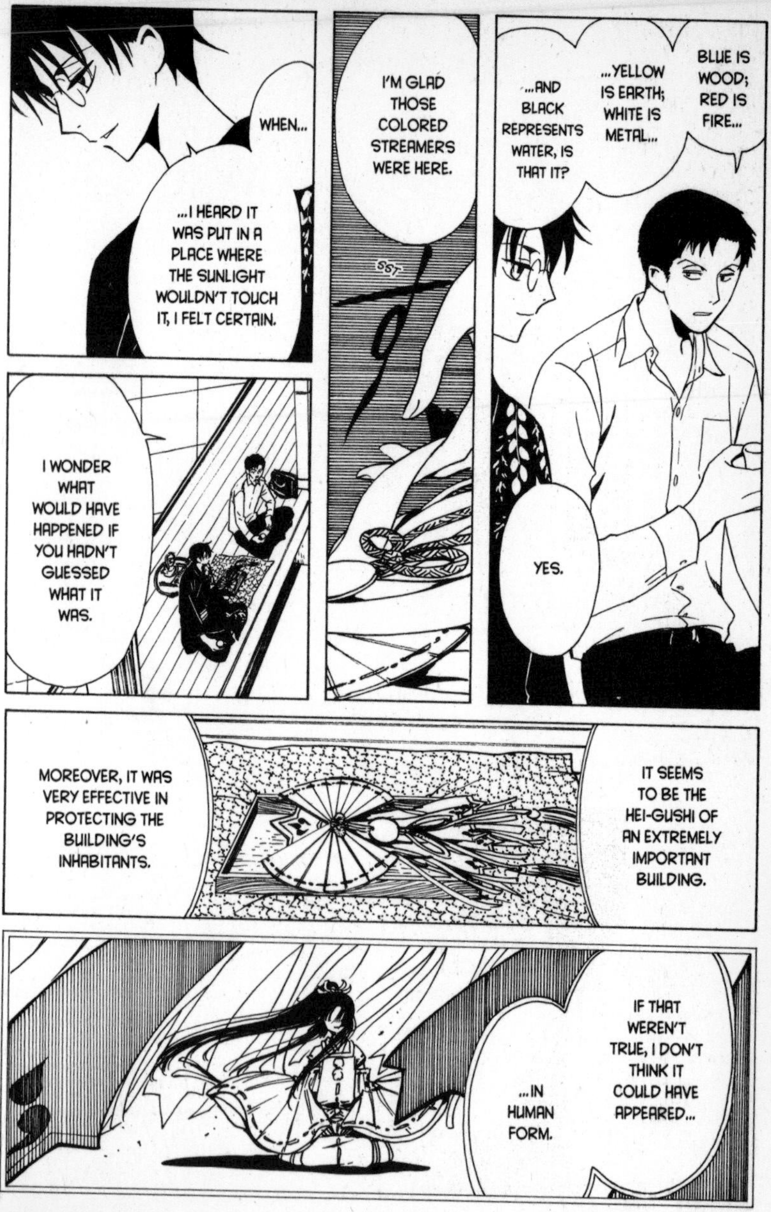
BLUE IS WOOD; RED IS FIRE...
...YELLOW IS EARTH; WHITE IS METAL...
...AND BLACK REPRESENTS WATER, IS THAT IT?
YES.
I'M GLAD THOSE COLORED STREAMERS WERE HERE.
SST
WHEN...
...I HEARD IT WAS PUT IN A PLACE WHERE THE SUNLIGHT WOULDN'T TOUCH IT, I FELT CERTAIN.
I WONDER WHAT WOULD HAVE HAPPENED IF YOU HADN'T GUESSED WHAT IT WAS.
IT SEEMS TO BE THE HEI-GUSHI OF AN EXTREMELY IMPORTANT BUILDING.
MOREOVER, IT WAS VERY EFFECTIVE IN PROTECTING THE BUILDING'S INHABITANTS.
IF THAT WEREN'T TRUE, I DON'T THINK IT COULD HAVE APPEARED...
...IN HUMAN FORM.

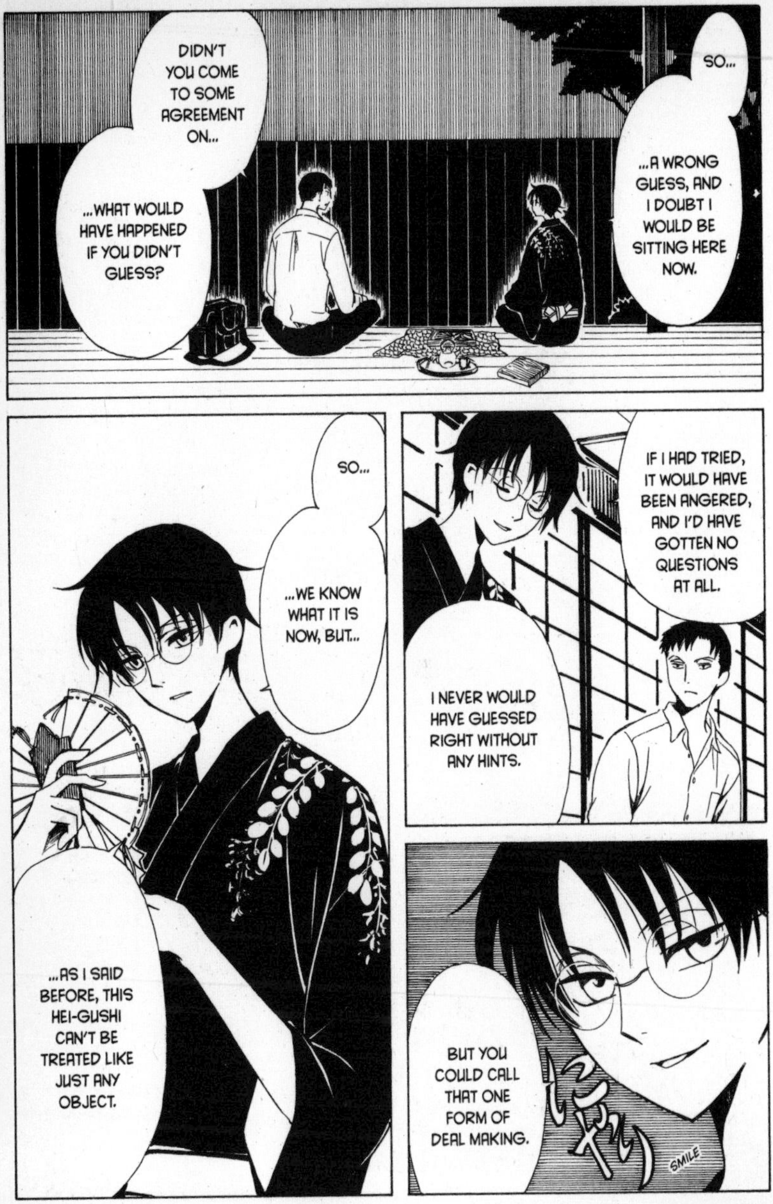
SO...
...A WRONG GUESS, AND I DOUBT I WOULD BE SITTING HERE NOW.
DIDN'T YOU COME TO SOME AGREEMENT ON...
...WHAT WOULD HAVE HAPPENED IF YOU DIDN'T GUESS?
IF I HAD TRIED, IT WOULD HAVE BEEN ANGERED, AND I'D HAVE GOTTEN NO QUESTIONS AT ALL.
I NEVER WOULD HAVE GUESSED RIGHT WITHOUT ANY HINTS.
BUT YOU COULD CALL THAT ONE FORM OF DEAL MAKING.
SMILE
SO...
...WE KNOW WHAT IT IS NOW, BUT...
...AS I SAID BEFORE, THIS HEI-GUSHI CAN'T BE TREATED LIKE JUST ANY OBJECT.

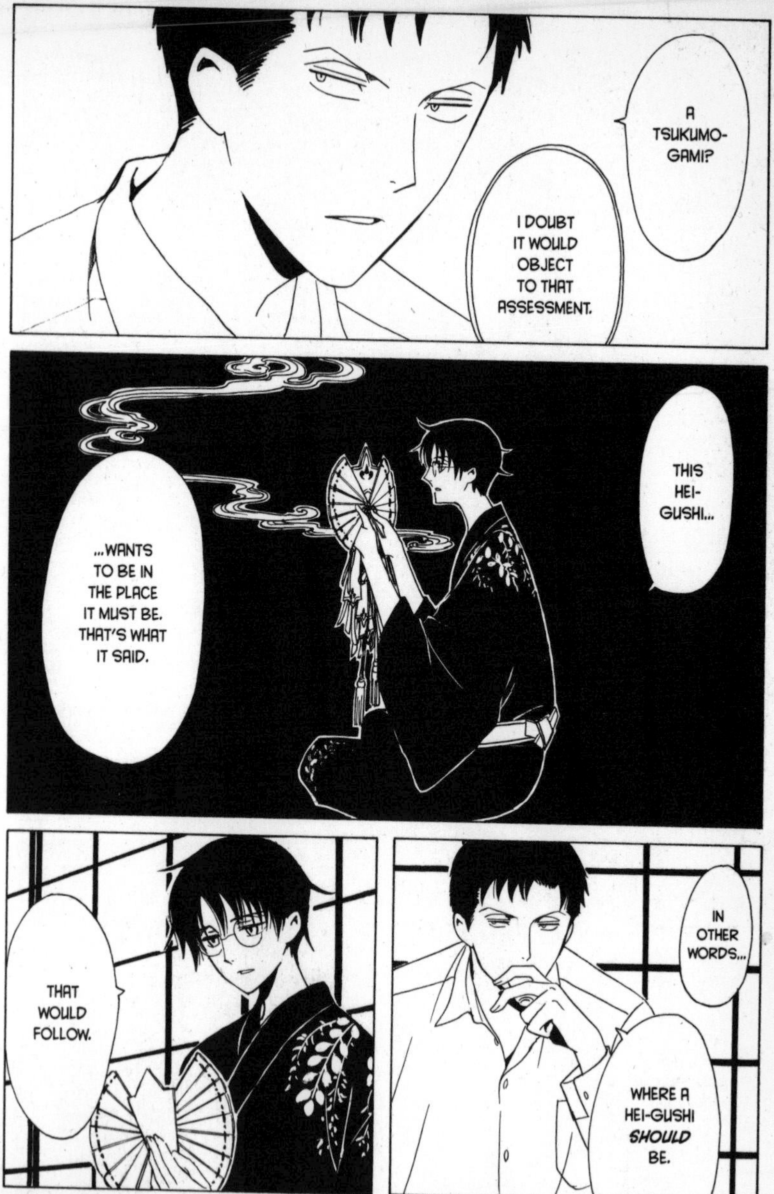
A TSUKUMO-GAMI?
I DOUBT IT WOULD OBJECT TO THAT ASSESSMENT.
THIS HEI-GUSHI...
...WANTS TO BE IN THE PLACE IT MUST BE. THAT'S WHAT IT SAID.
IN OTHER WORDS...
WHERE A HEI-GUSHI *SHOULD* BE.
THAT WOULD FOLLOW.

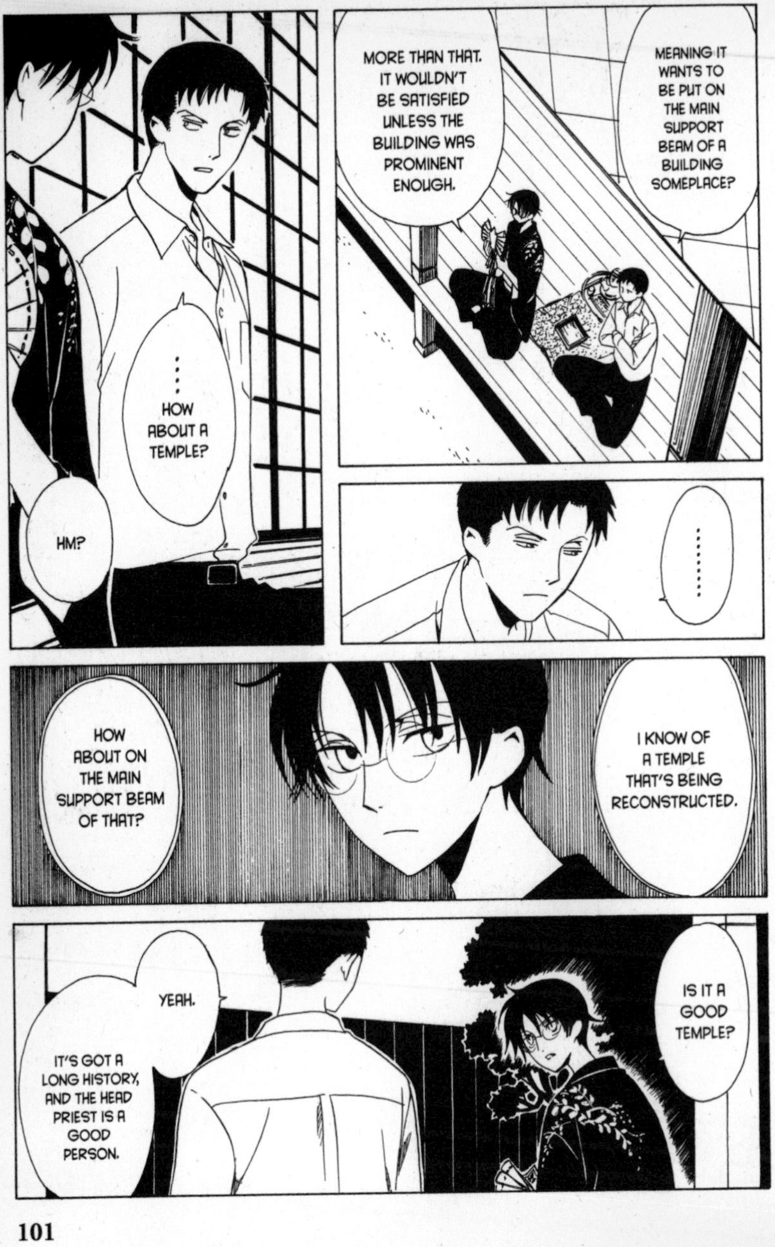
MEANING IT WANTS TO BE PUT ON THE MAIN SUPPORT BEAM OF A BUILDING SOMEPLACE?
MORE THAN THAT. IT WOULDN'T BE SATISFIED UNLESS THE BUILDING WAS PROMINENT ENOUGH.
......
... HOW ABOUT A TEMPLE?
HM?
I KNOW OF A TEMPLE THAT'S BEING RECONSTRUCTED.
HOW ABOUT ON THE MAIN SUPPORT BEAM OF THAT?
IS IT A GOOD TEMPLE?
YEAH.
IT'S GOT A LONG HISTORY, AND THE HEAD PRIEST IS A GOOD PERSON.

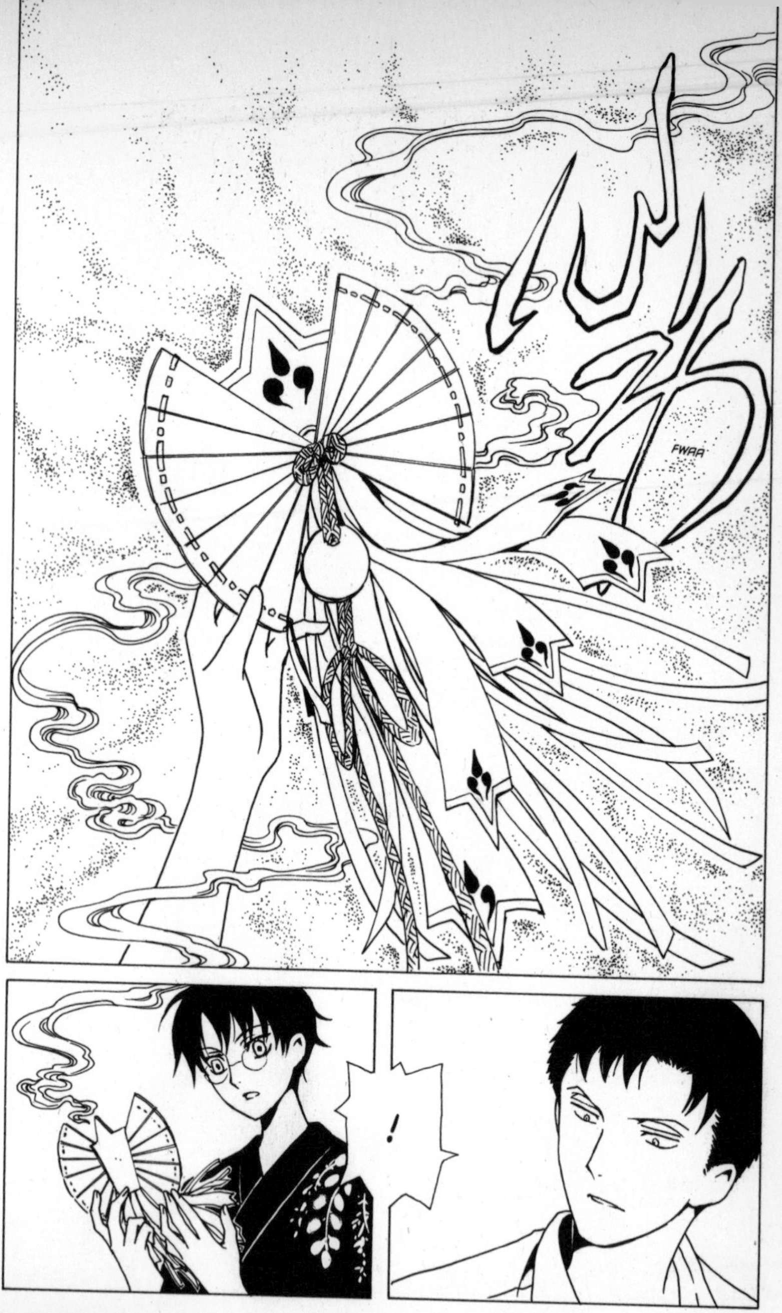
FWAA
!

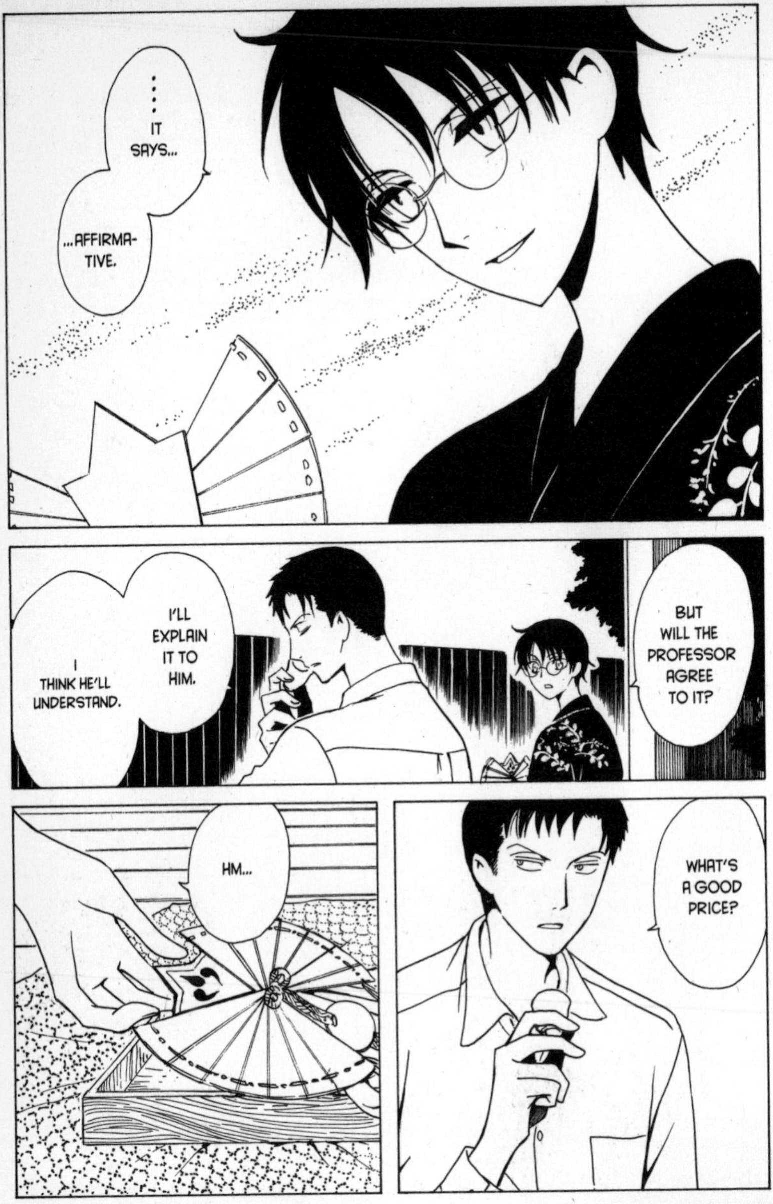
.....
IT SAYS...
...AFFIRMA-TIVE.
BUT WILL THE PROFESSOR AGREE TO IT?
I'LL EXPLAIN IT TO HIM.
I THINK HE'LL UNDERSTAND.
WHAT'S A GOOD PRICE?
HM...

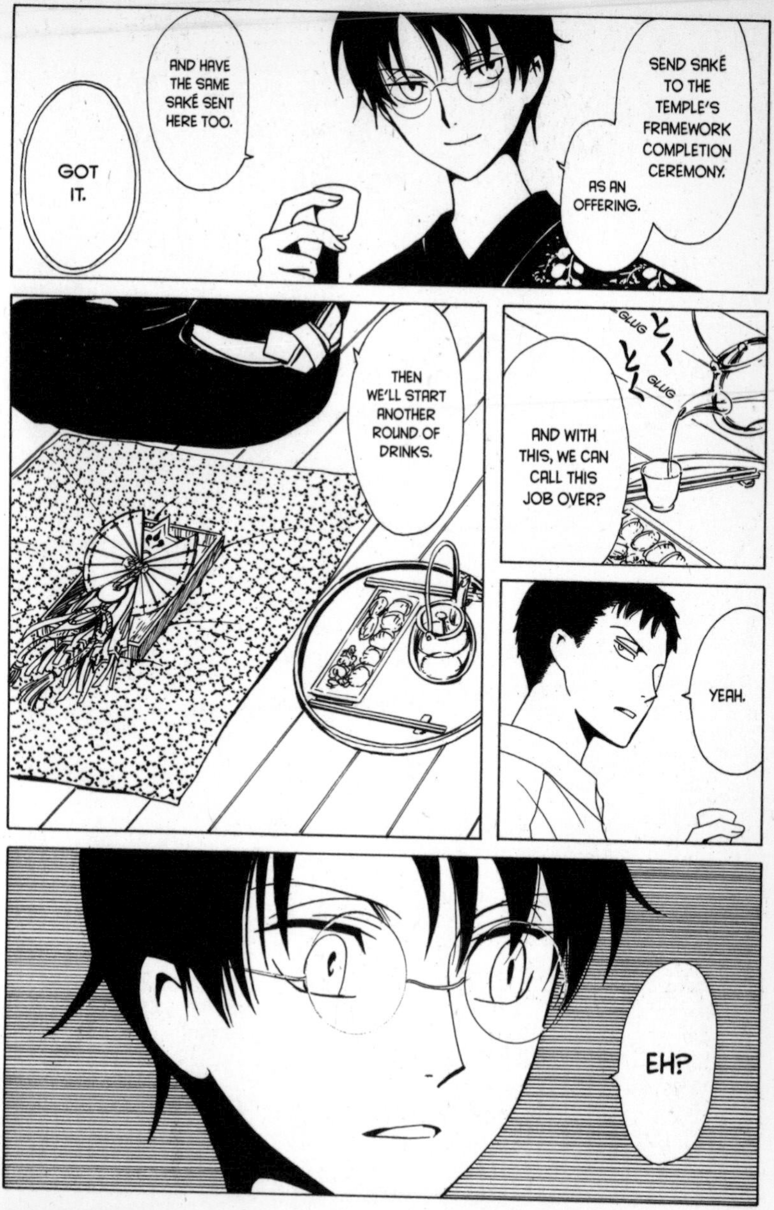
SEND SAKÉ TO THE TEMPLE'S FRAMEWORK COMPLETION CEREMONY.
AS AN OFFERING.
AND HAVE THE SAME SAKÉ SENT HERE TOO.
GOT IT.
GLUG
GLUG
AND WITH THIS, WE CAN CALL THIS JOB OVER?
YEAH.
THEN WE'LL START ANOTHER ROUND OF DRINKS.
EH?

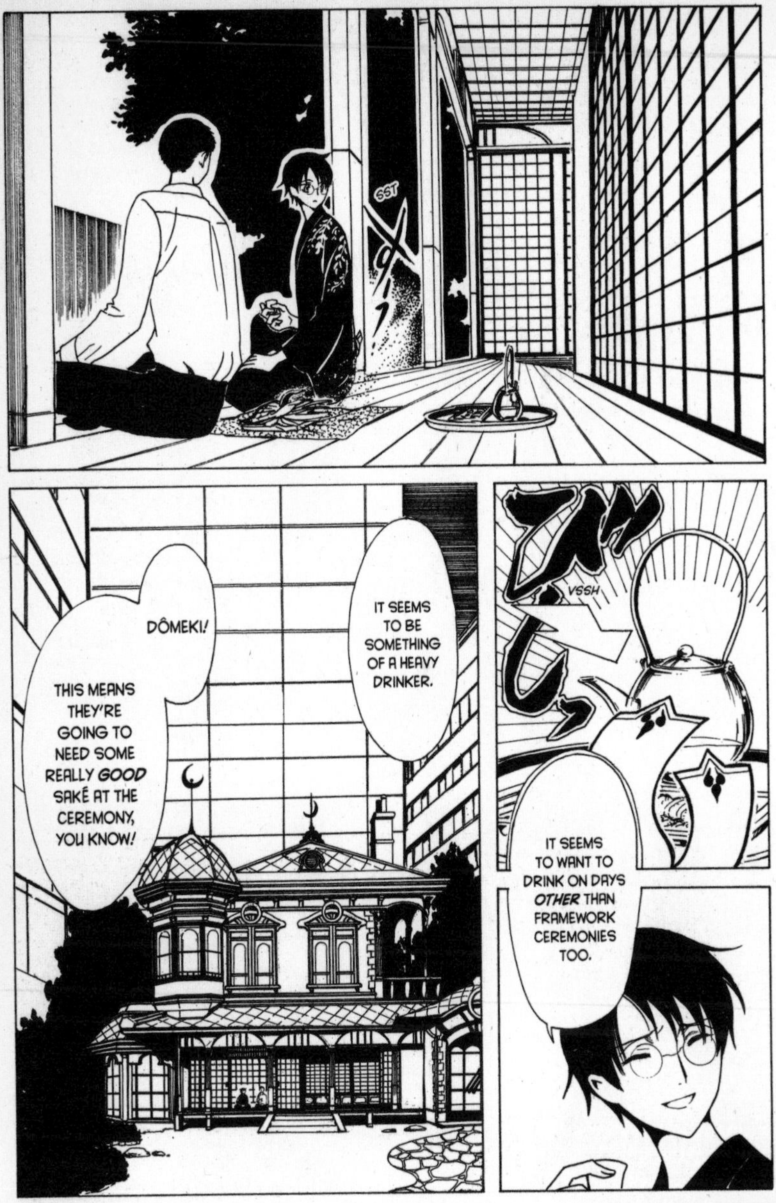
SST
VSSH
IT SEEMS TO WANT TO DRINK ON DAYS *OTHER* THAN FRAMEWORK CEREMONIES TOO.
IT SEEMS TO BE SOMETHING OF A HEAVY DRINKER.
DÔMEKI!
THIS MEANS THEY'RE GOING TO NEED SOME REALLY *GOOD* SAKÉ AT THE CEREMONY, YOU KNOW!

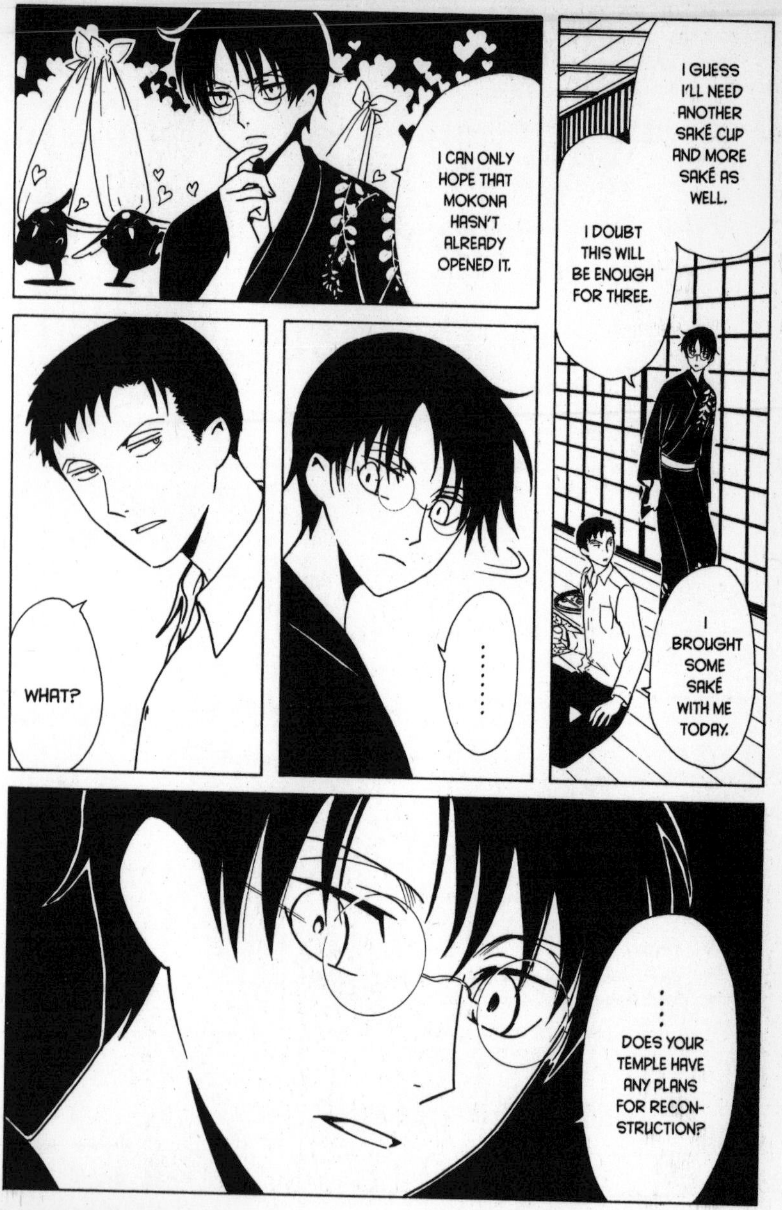
I GUESS I'LL NEED ANOTHER SAKÉ CUP AND MORE SAKÉ AS WELL.
I DOUBT THIS WILL BE ENOUGH FOR THREE.
I BROUGHT SOME SAKÉ WITH ME TODAY.
I CAN ONLY HOPE THAT MOKONA HASN'T ALREADY OPENED IT.
......
WHAT?
... DOES YOUR TEMPLE HAVE ANY PLANS FOR RECON-STRUCTION?

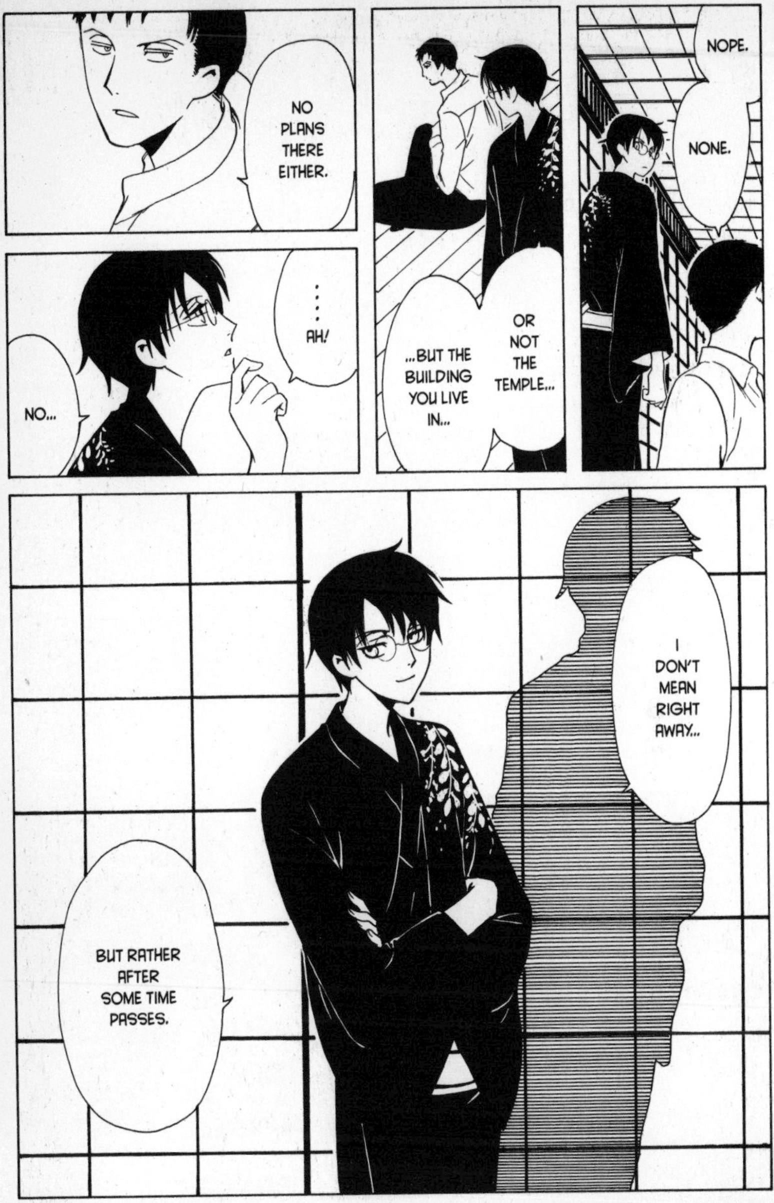
NOPE.
NONE.
OR NOT THE TEMPLE...
...BUT THE BUILDING YOU LIVE IN...
NO PLANS THERE EITHER.
... AH!
NO...
I DON'T MEAN RIGHT AWAY...
BUT RATHER AFTER SOME TIME PASSES.

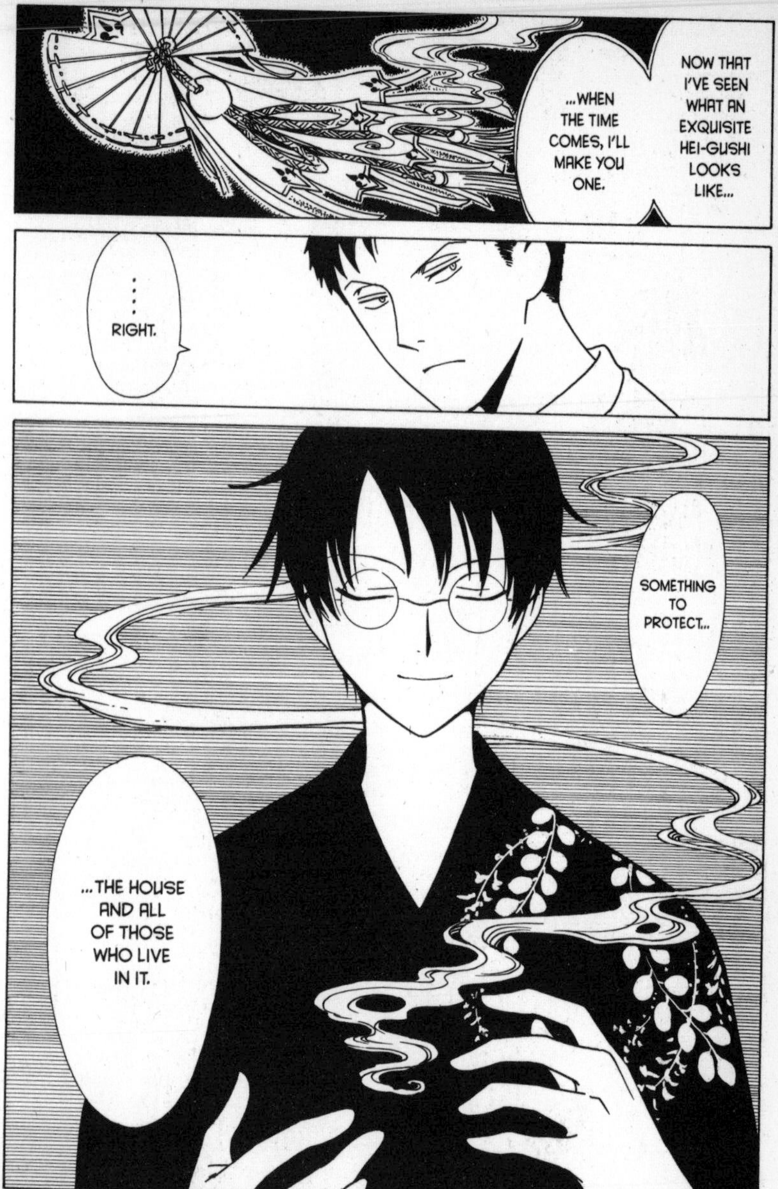
NOW THAT I'VE SEEN WHAT AN EXQUISITE HEI-GUSHI LOOKS LIKE...
...WHEN THE TIME COMES, I'LL MAKE YOU ONE.
.....
RIGHT.
SOMETHING TO PROTECT...
...THE HOUSE AND ALL OF THOSE WHO LIVE IN IT.

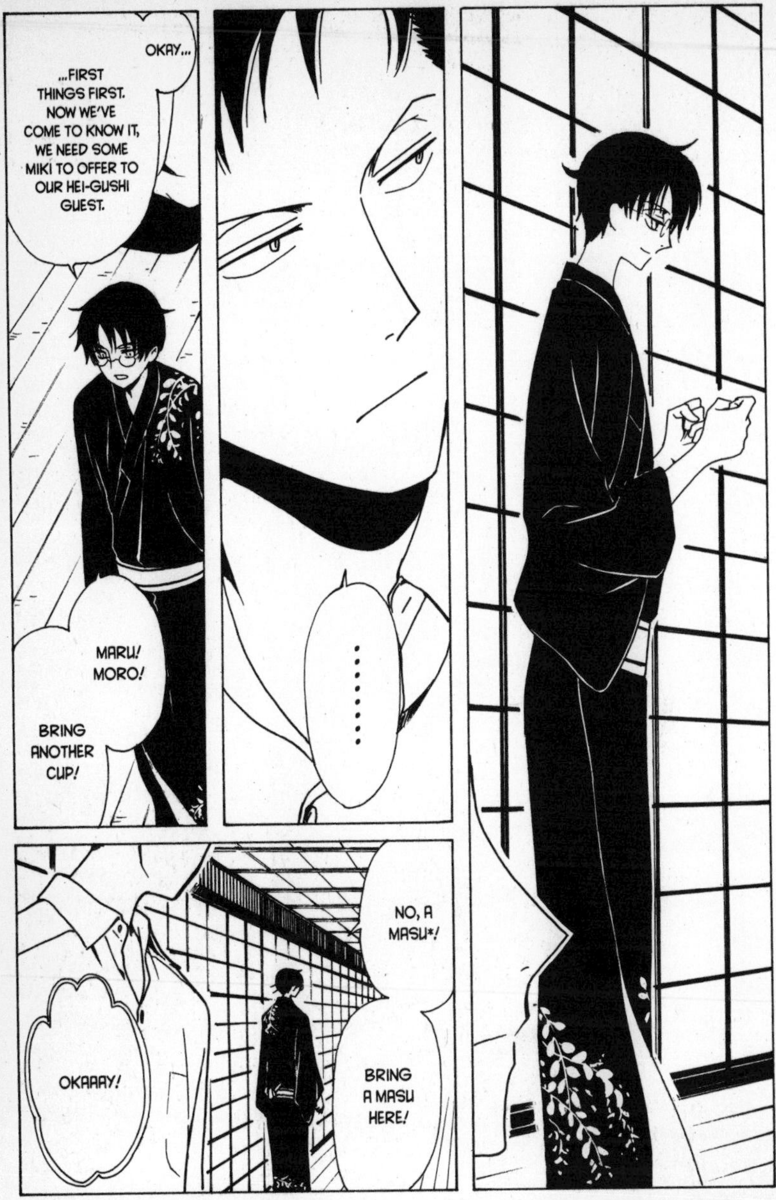
......
OKAY...
...FIRST THINGS FIRST. NOW WE'VE COME TO KNOW IT, WE NEED SOME MIKI TO OFFER TO OUR HEI-GUSHI GUEST.
MARU! MORO!
BRING ANOTHER CUP!
NO, A MASU*!
BRING A MASU HERE!
OKAAAY!

*MASU = 5-LITER MEASURING CUP

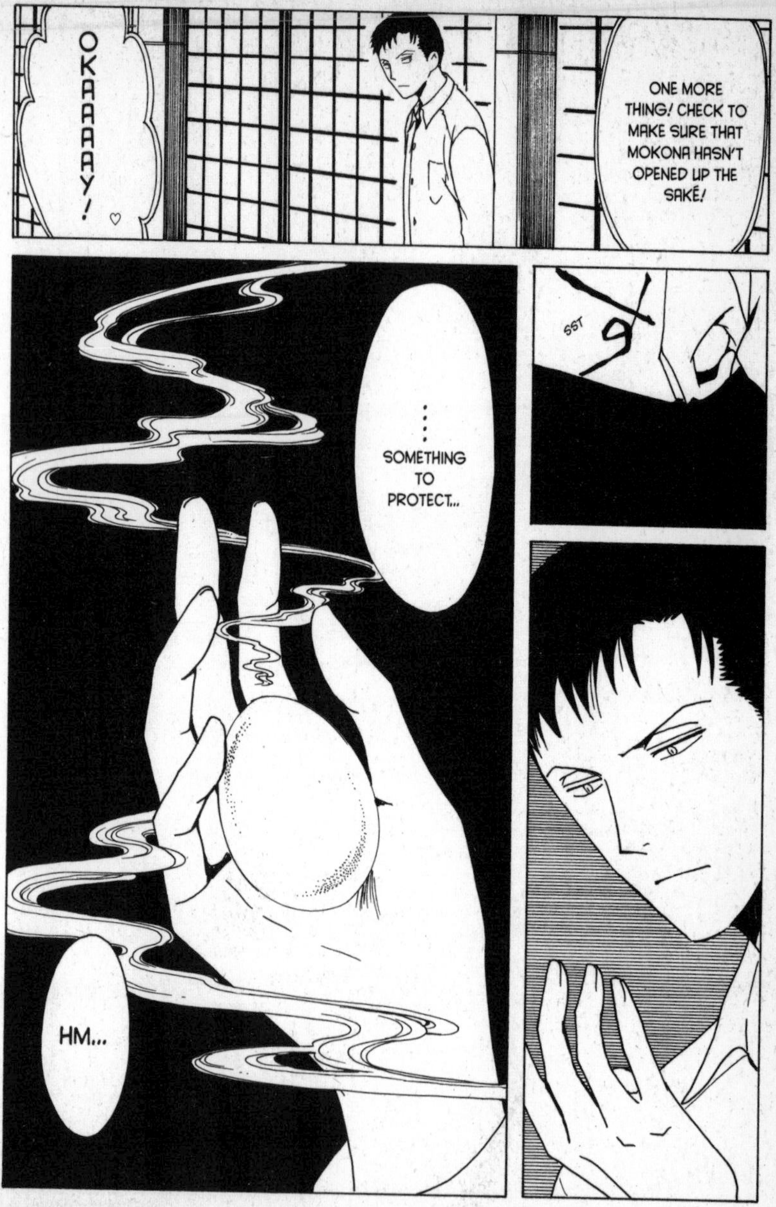
ONE MORE THING! CHECK TO MAKE SURE THAT MOKONA HASN'T OPENED UP THE SAKÉ!
OKAAAAY! ♡
SST
...SOMETHING TO PROTECT...
HM...

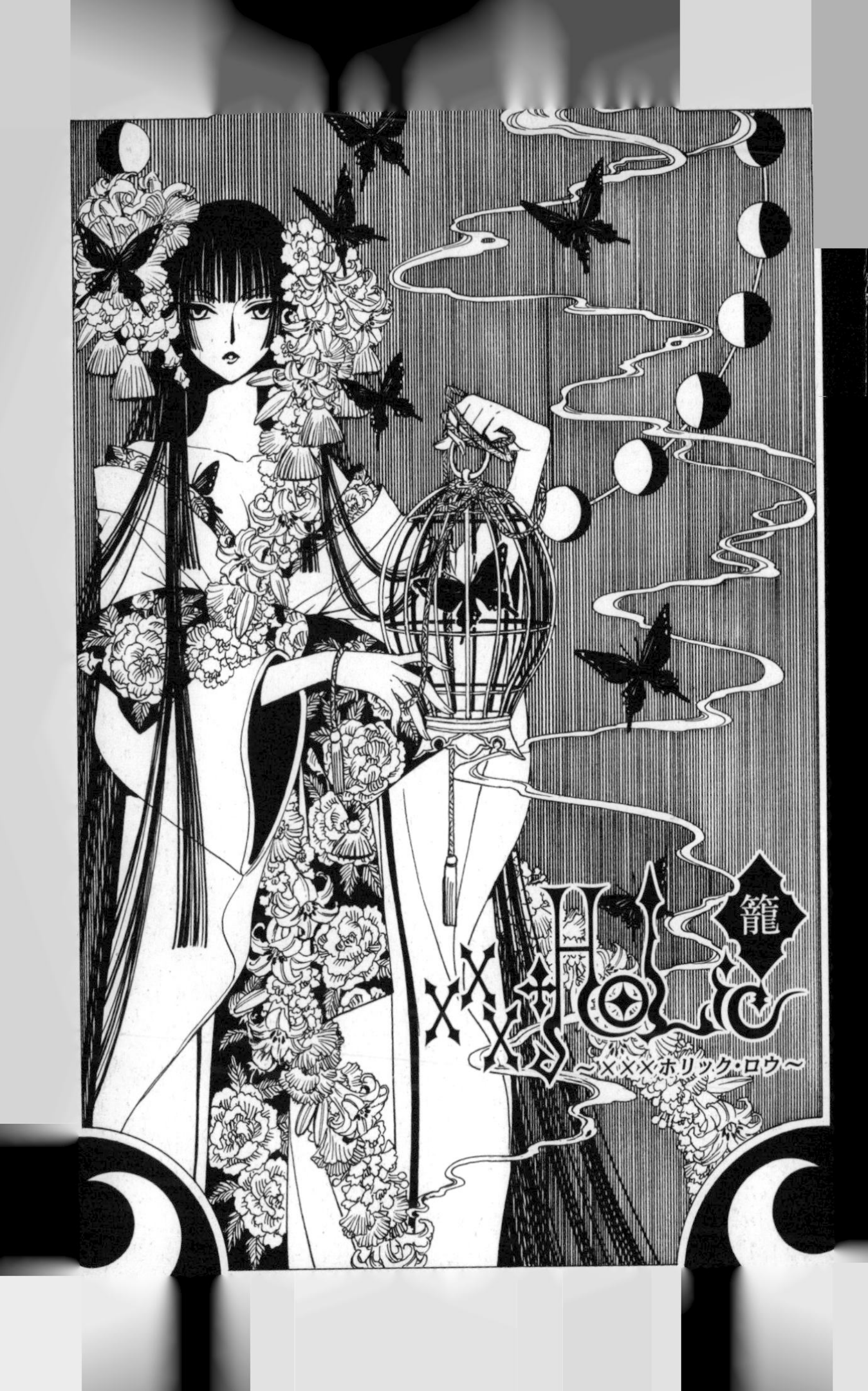
籠
xxxHOLiC
~×××ホリック・ロウ~

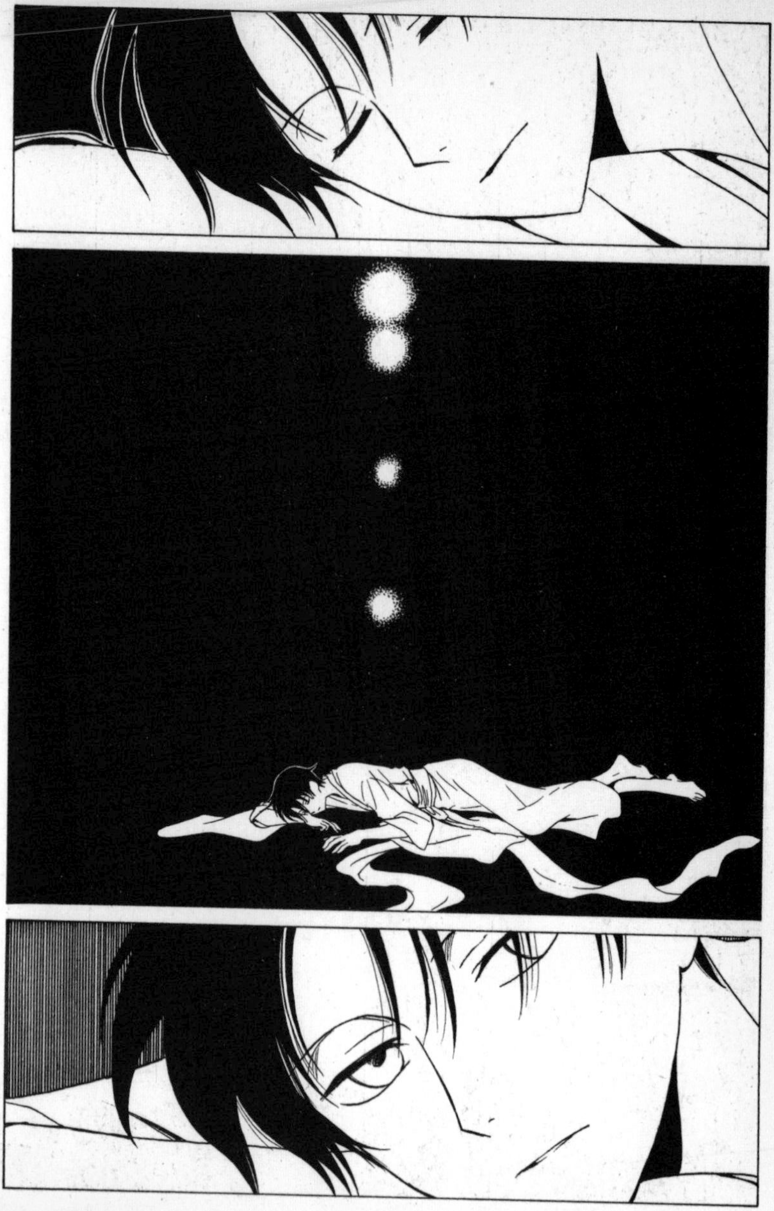

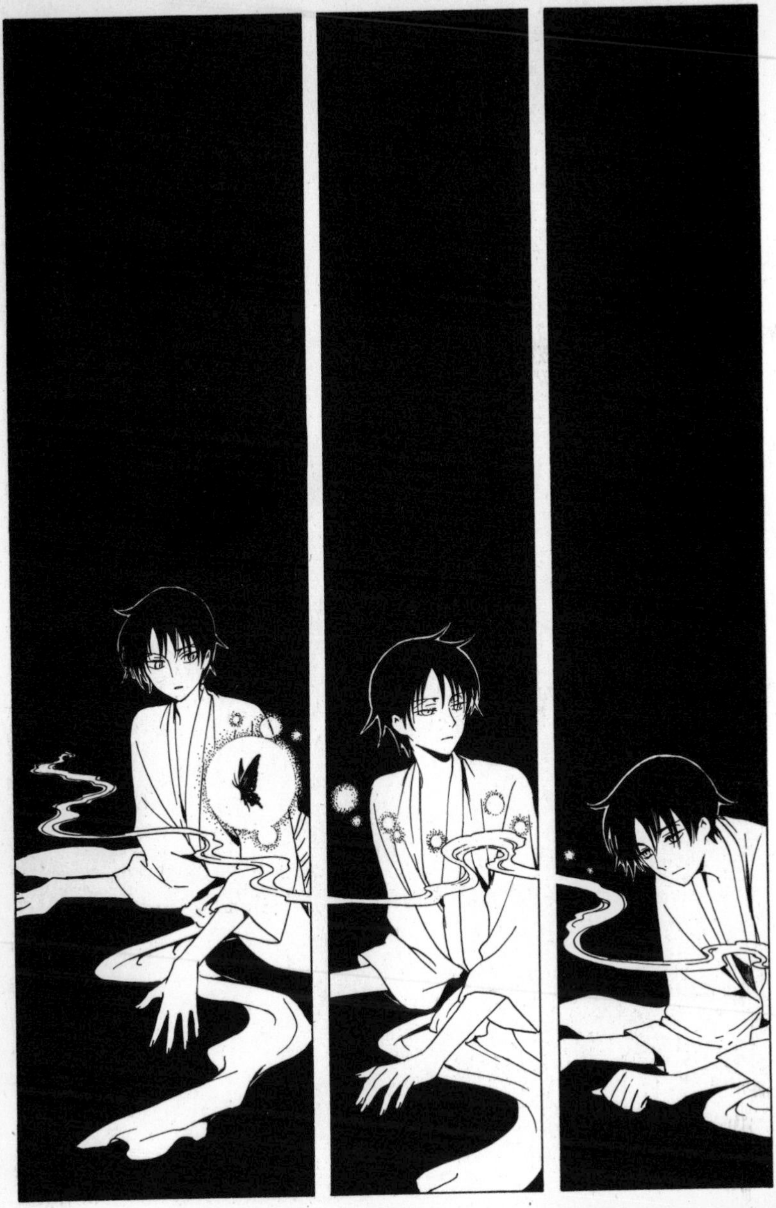

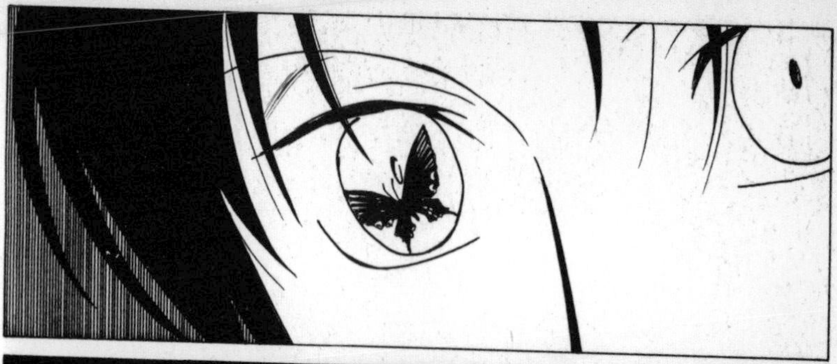
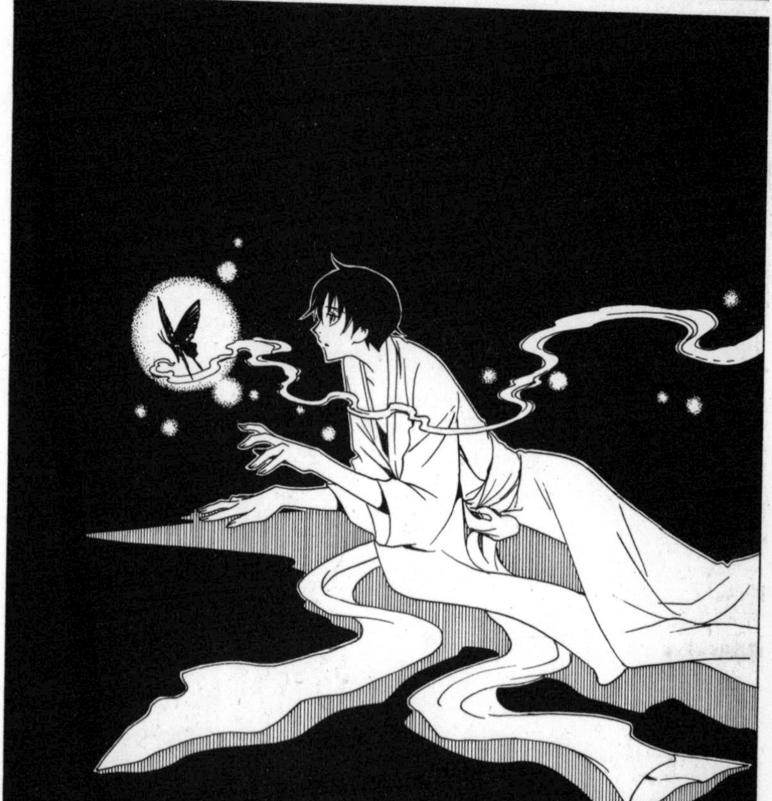

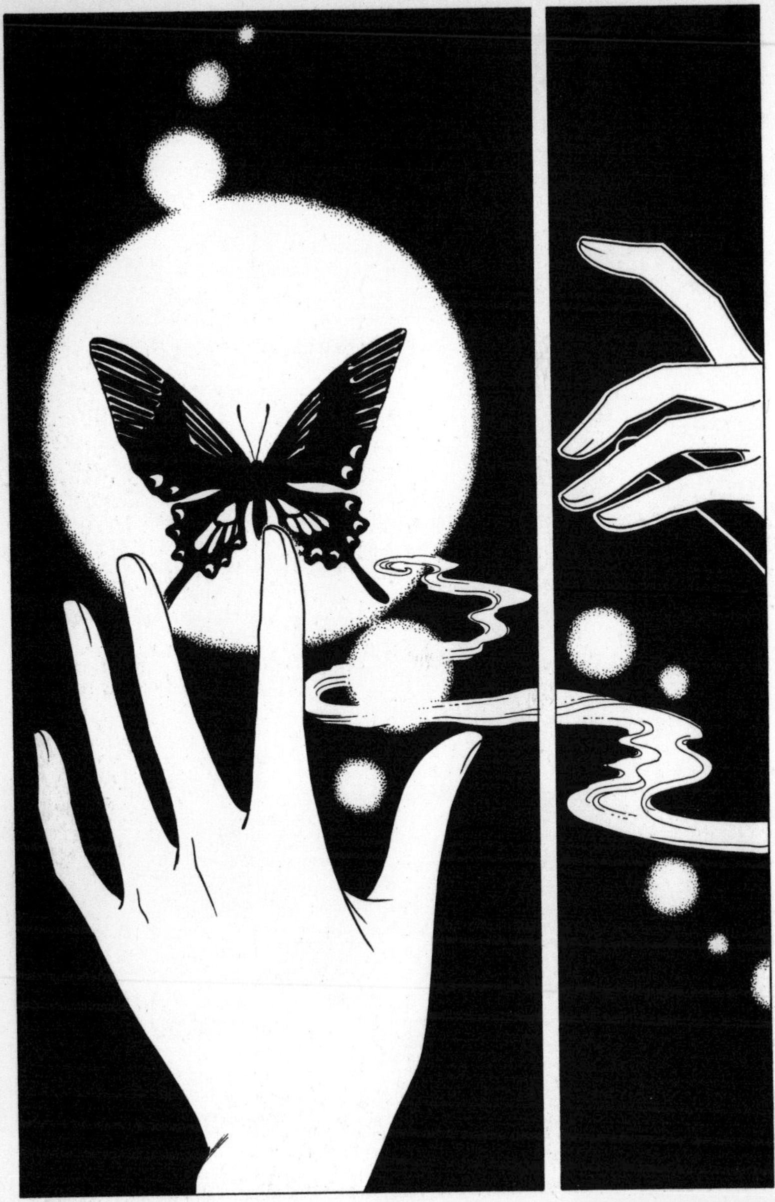

YEAH.

P-R-C-H-K

THAT'S WHEN YOU...

...WOKE UP?

PUT IT IN.

IT'S COOKED.

THOK

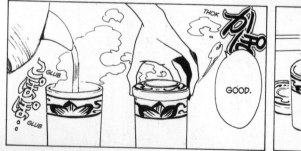

GLUB

GLUB

GOOD.

SST

118

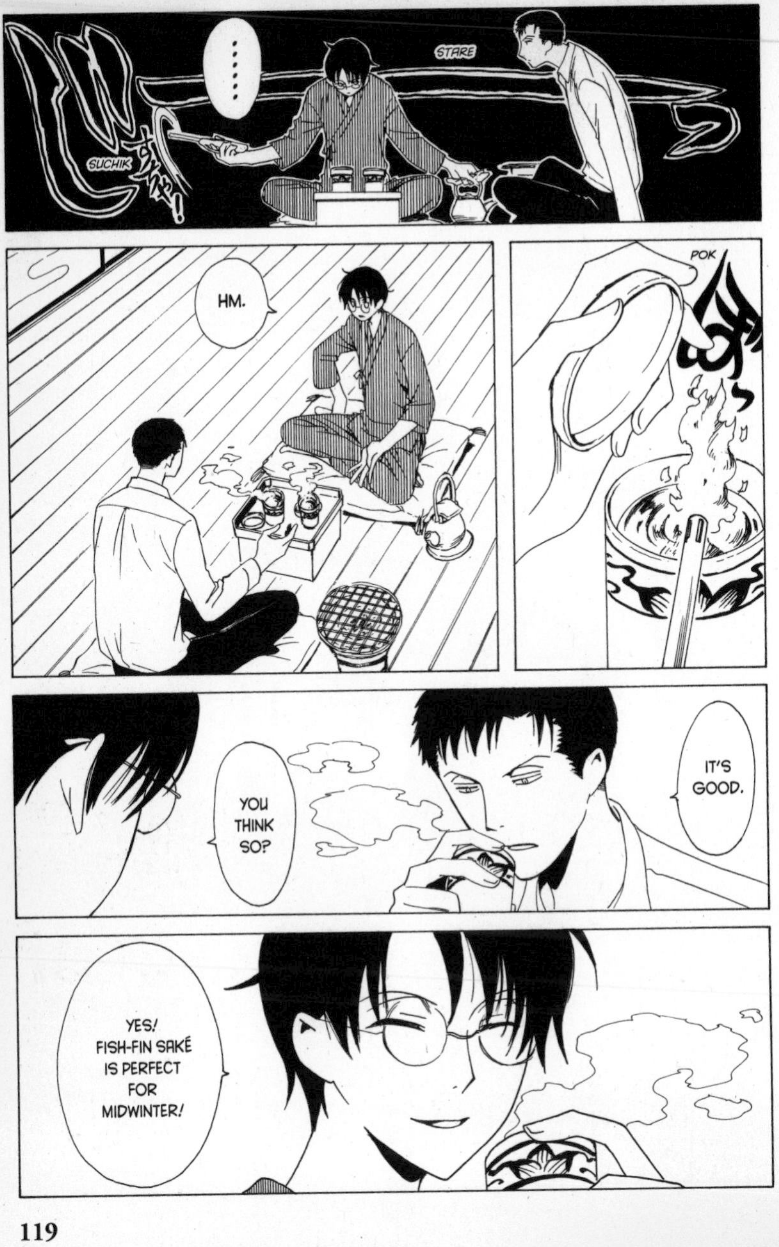
STARE
......
SUCHIK
POK
HM.
IT'S GOOD.
YOU THINK SO?
YES! FISH-FIN SAKÉ IS PERFECT FOR MIDWINTER!

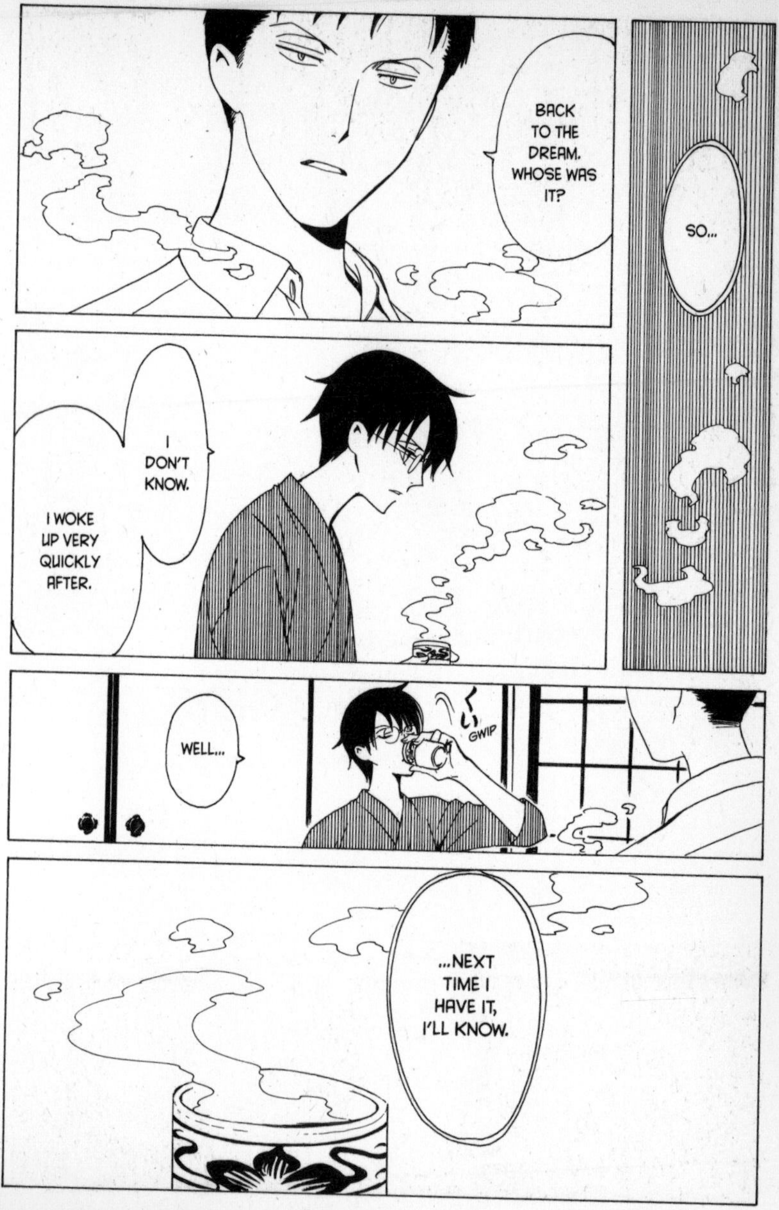
SO...
BACK TO THE DREAM. WHOSE WAS IT?
I DON'T KNOW.
I WOKE UP VERY QUICKLY AFTER.
GWIP
WELL...
...NEXT TIME I HAVE IT, I'LL KNOW.

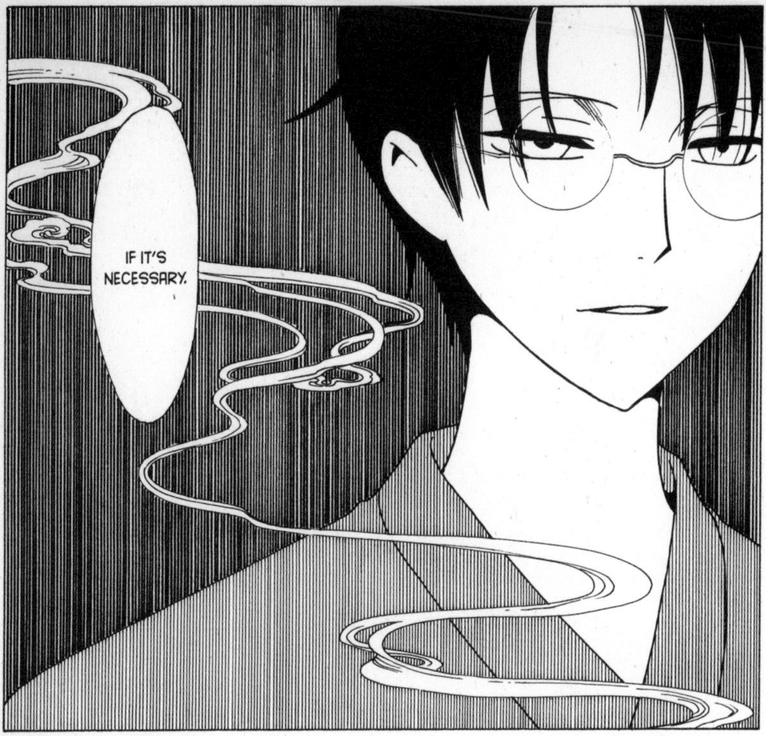
IF IT'S NECESSARY.

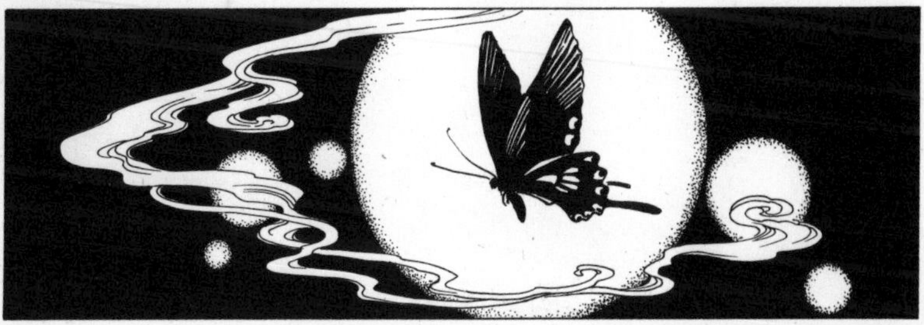

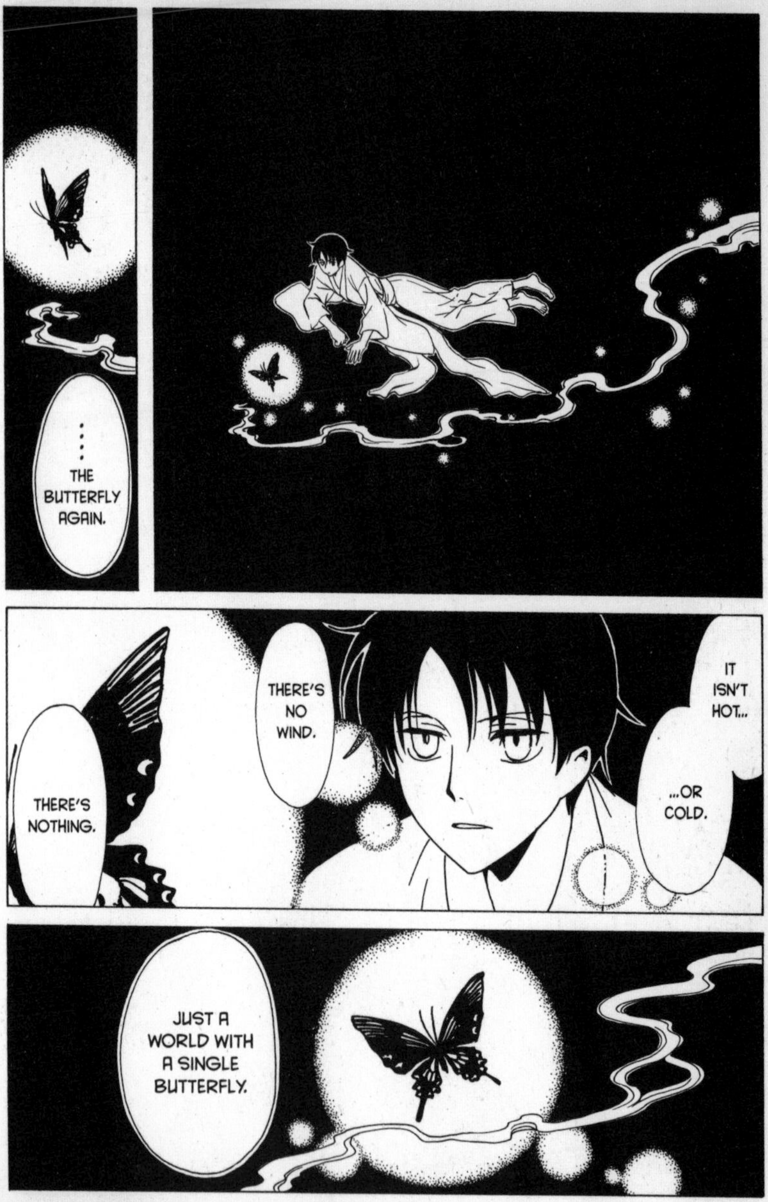
....
THE BUTTERFLY AGAIN.
IT ISN'T HOT...
...OR COLD.
THERE'S NO WIND.
THERE'S NOTHING.
JUST A WORLD WITH A SINGLE BUTTERFLY.

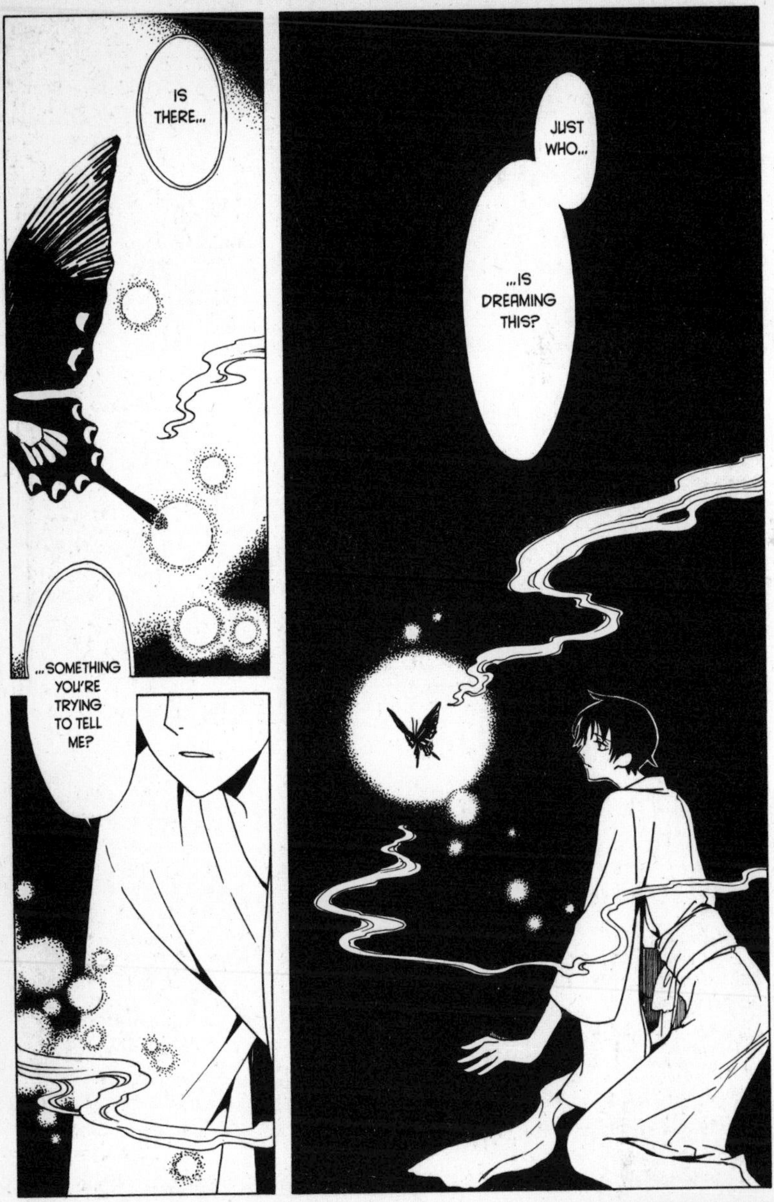
JUST WHO...
...IS DREAMING THIS?
IS THERE...
...SOMETHING YOU'RE TRYING TO TELL ME?

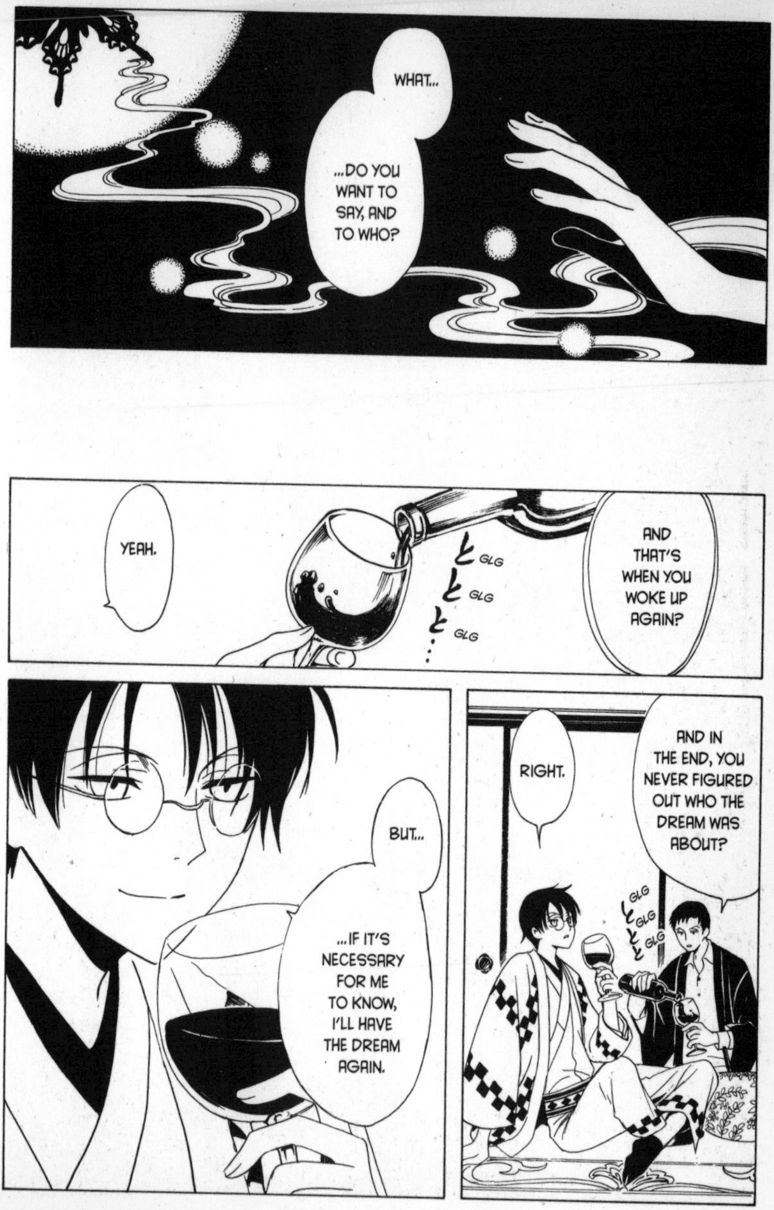
WHAT...
...DO YOU WANT TO SAY, AND TO WHO?
AND THAT'S WHEN YOU WOKE UP AGAIN?
と GLG
と GLG
と GLG
YEAH.
AND IN THE END, YOU NEVER FIGURED OUT WHO THE DREAM WAS ABOUT?
RIGHT.
と GLG
と GLG
と GLG
BUT...
...IF IT'S NECESSARY FOR ME TO KNOW, I'LL HAVE THE DREAM AGAIN.

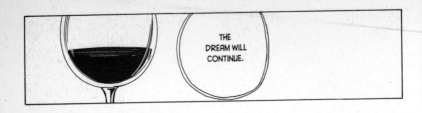

THE
DREAM WILL
CONTINUE.

THE
BUTTERFLY
AGAIN.

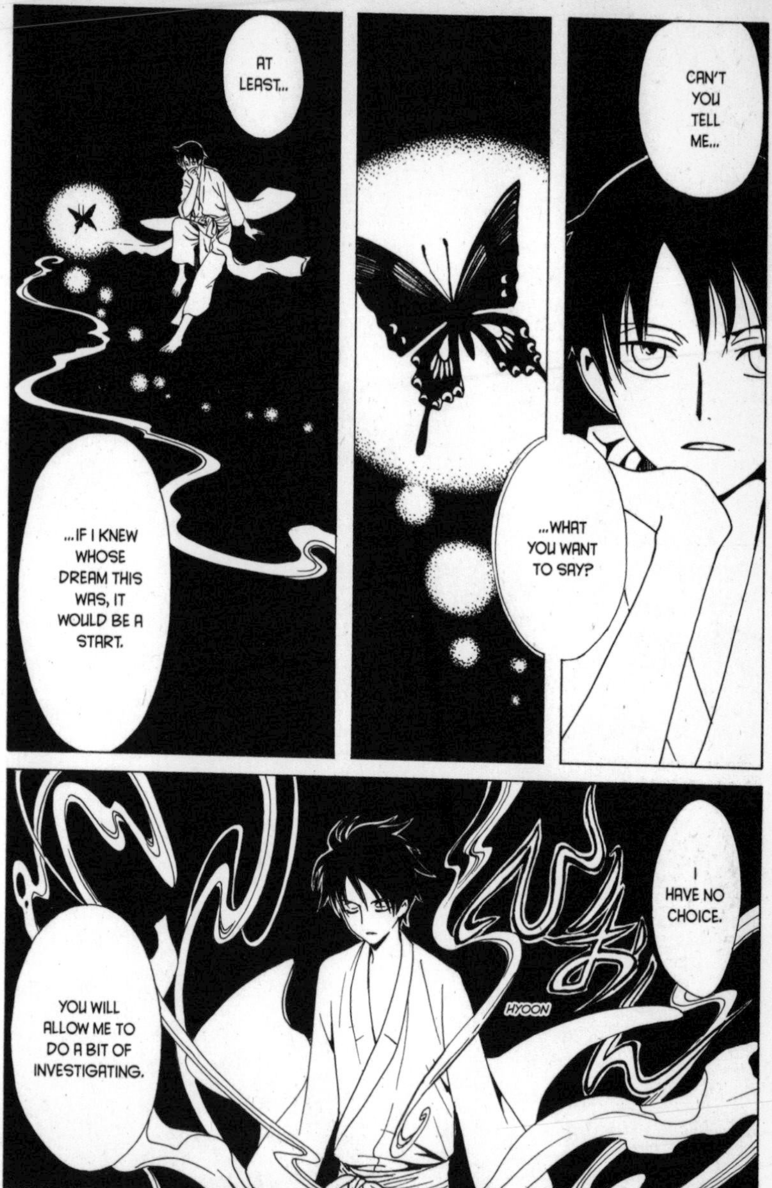
CAN'T YOU TELL ME...
...WHAT YOU WANT TO SAY?
AT LEAST...
...IF I KNEW WHOSE DREAM THIS WAS, IT WOULD BE A START.
I HAVE NO CHOICE.
HYOON
YOU WILL ALLOW ME TO DO A BIT OF INVESTIGATING.

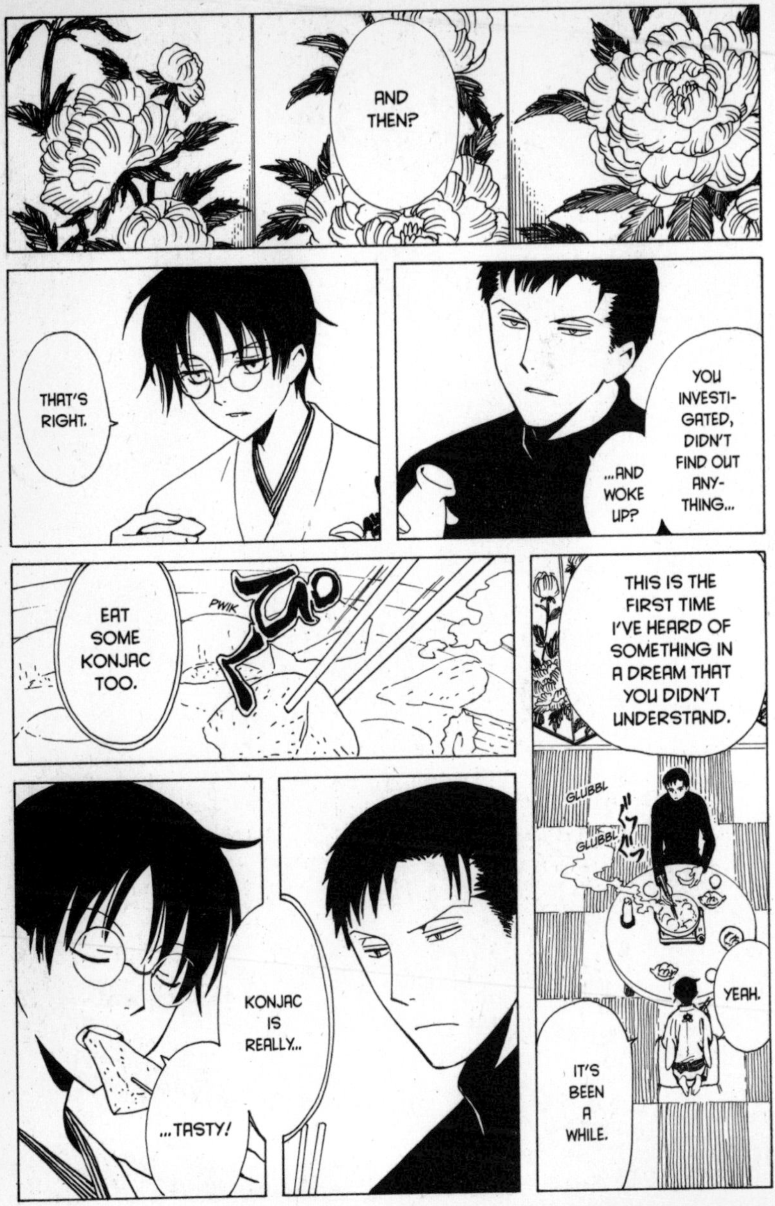
AND THEN?
YOU INVESTIGATED, DIDN'T FIND OUT ANYTHING...
...AND WOKE UP?
THAT'S RIGHT.
THIS IS THE FIRST TIME I'VE HEARD OF SOMETHING IN A DREAM THAT YOU DIDN'T UNDERSTAND.
GLUBBL
GLUBBL
YEAH.
IT'S BEEN A WHILE.
EAT SOME KONJAC TOO.
PWIK
KONJAC IS REALLY...
...TASTY!

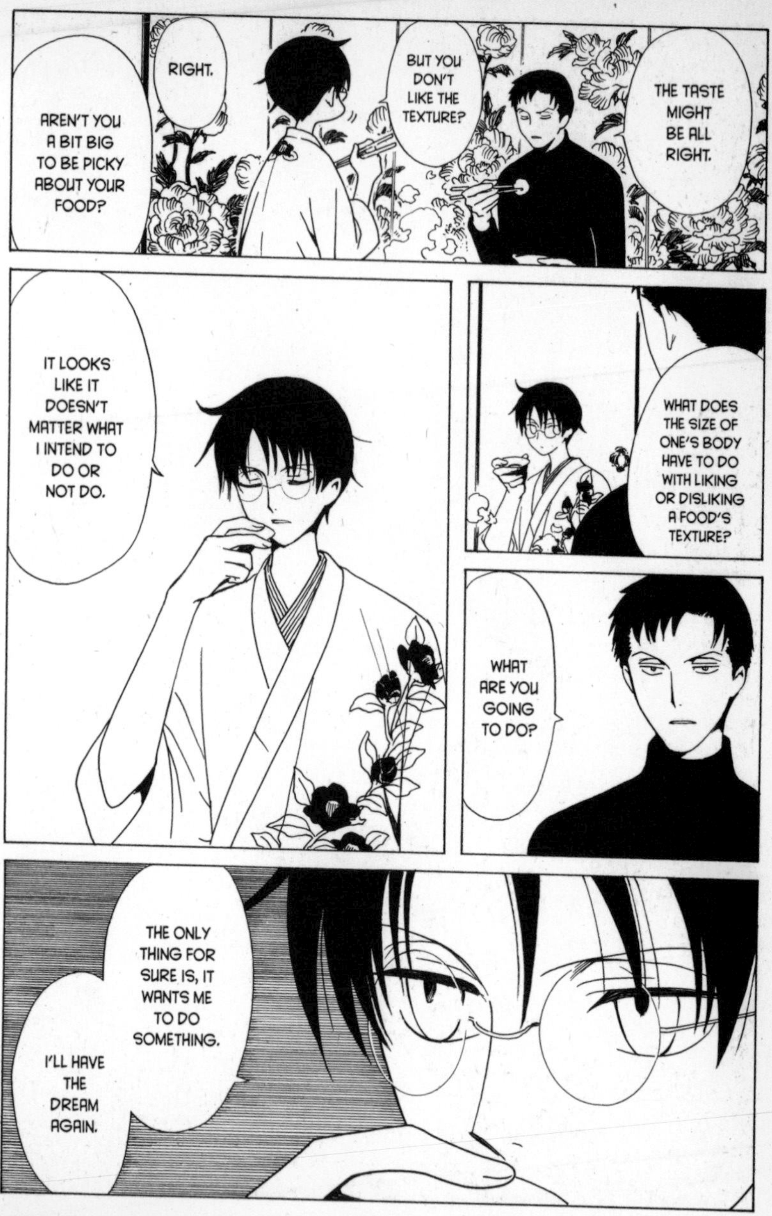
THE TASTE MIGHT BE ALL RIGHT.
BUT YOU DON'T LIKE THE TEXTURE?
RIGHT.
AREN'T YOU A BIT BIG TO BE PICKY ABOUT YOUR FOOD?
WHAT DOES THE SIZE OF ONE'S BODY HAVE TO DO WITH LIKING OR DISLIKING A FOOD'S TEXTURE?
WHAT ARE YOU GOING TO DO?
IT LOOKS LIKE IT DOESN'T MATTER WHAT I INTEND TO DO OR NOT DO.
THE ONLY THING FOR SURE IS, IT WANTS ME TO DO SOMETHING.
I'LL HAVE THE DREAM AGAIN.

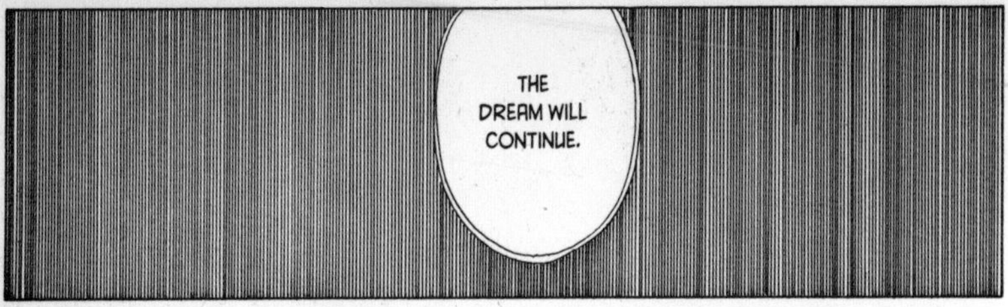
THE DREAM WILL CONTINUE.

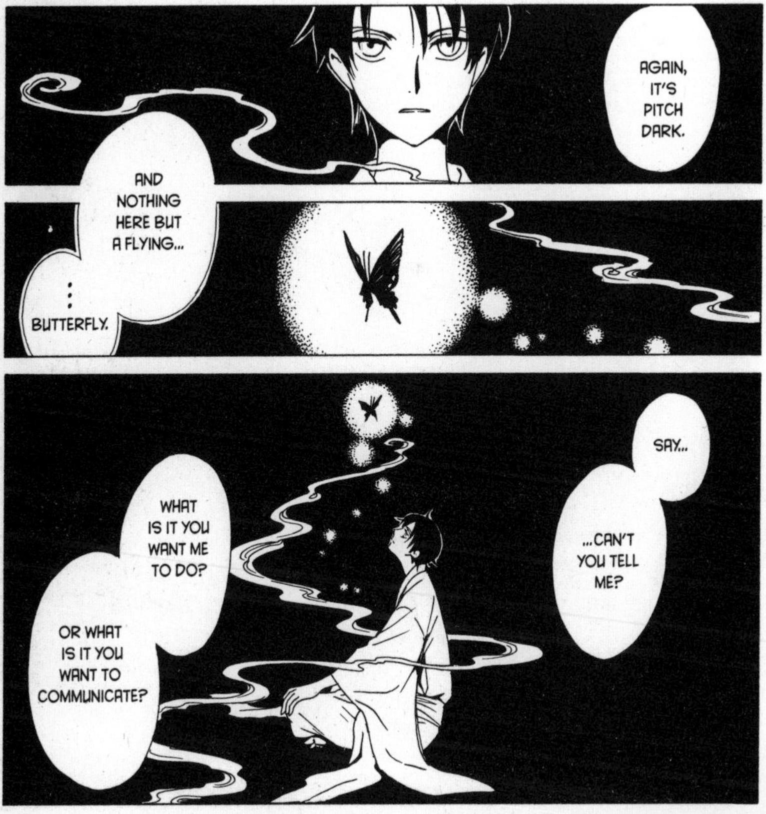
AGAIN, IT'S PITCH DARK.
AND NOTHING HERE BUT A FLYING...
...BUTTERFLY.
SAY...
...CAN'T YOU TELL ME?
WHAT IS IT YOU WANT ME TO DO?
OR WHAT IS IT YOU WANT TO COMMUNICATE?

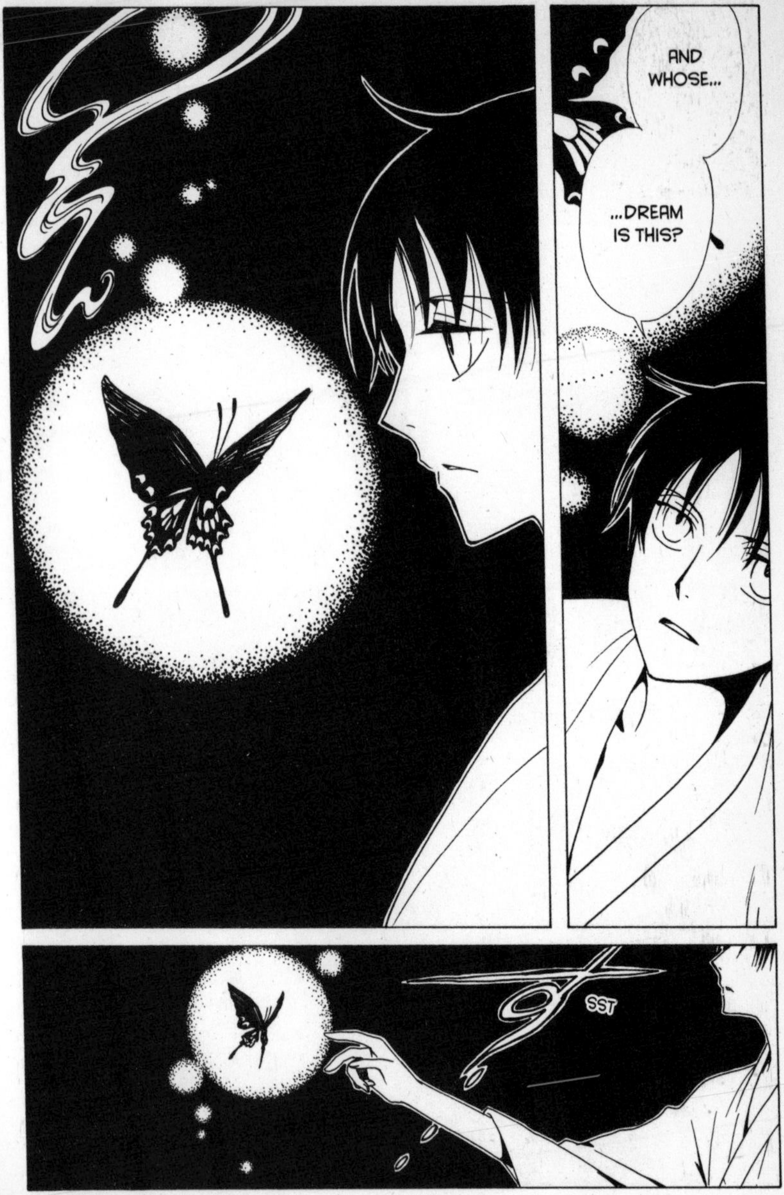
AND WHOSE...
...DREAM IS THIS?
SST

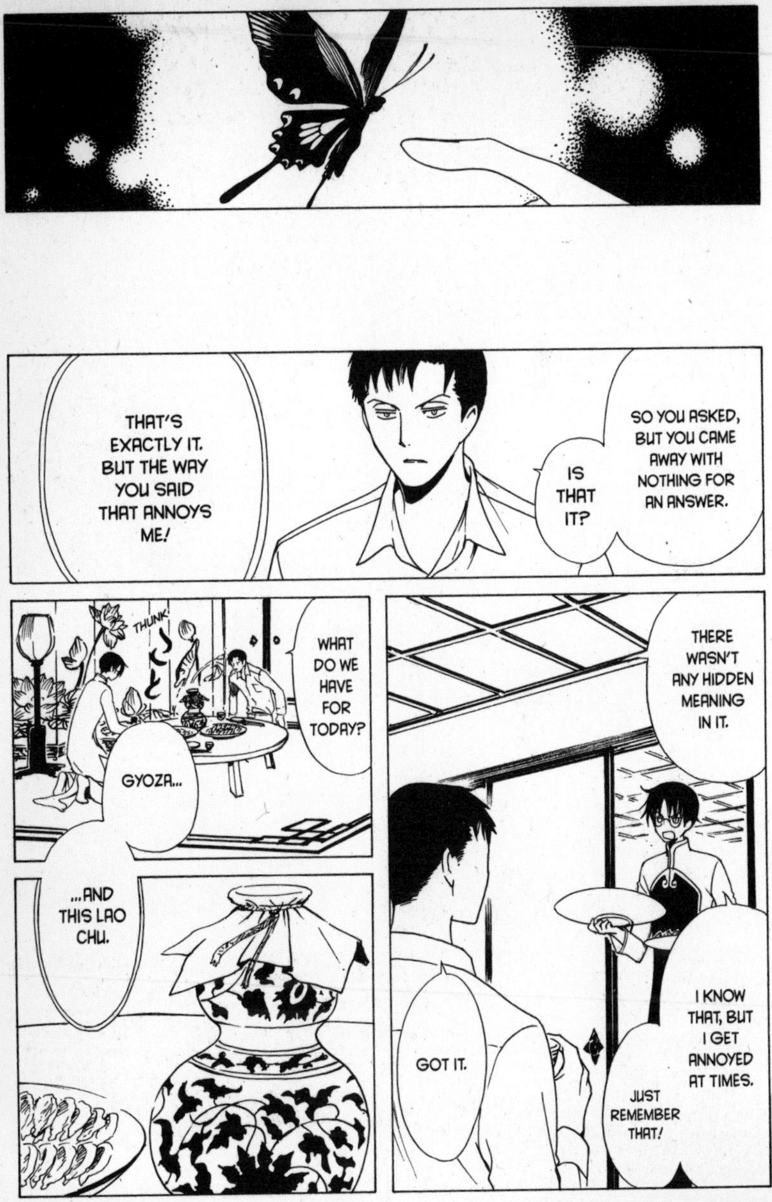
SO YOU ASKED, BUT YOU CAME AWAY WITH NOTHING FOR AN ANSWER.
IS THAT IT?
THAT'S EXACTLY IT. BUT THE WAY YOU SAID THAT ANNOYS ME!
THERE WASN'T ANY HIDDEN MEANING IN IT.
I KNOW THAT, BUT I GET ANNOYED AT TIMES.
JUST REMEMBER THAT!
GOT IT.
WHAT DO WE HAVE FOR TODAY?
THUNK
GYOZA...
...AND THIS LAO CHU.

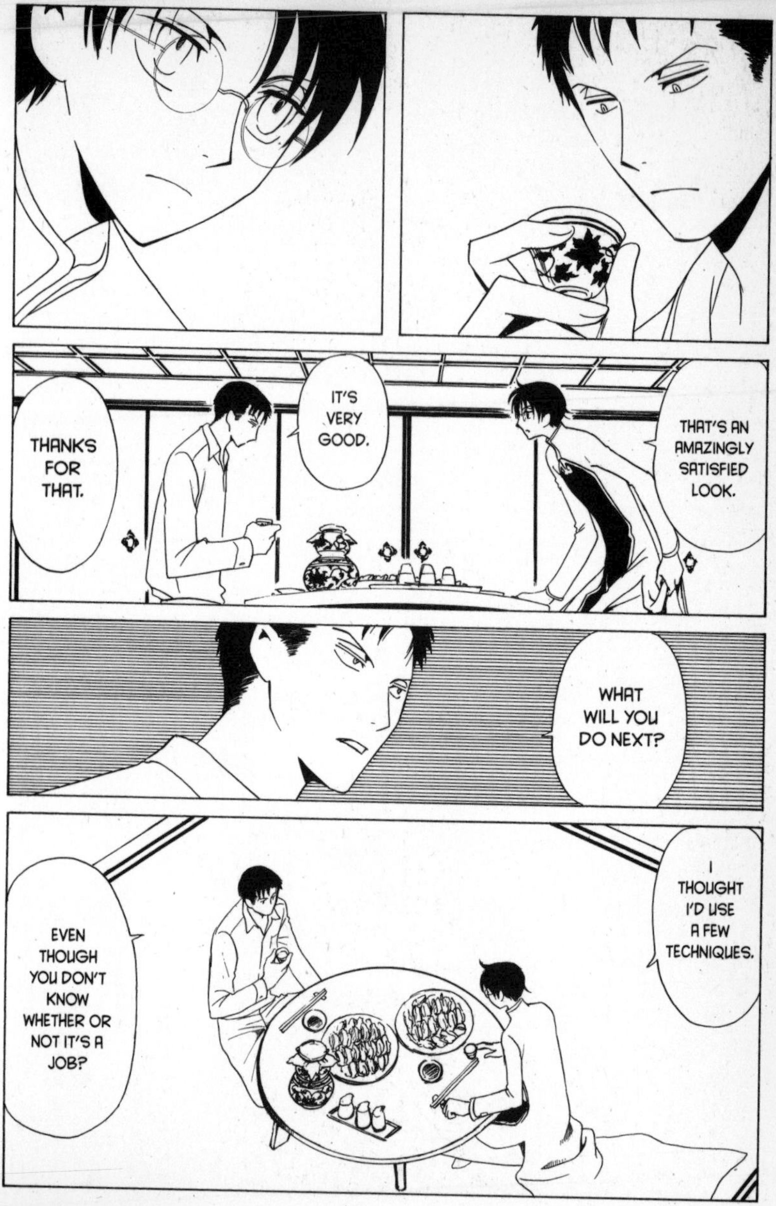
THAT'S AN AMAZINGLY SATISFIED LOOK.
IT'S VERY GOOD.
THANKS FOR THAT.
WHAT WILL YOU DO NEXT?
I THOUGHT I'D USE A FEW TECHNIQUES.
EVEN THOUGH YOU DON'T KNOW WHETHER OR NOT IT'S A JOB?

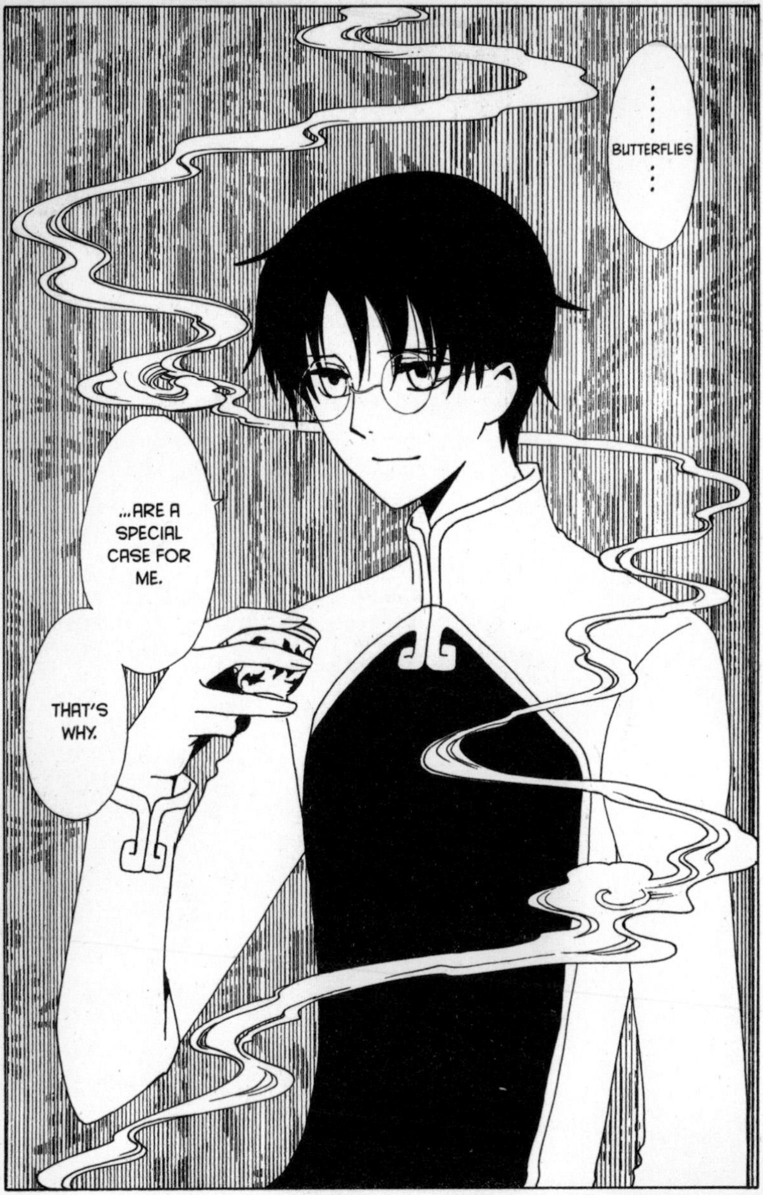
…BUTTERFLIES…
...ARE A SPECIAL CASE FOR ME.
THAT'S WHY.

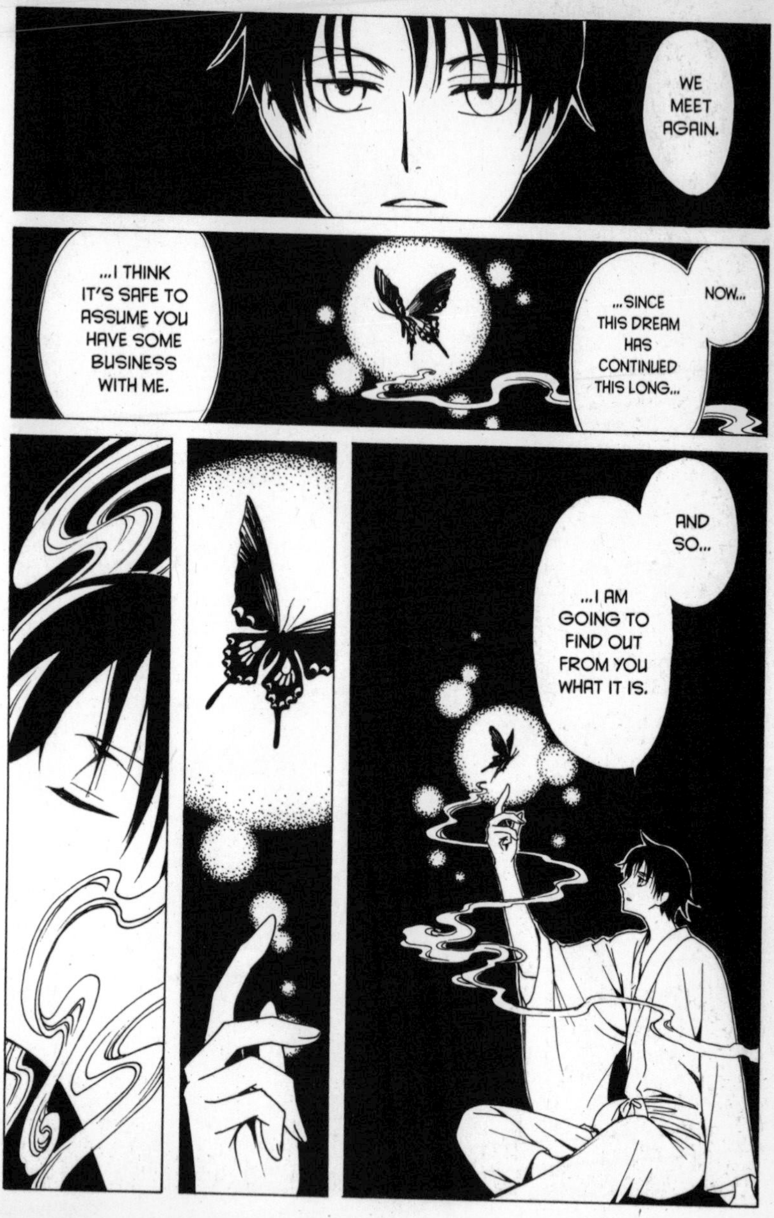
WE MEET AGAIN.
NOW...
...SINCE THIS DREAM HAS CONTINUED THIS LONG...
...I THINK IT'S SAFE TO ASSUME YOU HAVE SOME BUSINESS WITH ME.
AND SO...
...I AM GOING TO FIND OUT FROM YOU WHAT IT IS.

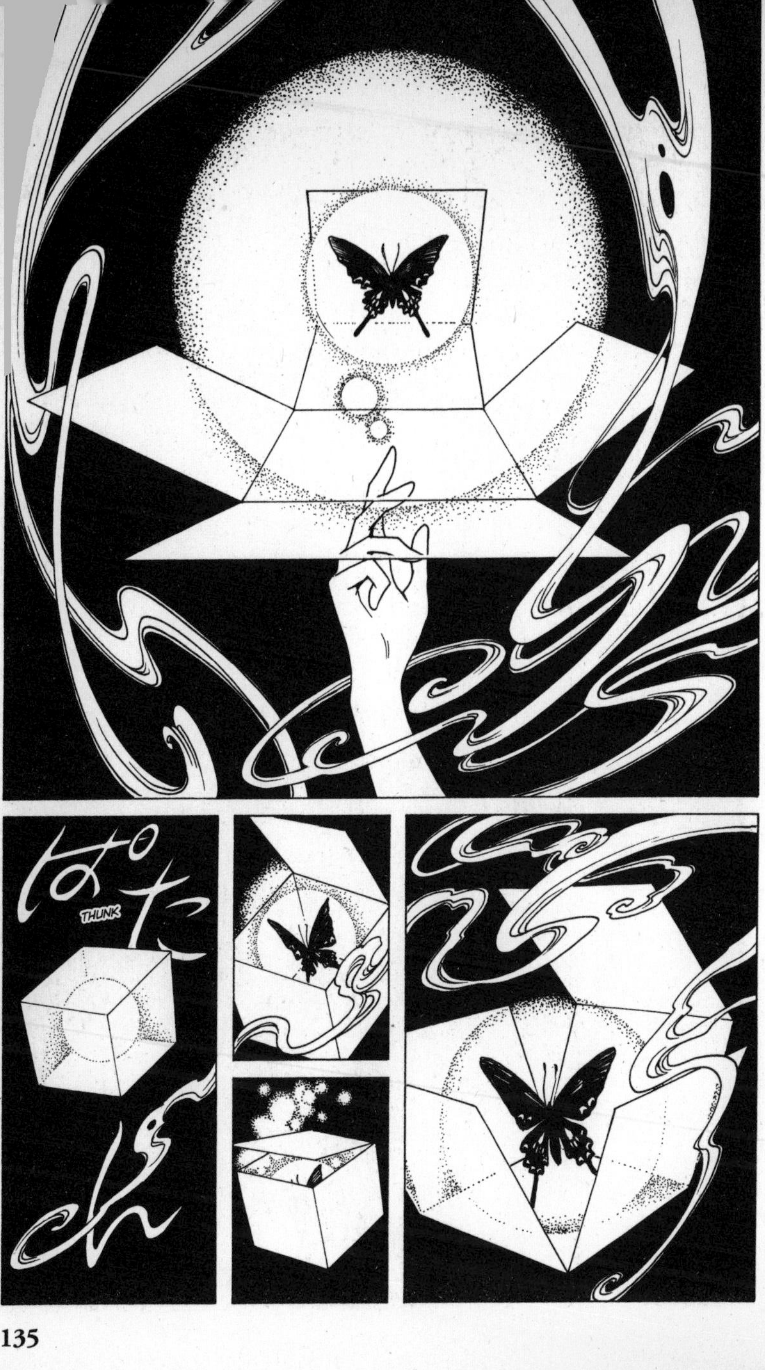
ぱたん
THUNK

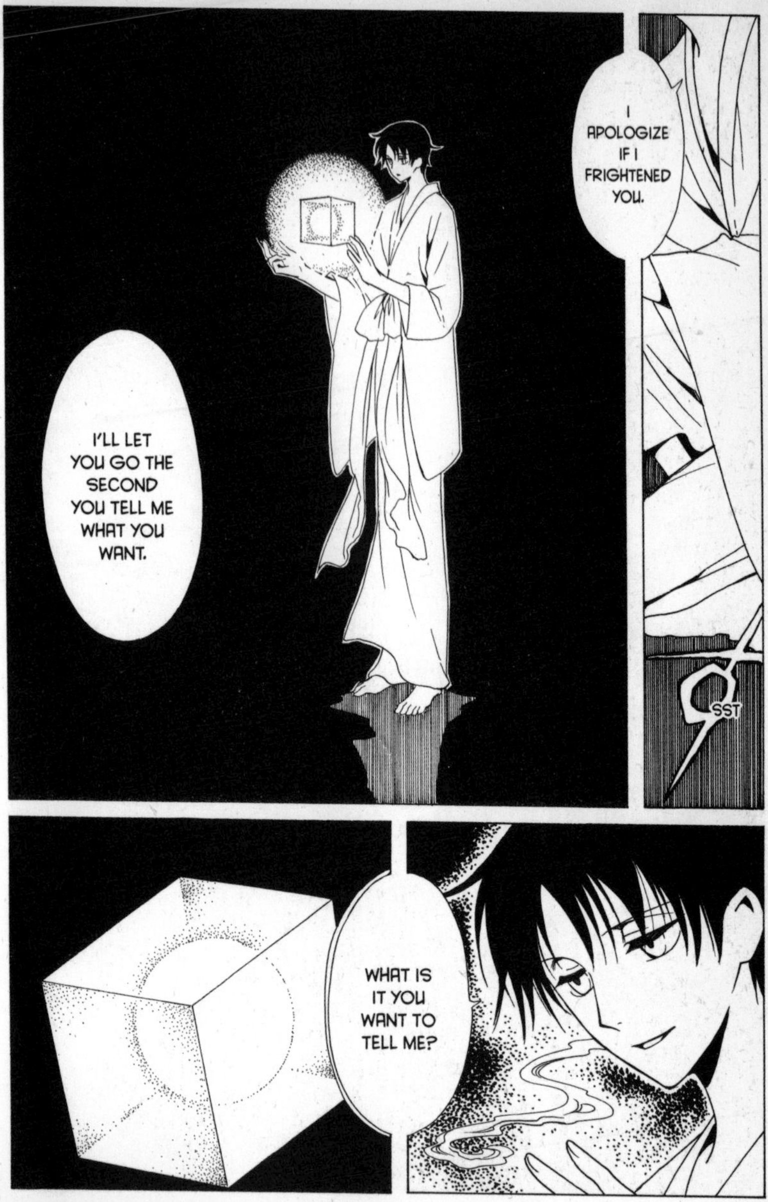
I APOLOGIZE IF I FRIGHTENED YOU.
SST
I'LL LET YOU GO THE SECOND YOU TELL ME WHAT YOU WANT.
WHAT IS IT YOU WANT TO TELL ME?

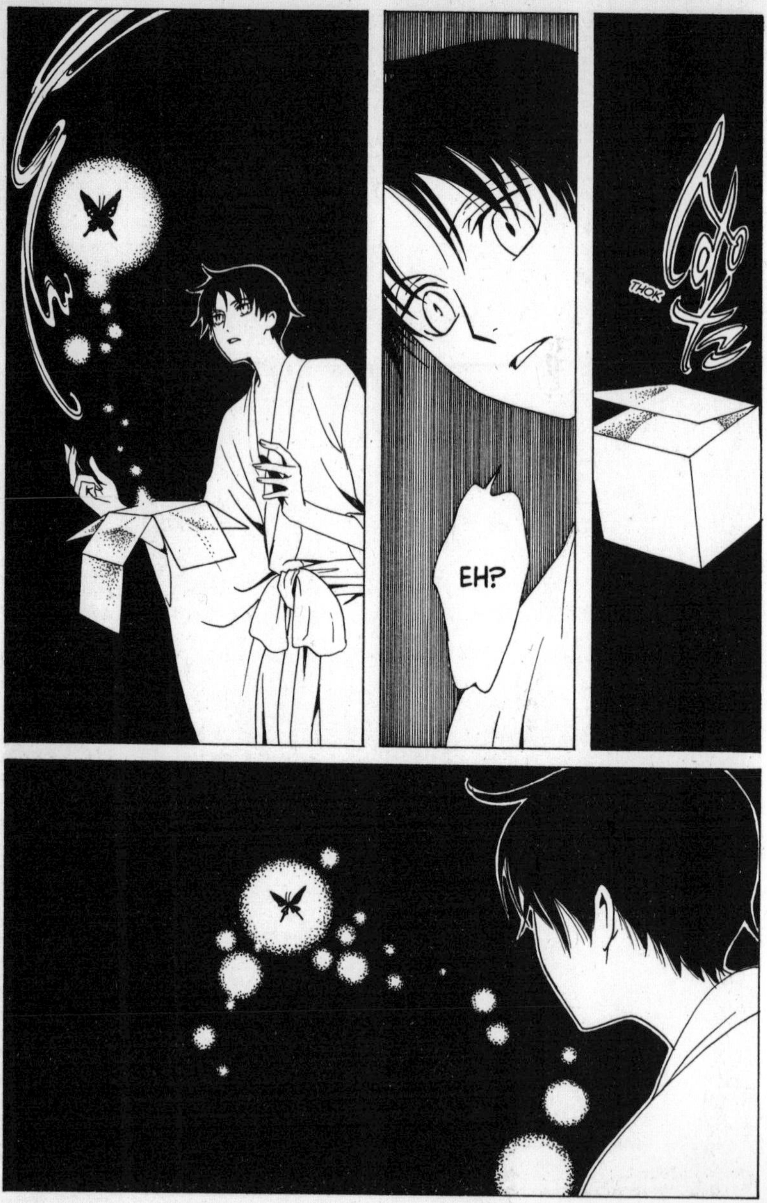
THOK
EH?

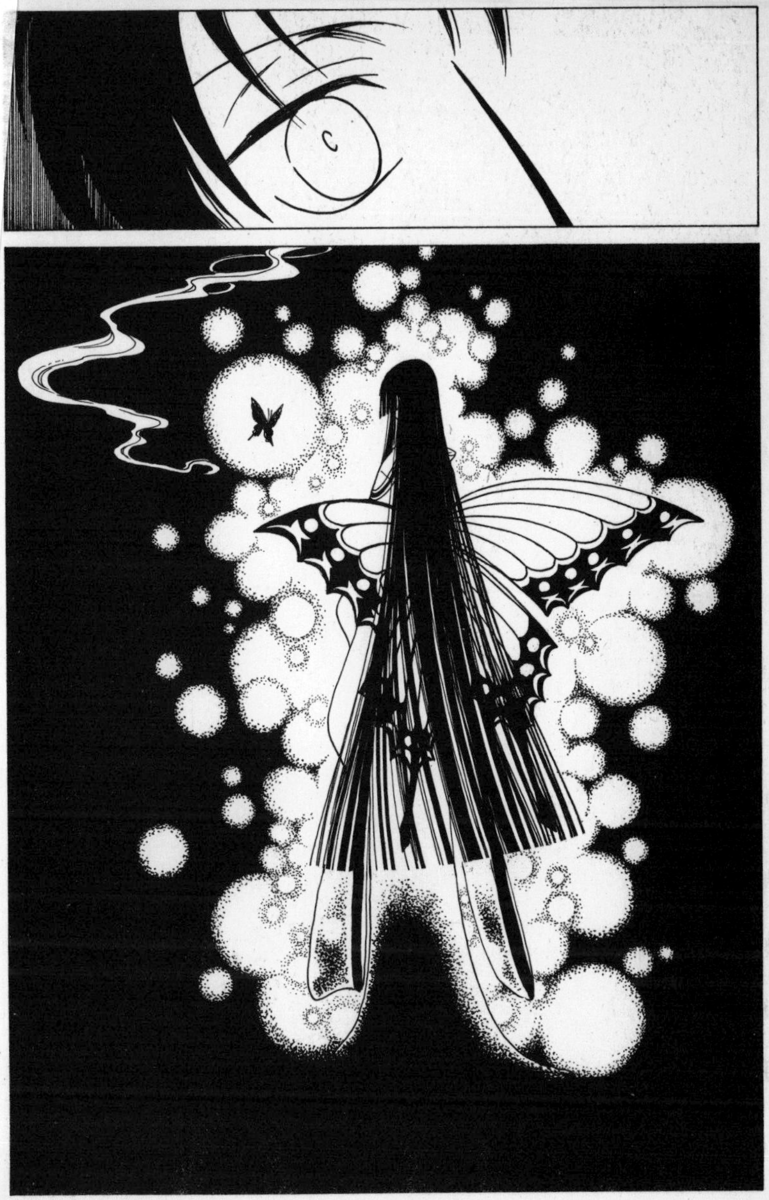

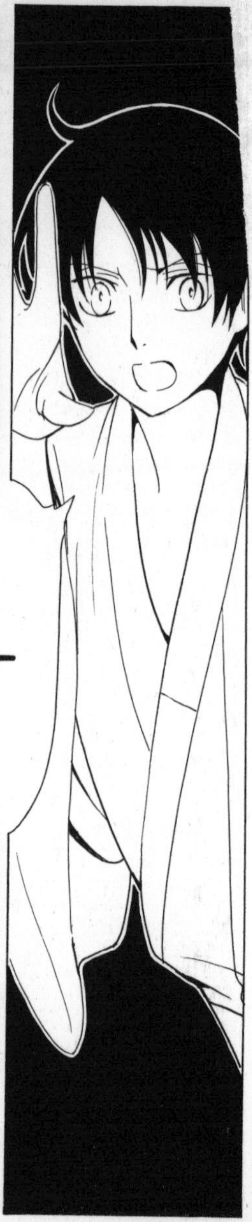
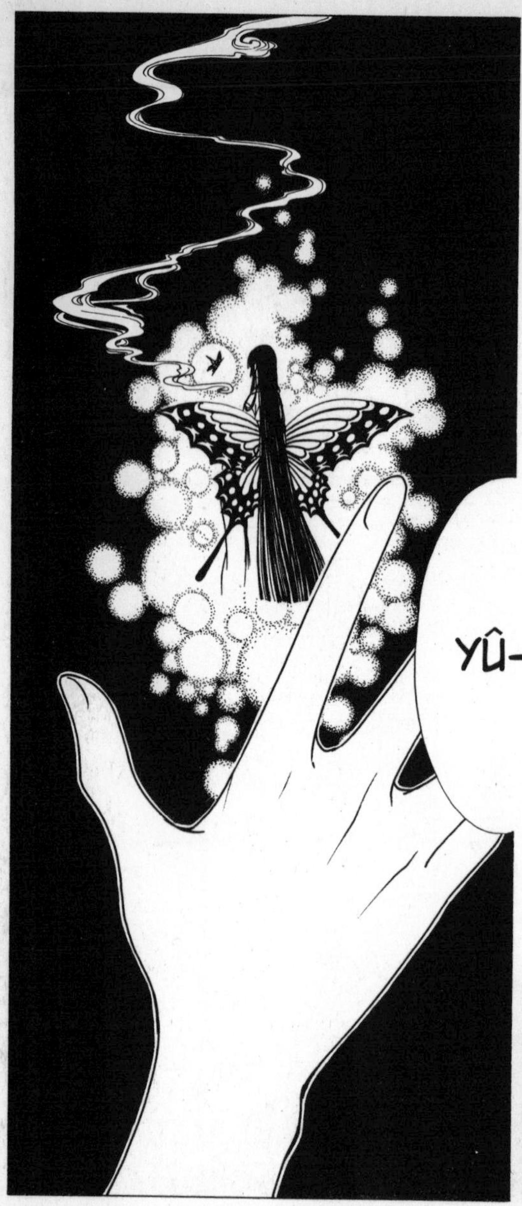
YÛ–

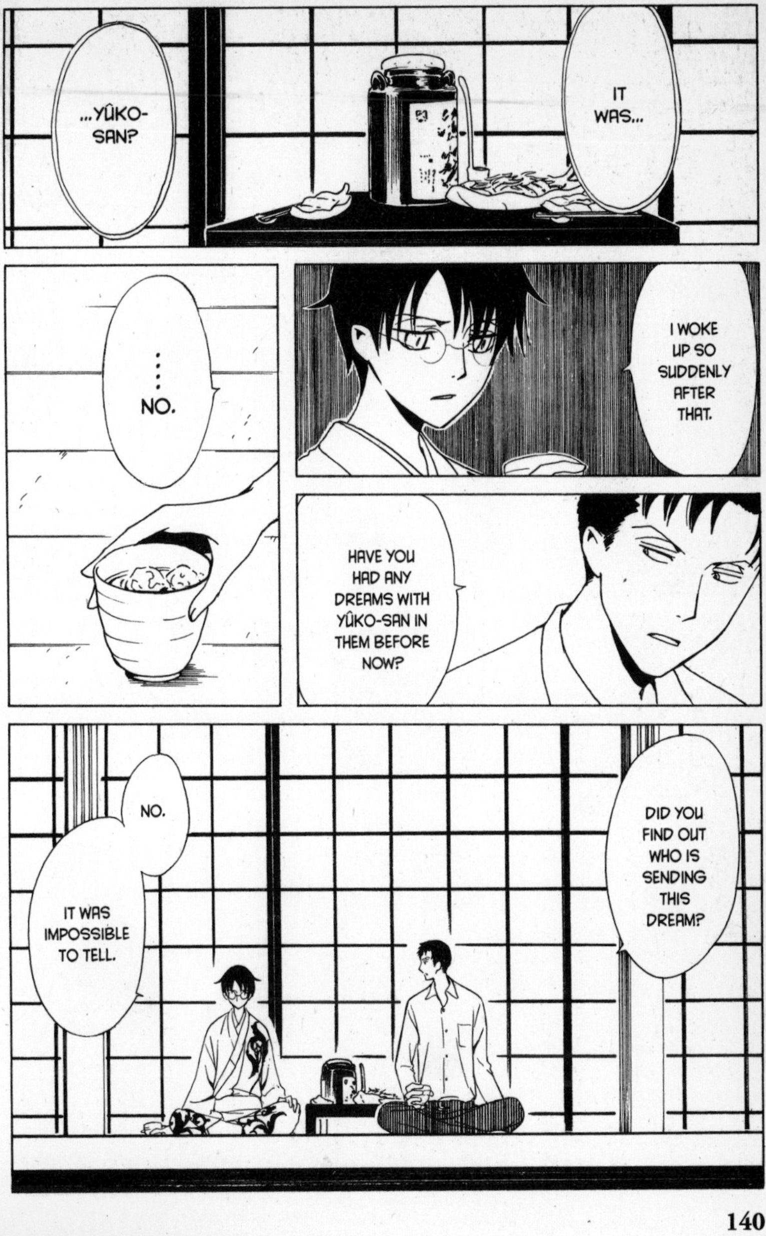
IT WAS...
...YÛKO-SAN?
I WOKE UP SO SUDDENLY AFTER THAT.
HAVE YOU HAD ANY DREAMS WITH YÛKO-SAN IN THEM BEFORE NOW?
....NO.
DID YOU FIND OUT WHO IS SENDING THIS DREAM?
NO.
IT WAS IMPOSSIBLE TO TELL.

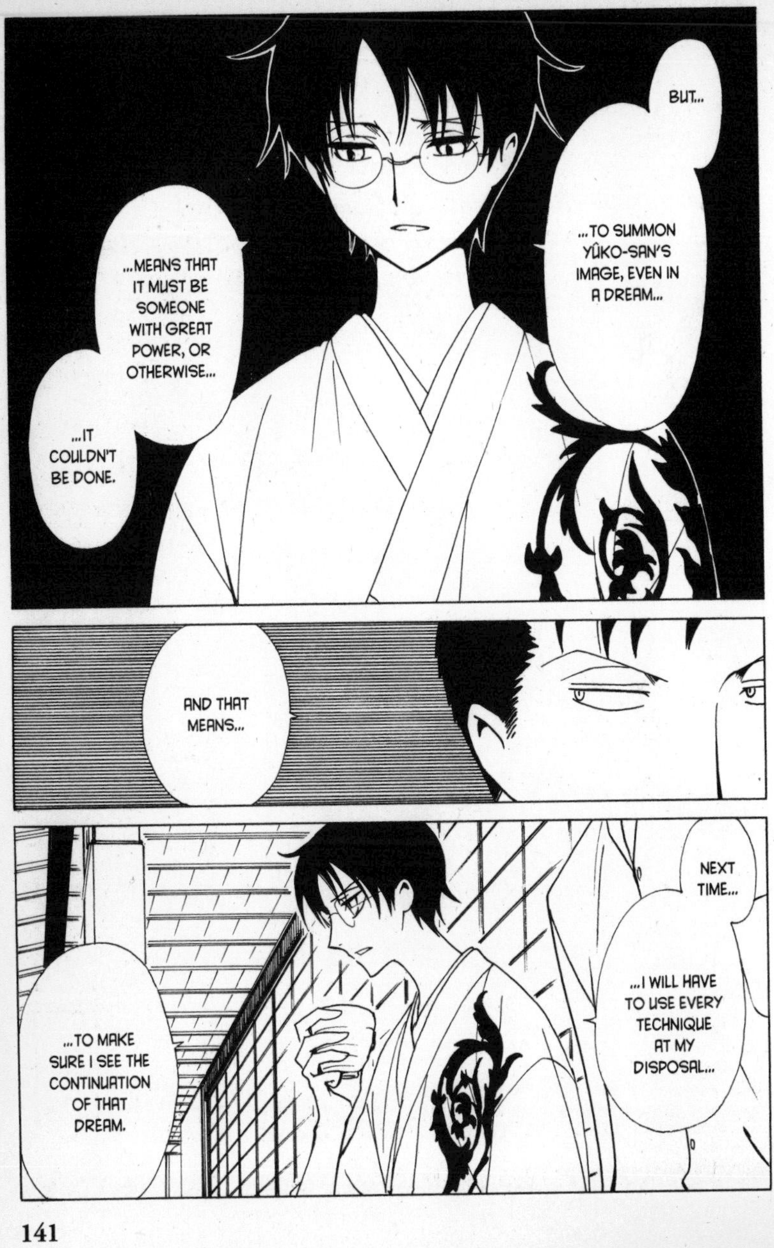
BUT...
...TO SUMMON YÛKO-SAN'S IMAGE, EVEN IN A DREAM...
...MEANS THAT IT MUST BE SOMEONE WITH GREAT POWER, OR OTHERWISE...
...IT COULDN'T BE DONE.
AND THAT MEANS...
NEXT TIME...
...I WILL HAVE TO USE EVERY TECHNIQUE AT MY DISPOSAL...
...TO MAKE SURE I SEE THE CONTINUATION OF THAT DREAM.

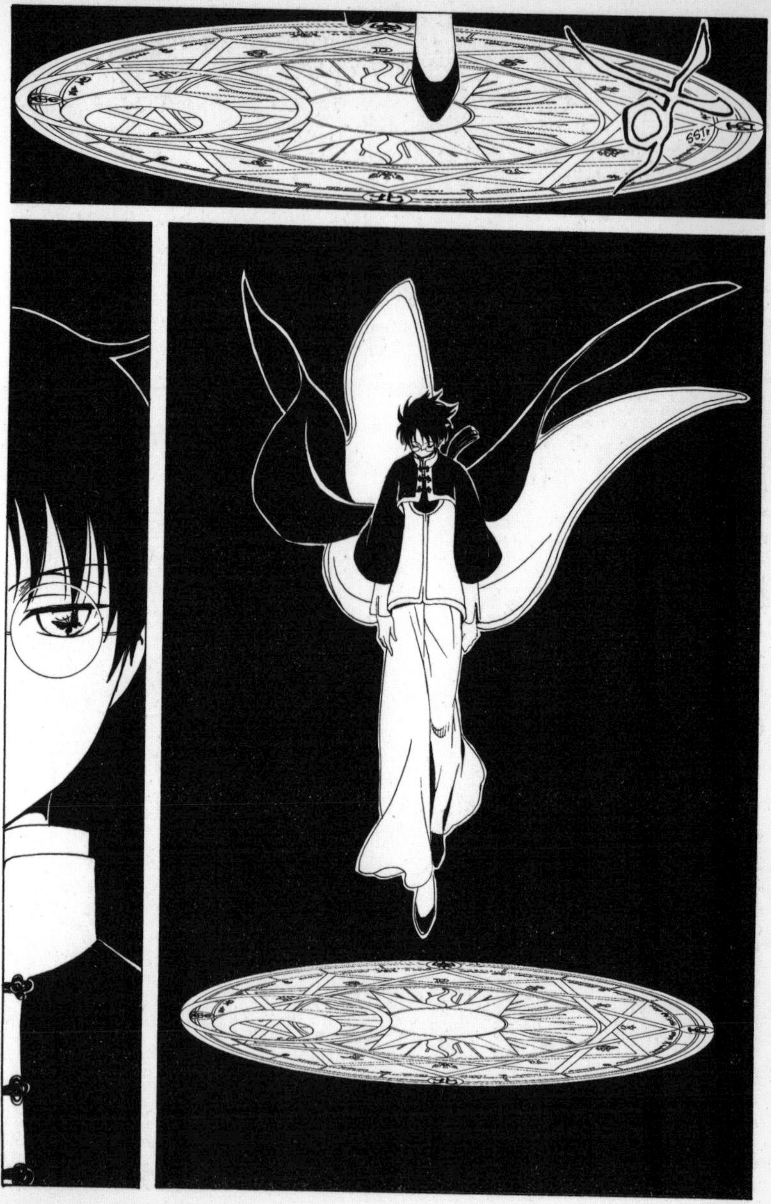
SST!

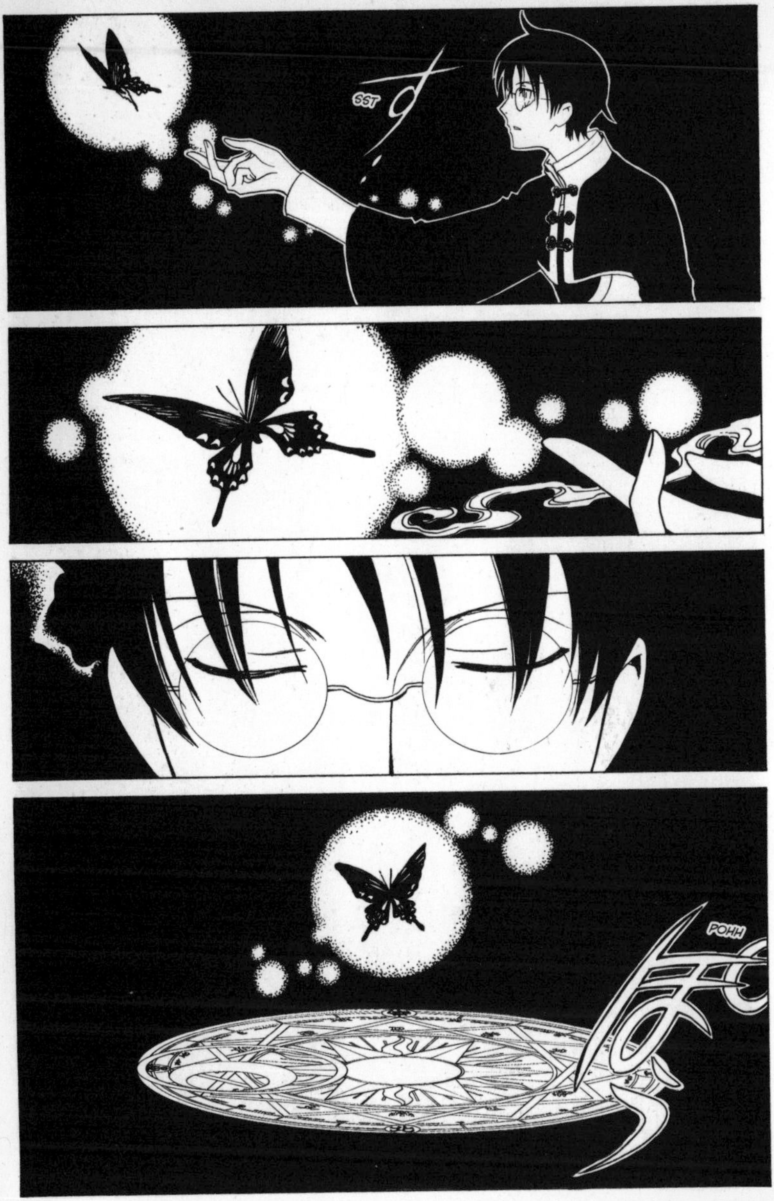
SST
POHH

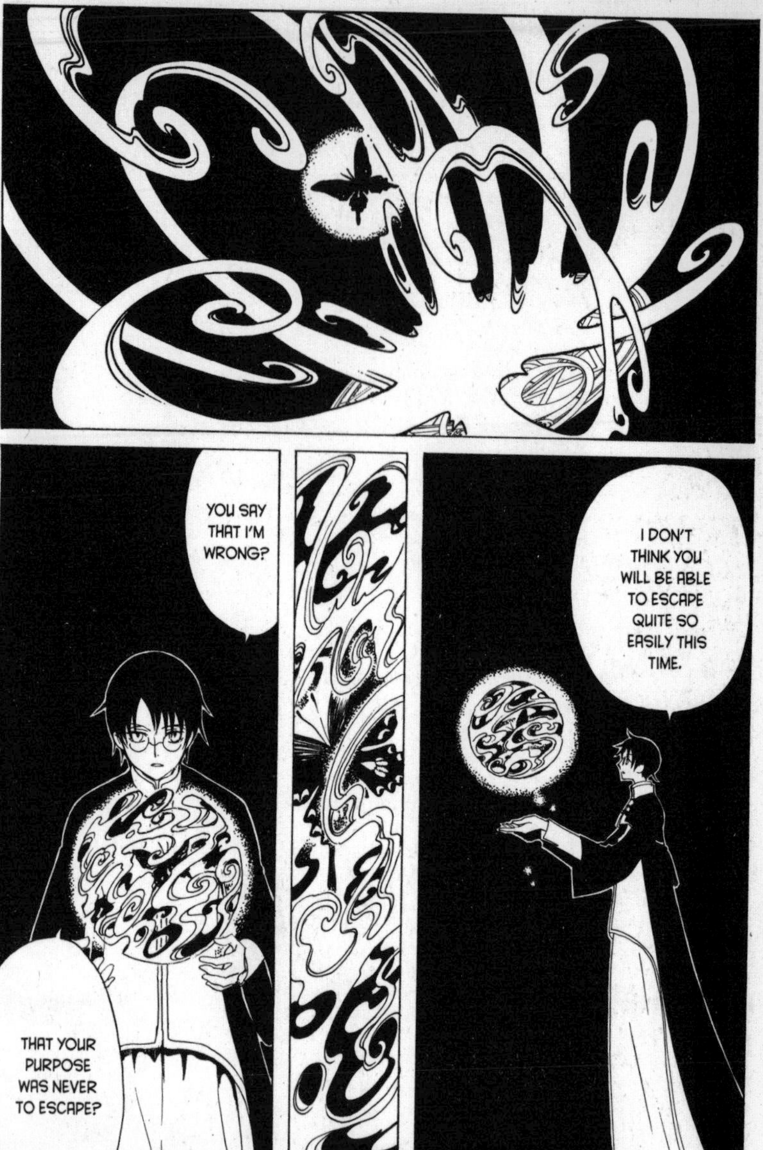
I DON'T THINK YOU WILL BE ABLE TO ESCAPE QUITE SO EASILY THIS TIME.
YOU SAY THAT I'M WRONG?
THAT YOUR PURPOSE WAS NEVER TO ESCAPE?

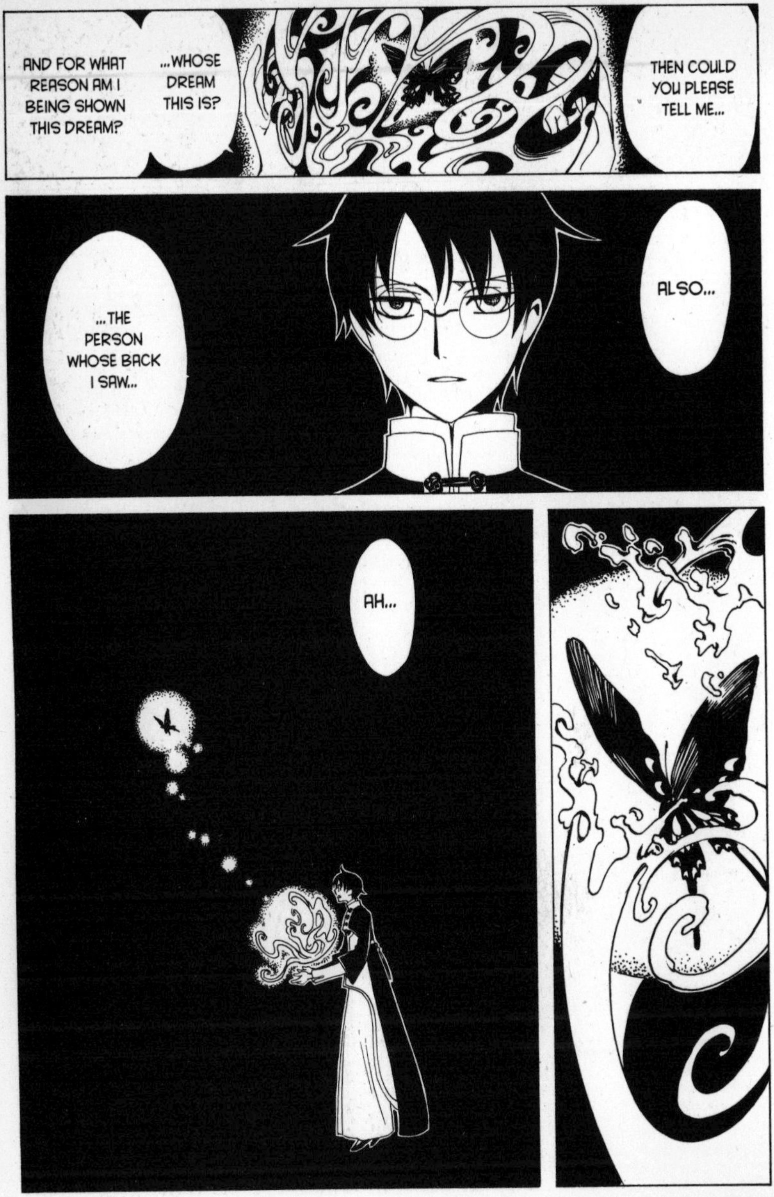
THEN COULD YOU PLEASE TELL ME...
...WHOSE DREAM THIS IS?
AND FOR WHAT REASON AM I BEING SHOWN THIS DREAM?
ALSO...
...THE PERSON WHOSE BACK I SAW...
AH...

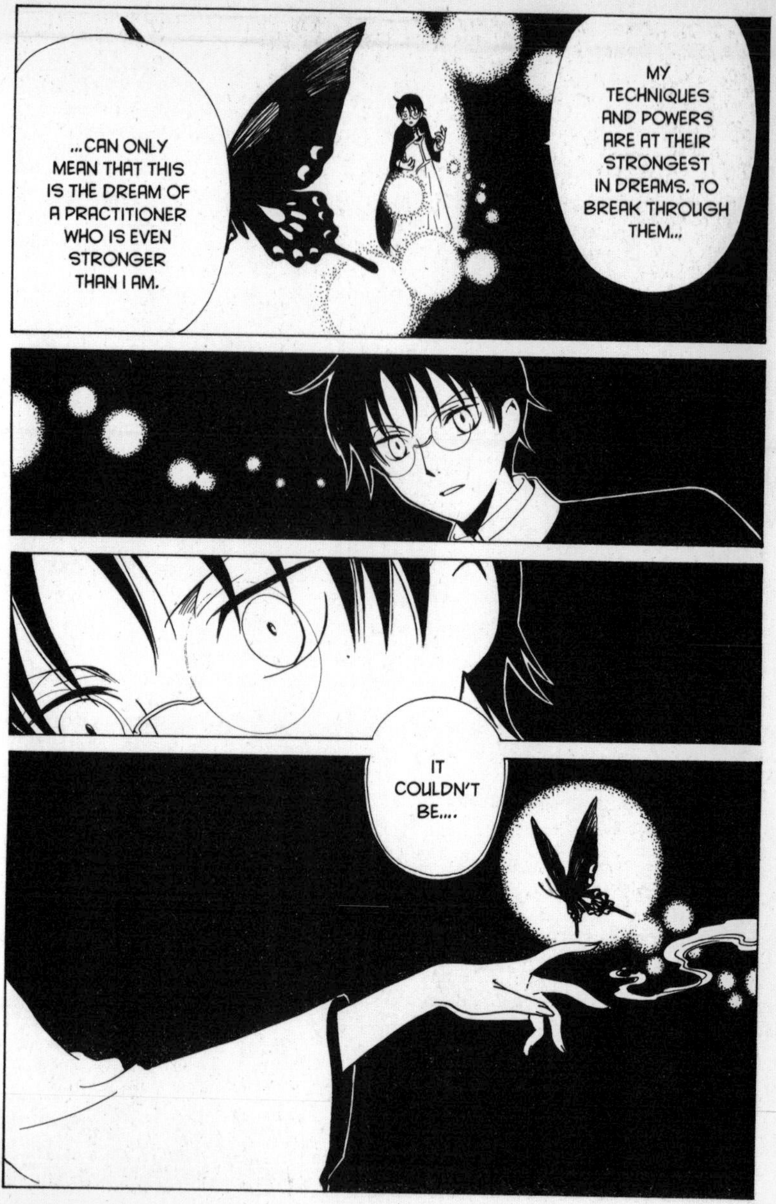
MY TECHNIQUES AND POWERS ARE AT THEIR STRONGEST IN DREAMS. TO BREAK THROUGH THEM...
...CAN ONLY MEAN THAT THIS IS THE DREAM OF A PRACTITIONER WHO IS EVEN STRONGER THAN I AM.
IT COULDN'T BE....

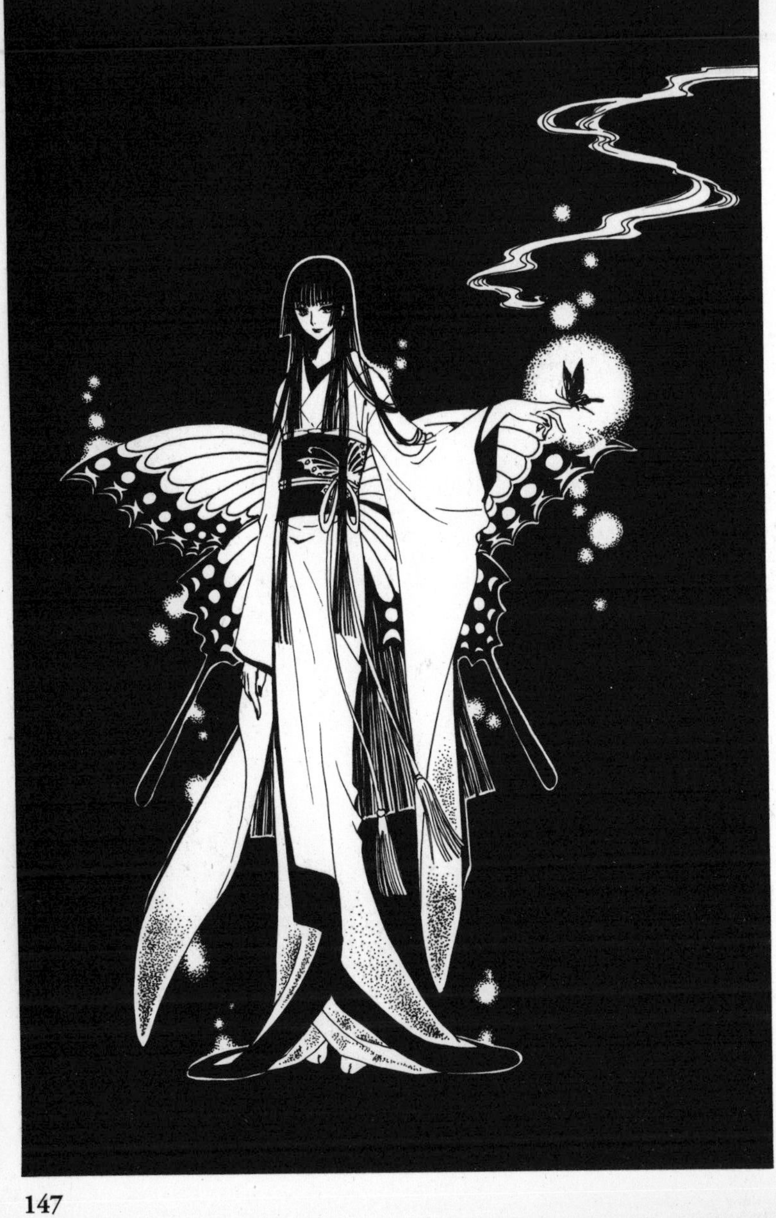

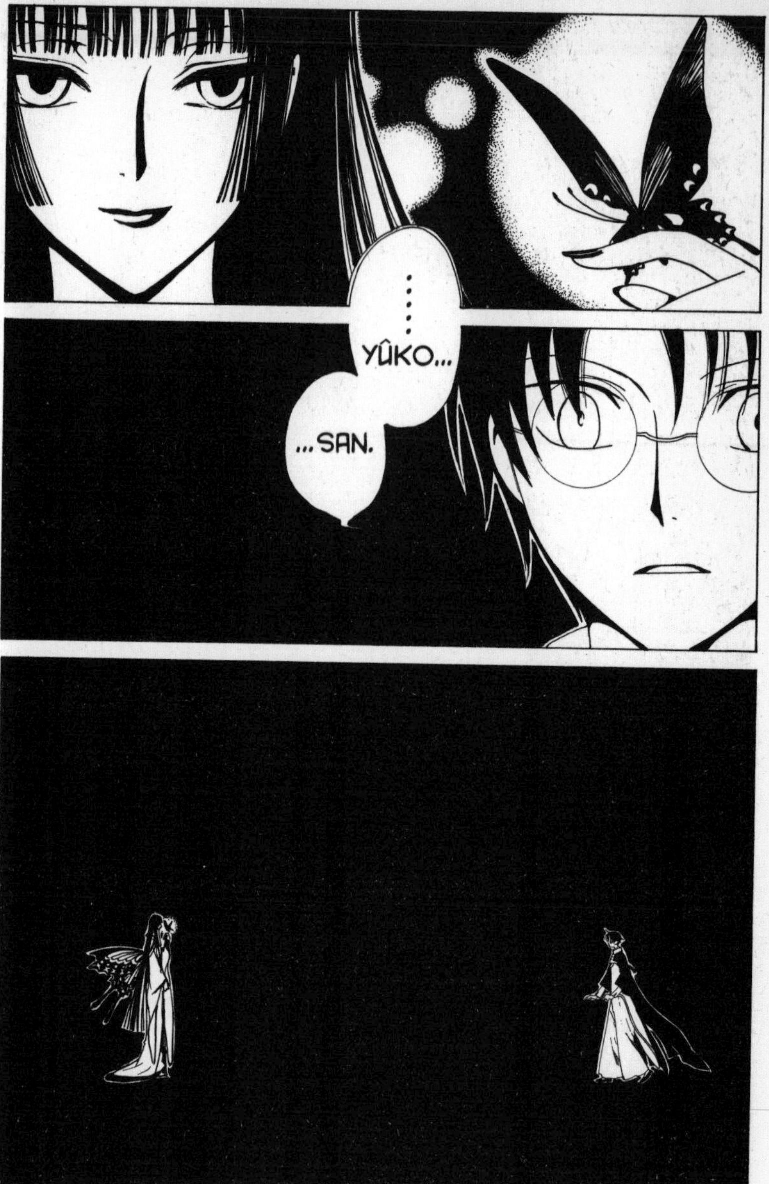
...
YÛKO...
...SAN.

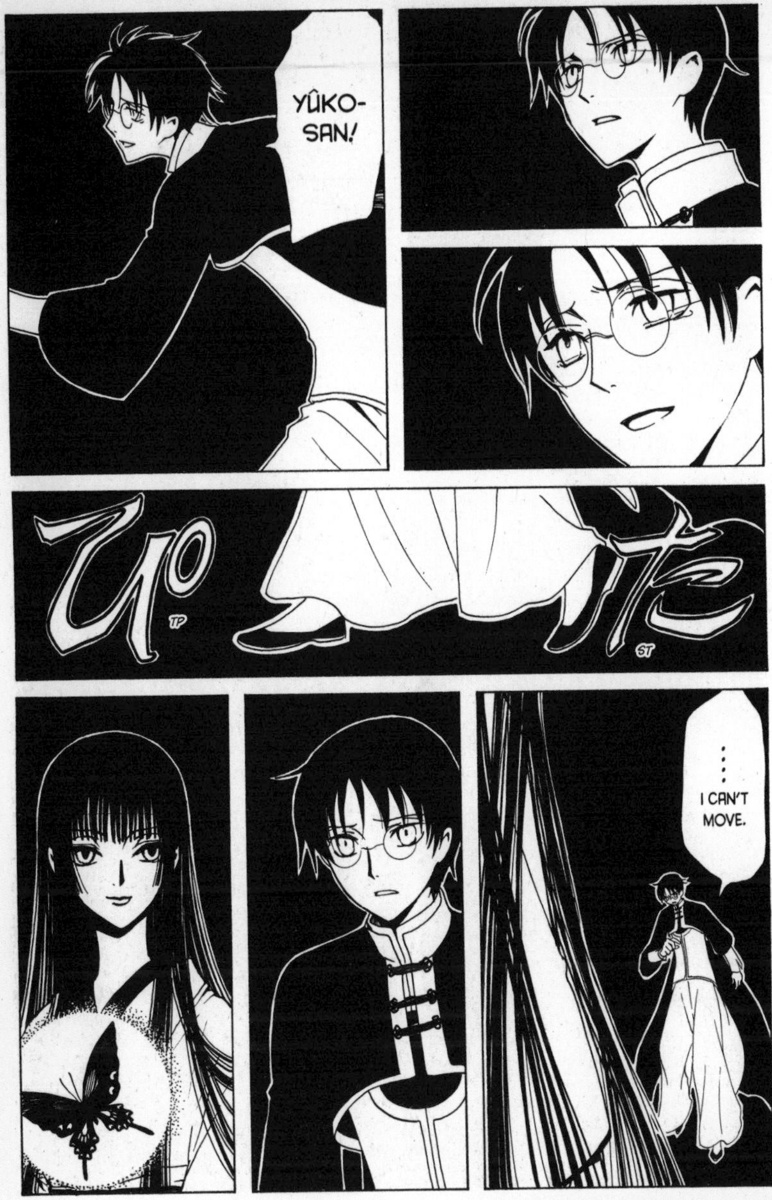
YÛKO-SAN!
ぴ
TP
た
ST
....
I CAN'T MOVE.

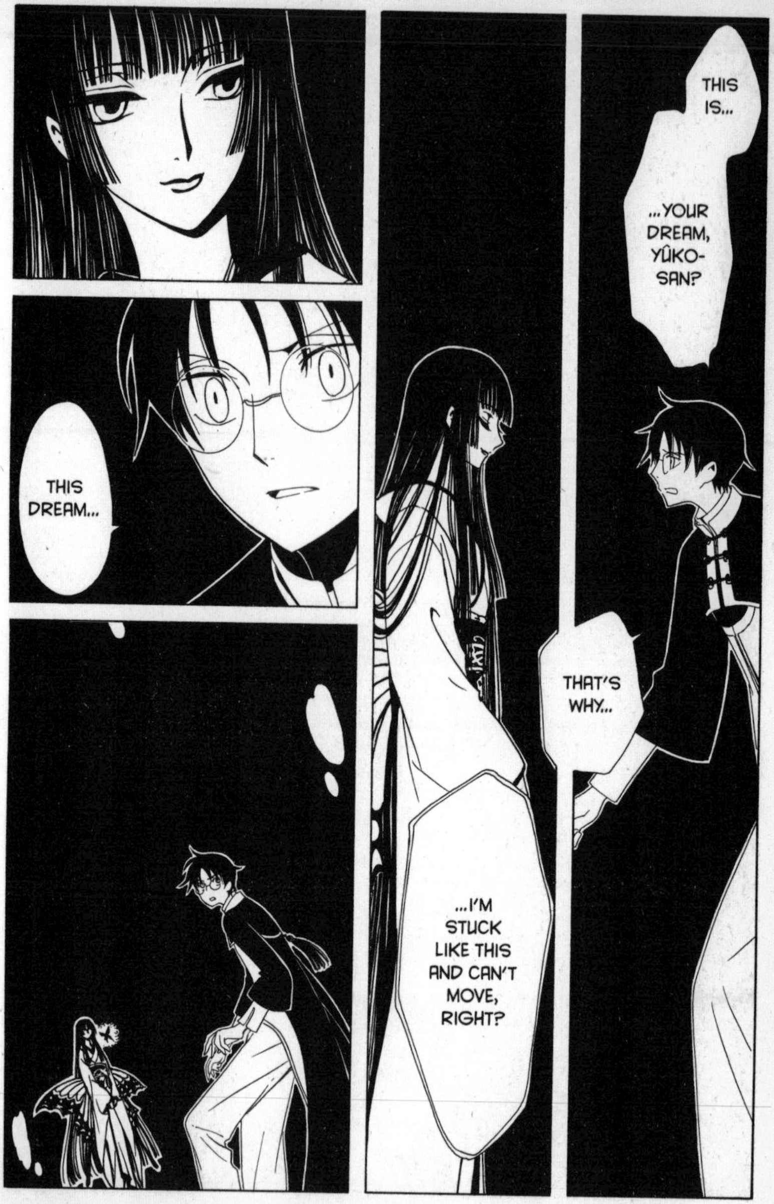
THIS IS...
...YOUR DREAM, YÛKO-SAN?
THAT'S WHY...
...I'M STUCK LIKE THIS AND CAN'T MOVE, RIGHT?
THIS DREAM...

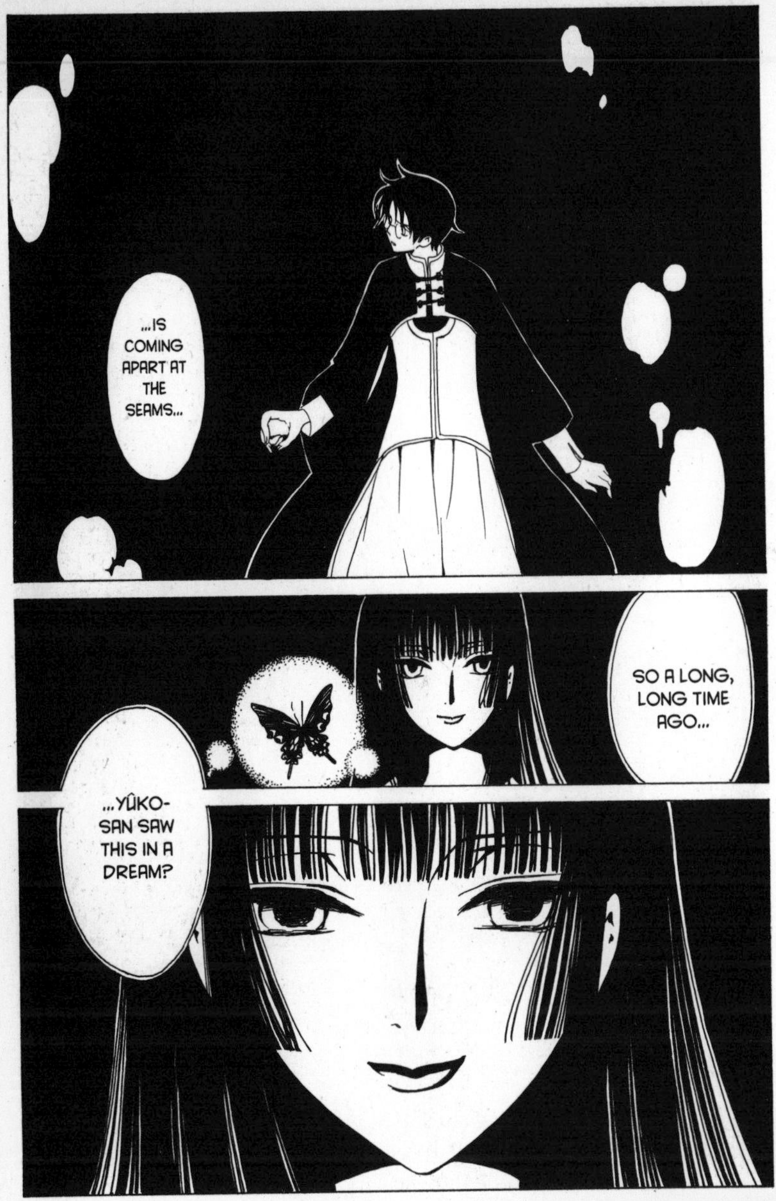
...IS COMING APART AT THE SEAMS...
SO A LONG, LONG TIME AGO...
...YÛKO-SAN SAW THIS IN A DREAM?

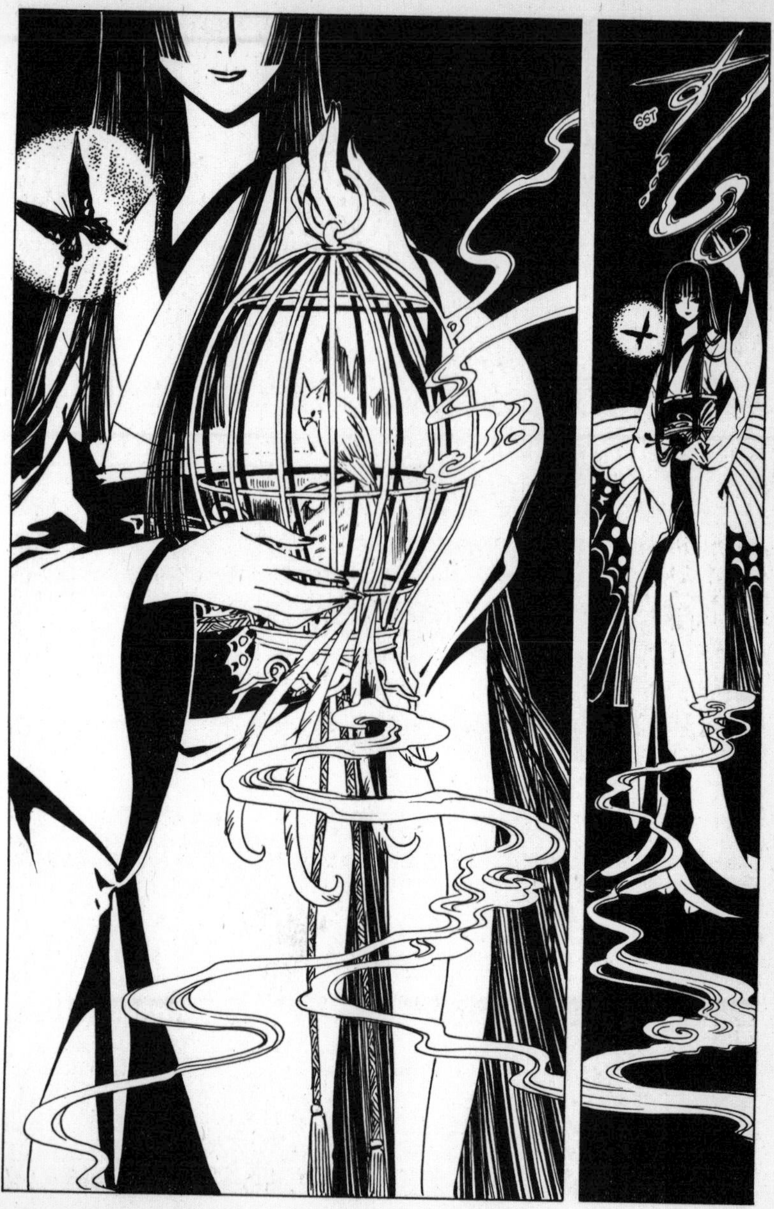
SST

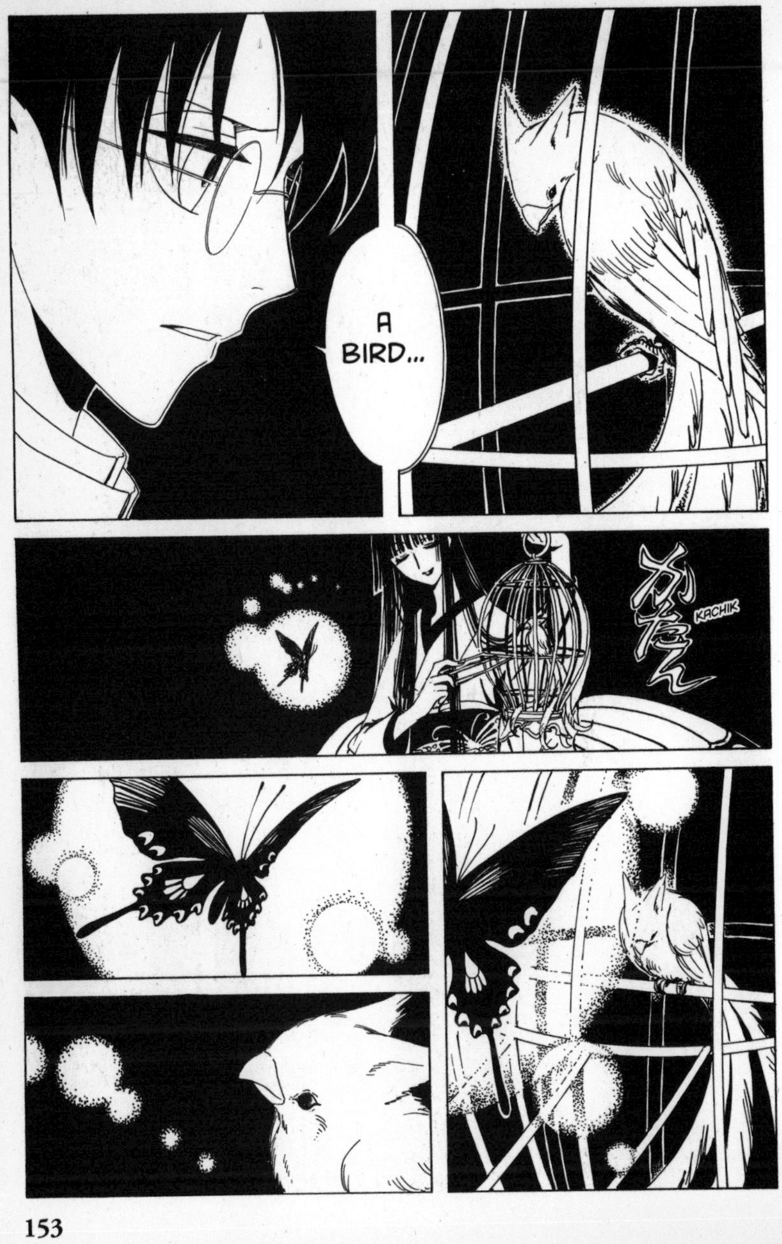
A BIRD...
かたん
KACHIK

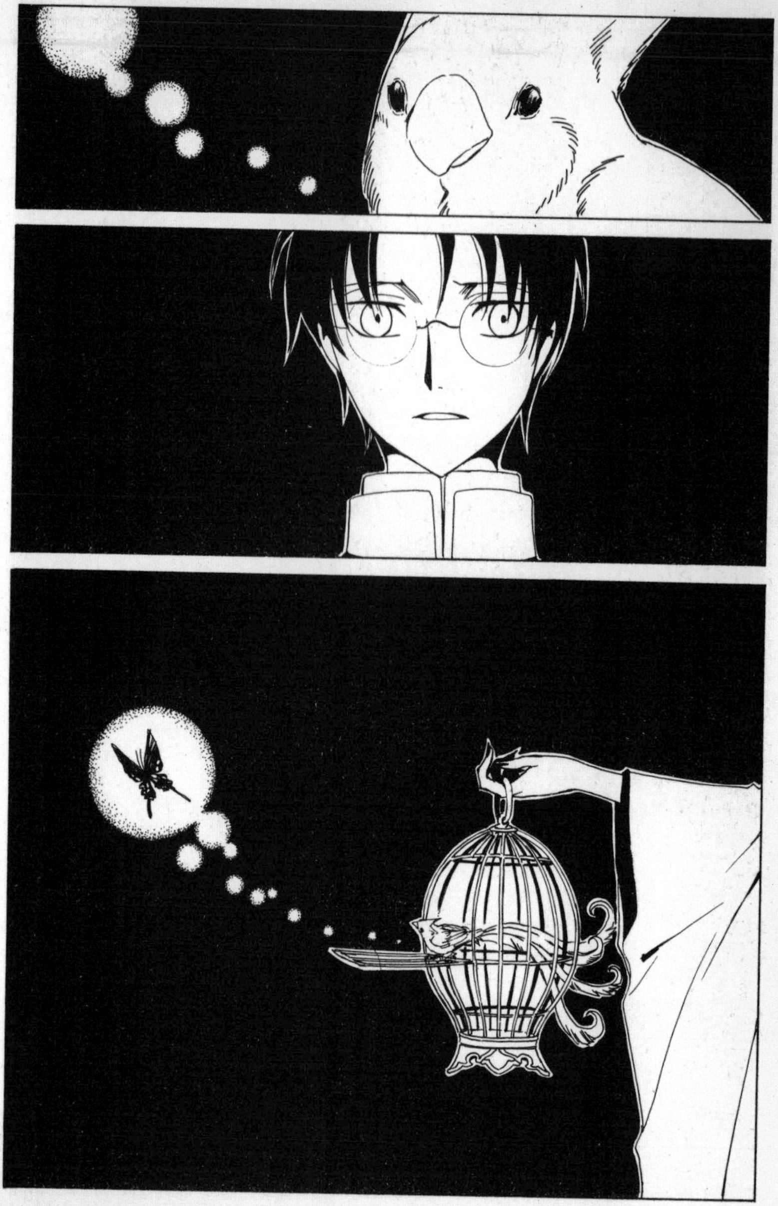

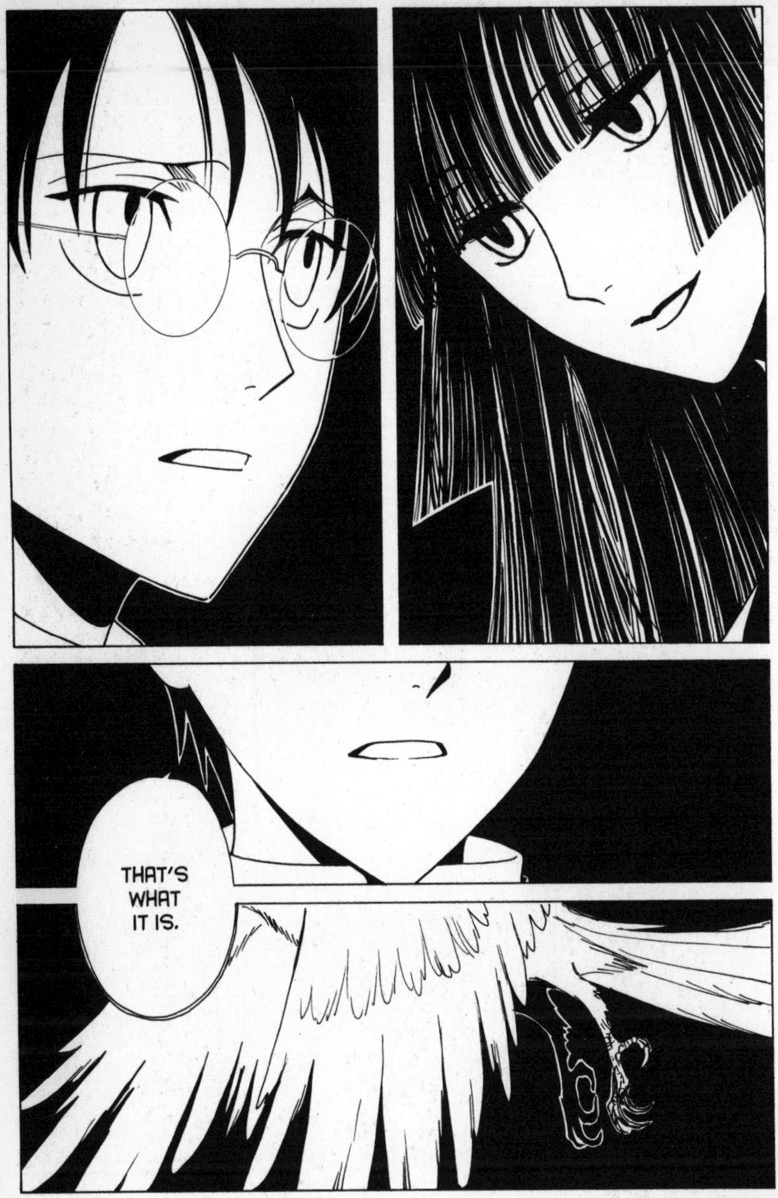
THAT'S WHAT IT IS.

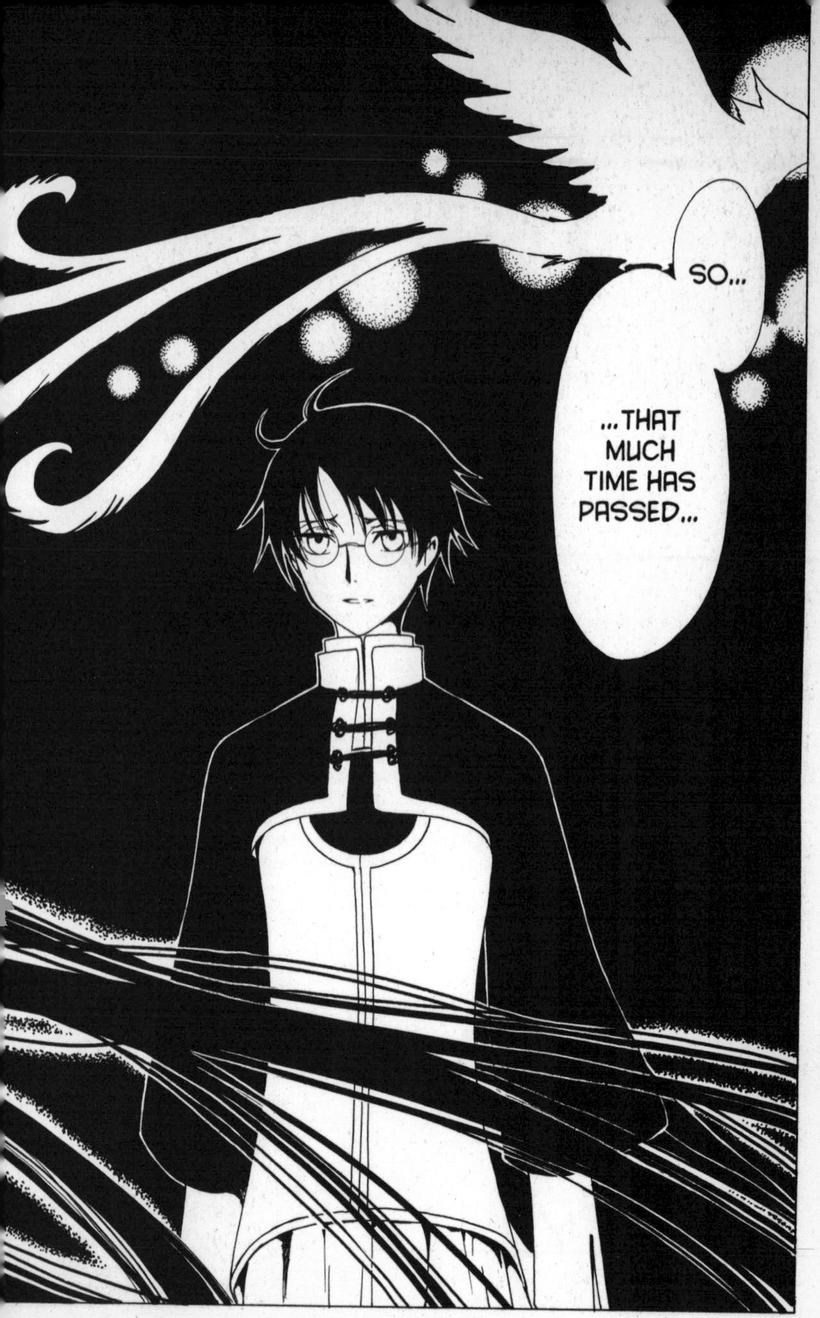
SO...
...THAT MUCH TIME HAS PASSED...

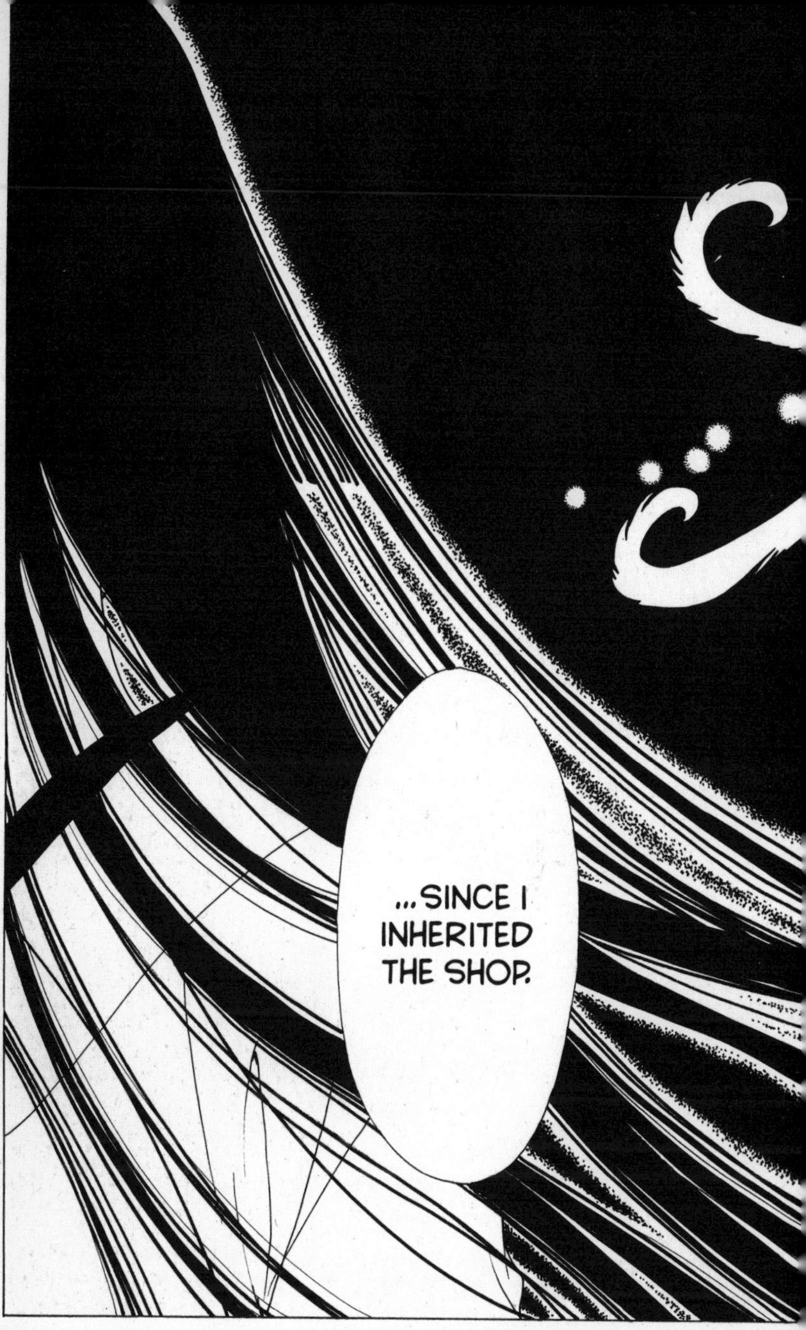
...SINCE I INHERITED THE SHOP.

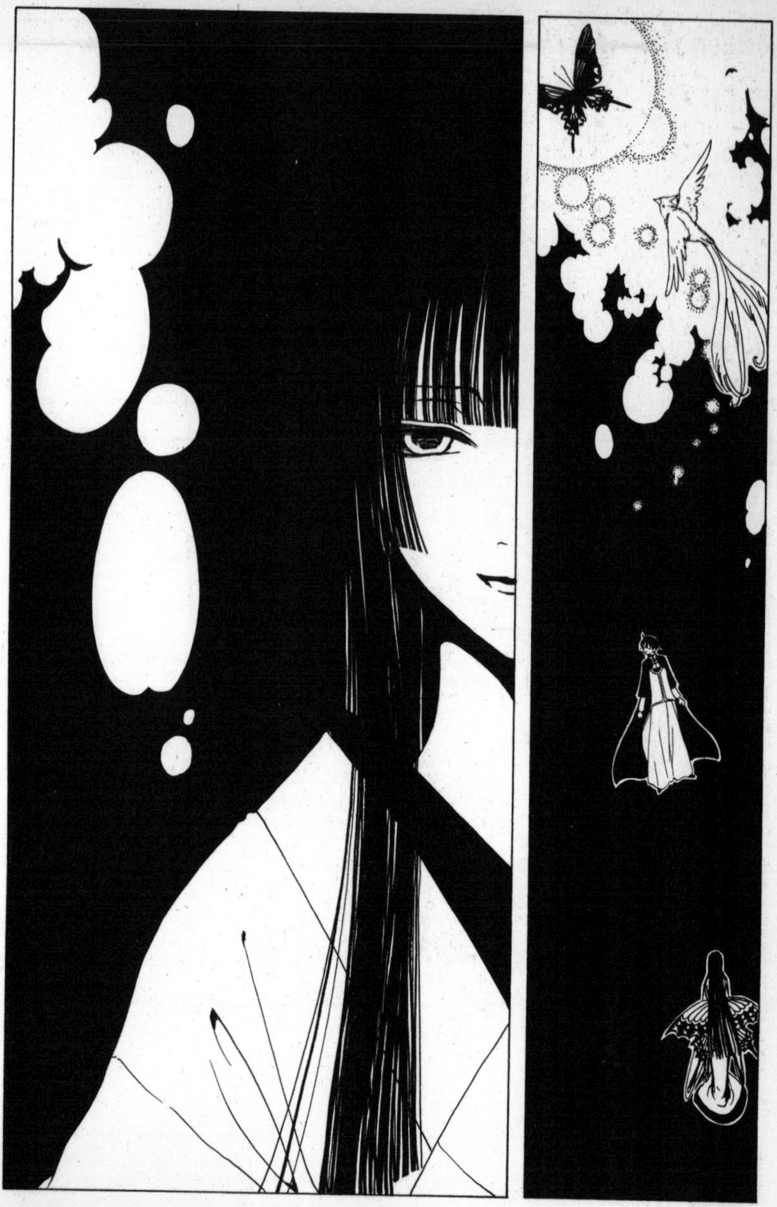

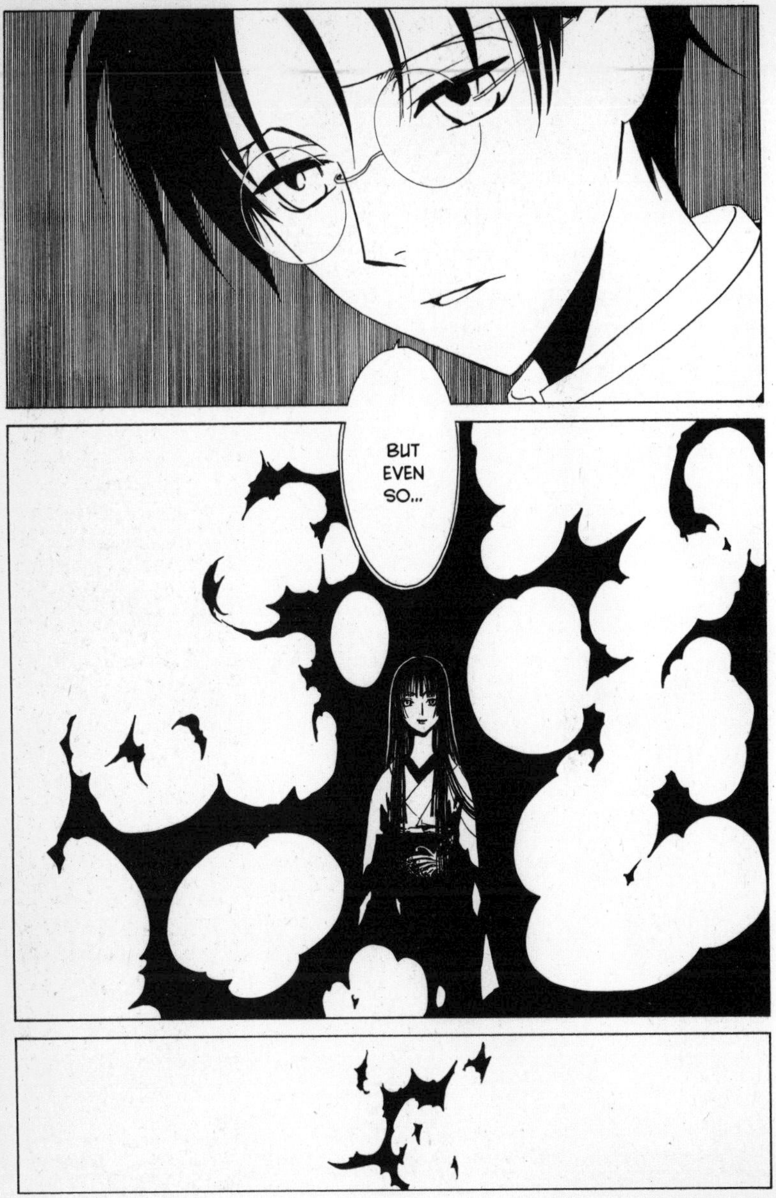
BUT EVEN SO...

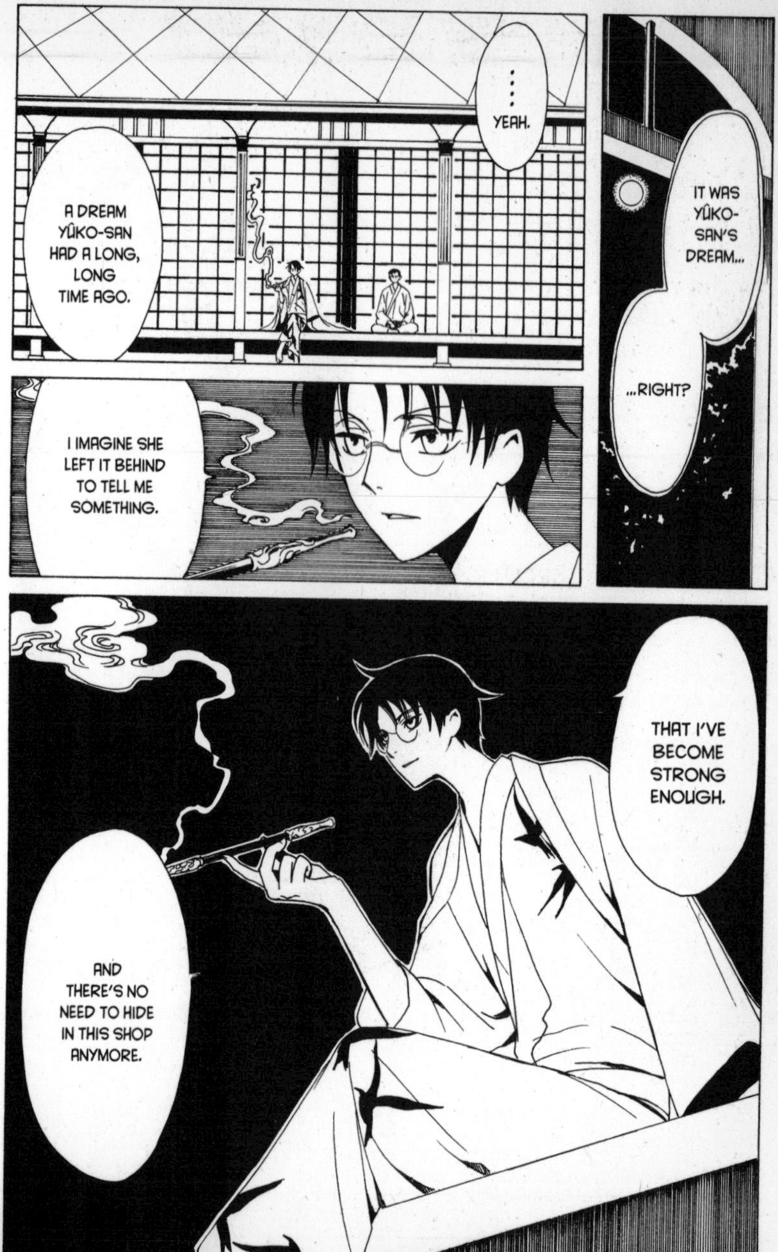
IT WAS YÛKO-SAN'S DREAM...
...RIGHT?
...
YEAH.
A DREAM YÛKO-SAN HAD A LONG, LONG TIME AGO.
I IMAGINE SHE LEFT IT BEHIND TO TELL ME SOMETHING.
THAT I'VE BECOME STRONG ENOUGH.
AND THERE'S NO NEED TO HIDE IN THIS SHOP ANYMORE.

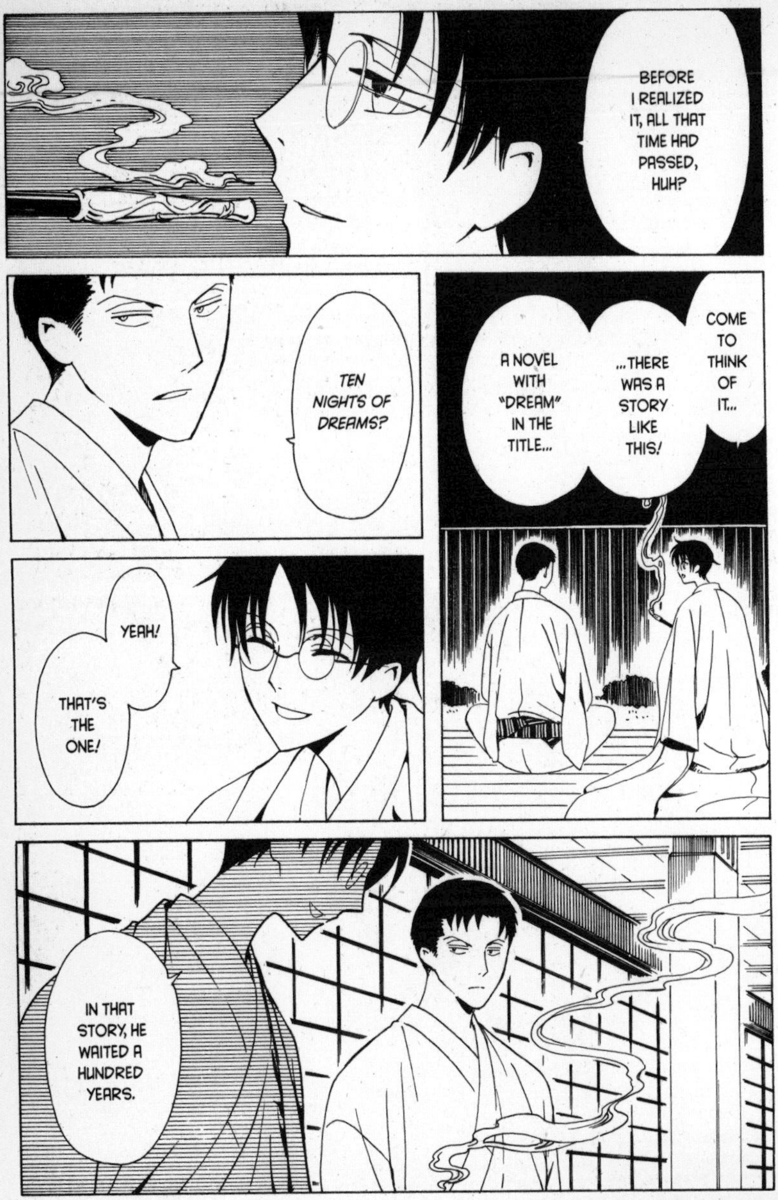
BEFORE I REALIZED IT, ALL THAT TIME HAD PASSED, HUH?
COME TO THINK OF IT...
...THERE WAS A STORY LIKE THIS!
A NOVEL WITH "DREAM" IN THE TITLE...
TEN NIGHTS OF DREAMS?
YEAH!
THAT'S THE ONE!
IN THAT STORY, HE WAITED A HUNDRED YEARS.

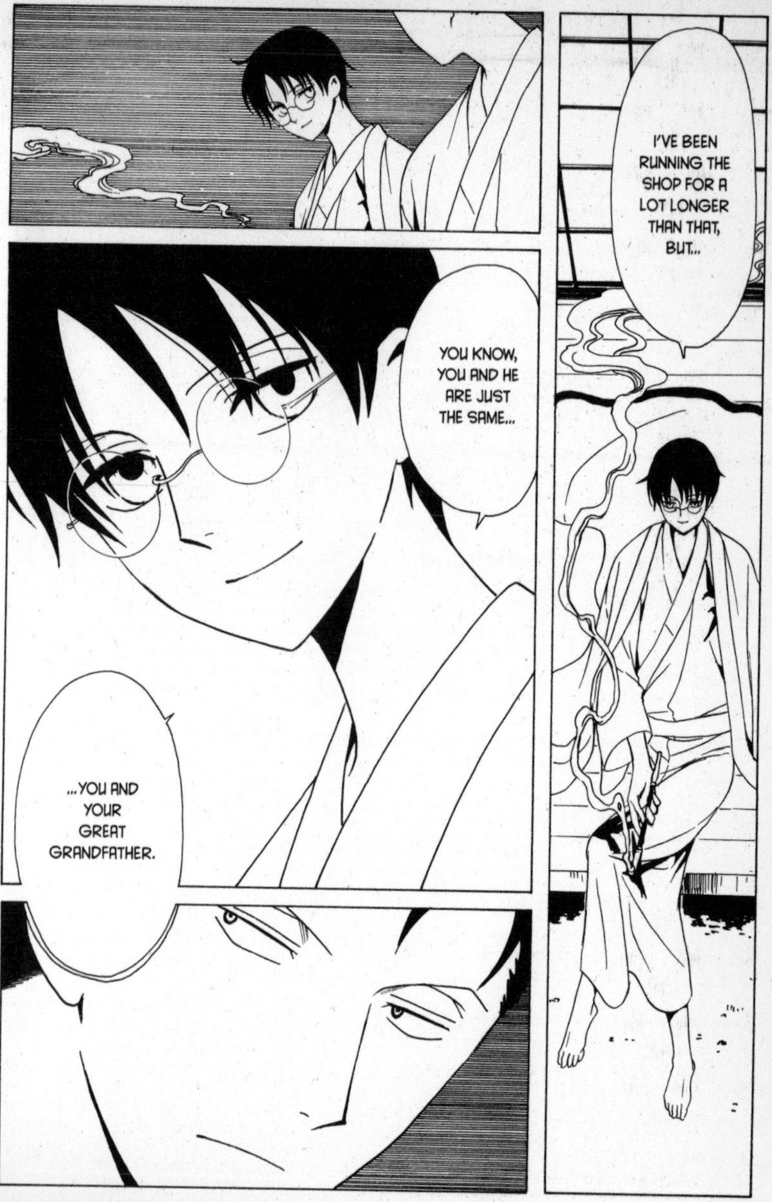
I'VE BEEN RUNNING THE SHOP FOR A LOT LONGER THAN THAT, BUT...
YOU KNOW, YOU AND HE ARE JUST THE SAME...
...YOU AND YOUR GREAT GRANDFATHER.

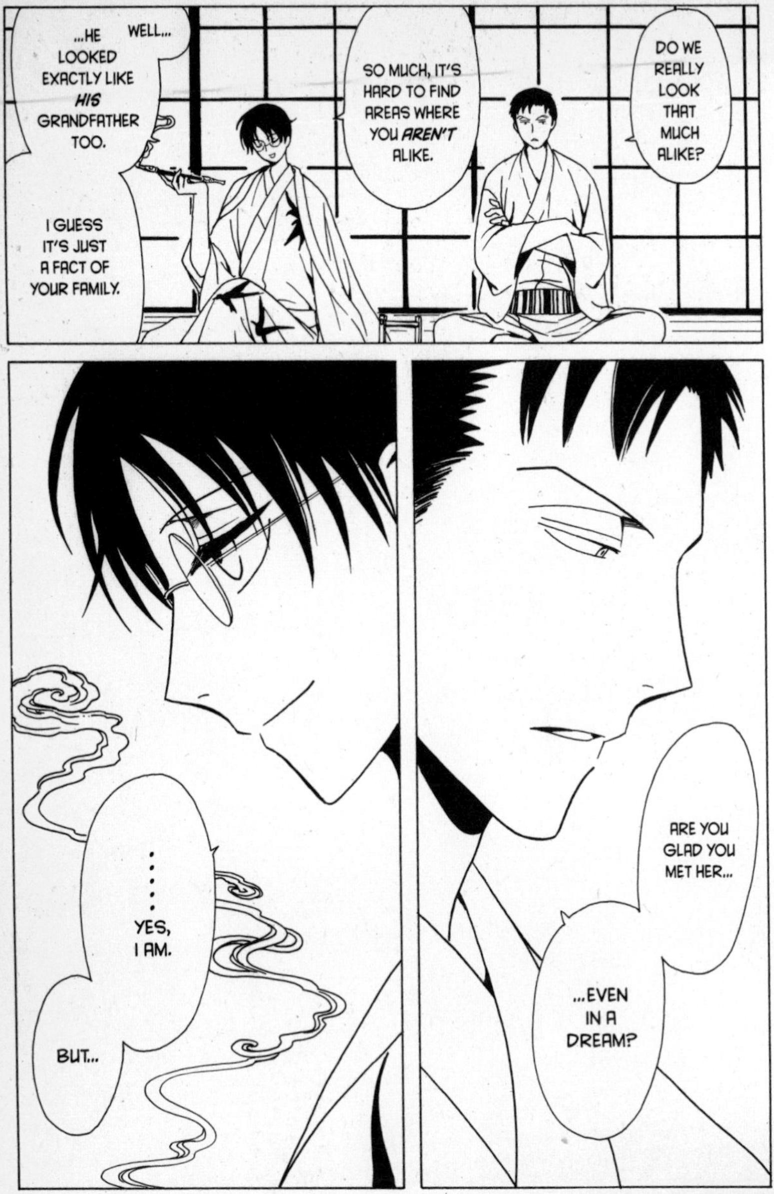
DO WE REALLY LOOK THAT MUCH ALIKE?
SO MUCH, IT'S HARD TO FIND AREAS WHERE YOU *AREN'T* ALIKE.
WELL...
...HE LOOKED EXACTLY LIKE *HIS* GRANDFATHER TOO.
I GUESS IT'S JUST A FACT OF YOUR FAMILY.
ARE YOU GLAD YOU MET HER...
...EVEN IN A DREAM?
......
YES, I AM.
BUT...

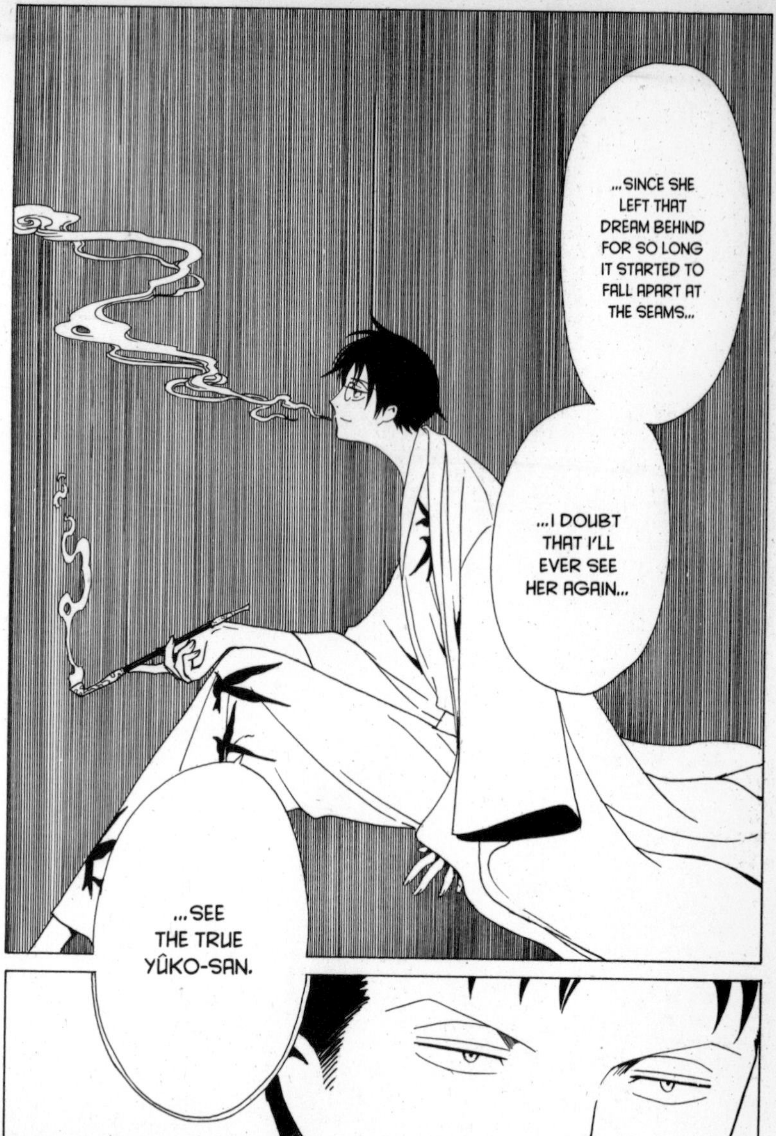
...SINCE SHE LEFT THAT DREAM BEHIND FOR SO LONG IT STARTED TO FALL APART AT THE SEAMS...
...I DOUBT THAT I'LL EVER SEE HER AGAIN...
...SEE THE TRUE YÛKO-SAN.

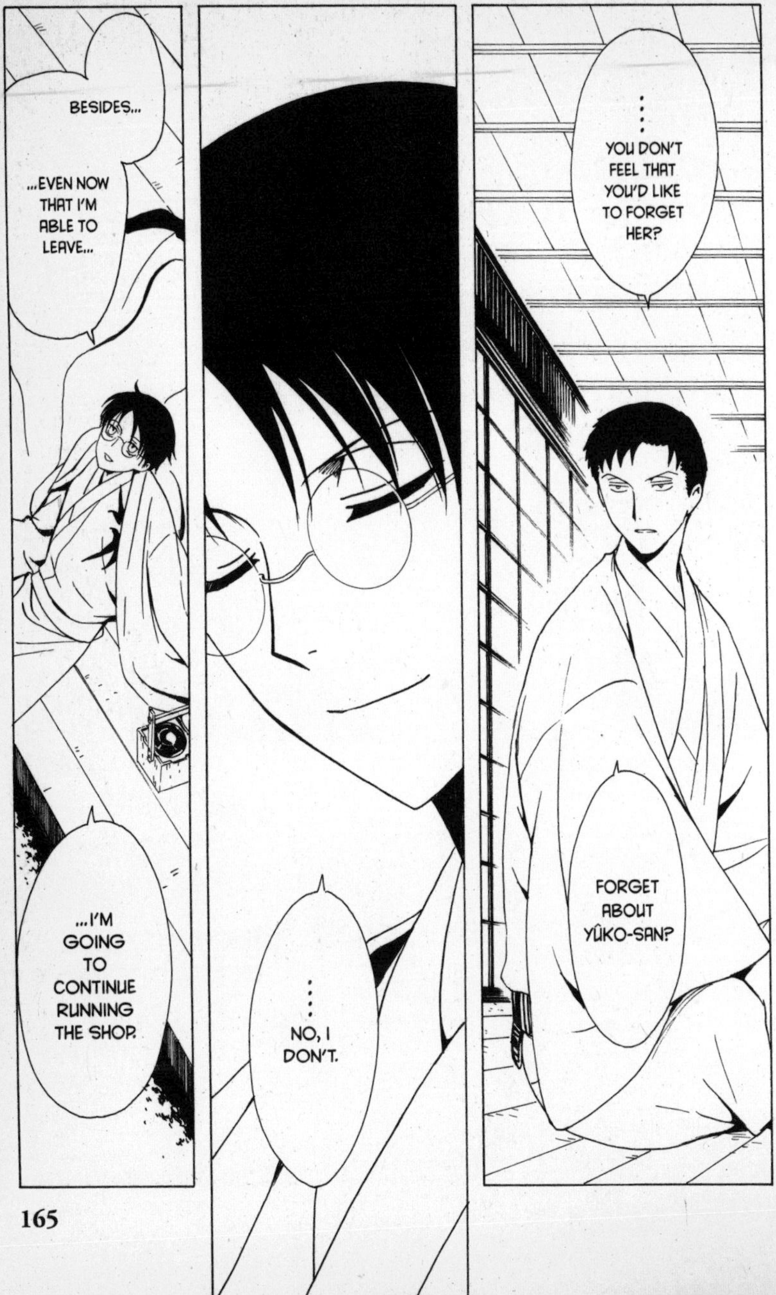
... YOU DON'T FEEL THAT YOU'D LIKE TO FORGET HER?
FORGET ABOUT YÛKO-SAN?
... NO, I DON'T.
BESIDES...
...EVEN NOW THAT I'M ABLE TO LEAVE...
...I'M GOING TO CONTINUE RUNNING THE SHOP.

SO I CAN WAIT FOR YÛKO-SAN.
.... IS THAT RIGHT?
NOW, DO YOU WANT A DRINK?
YEAH.
SST
I'LL HAVE WHISKEY...
...ON THE ROCKS.
GOT IT.

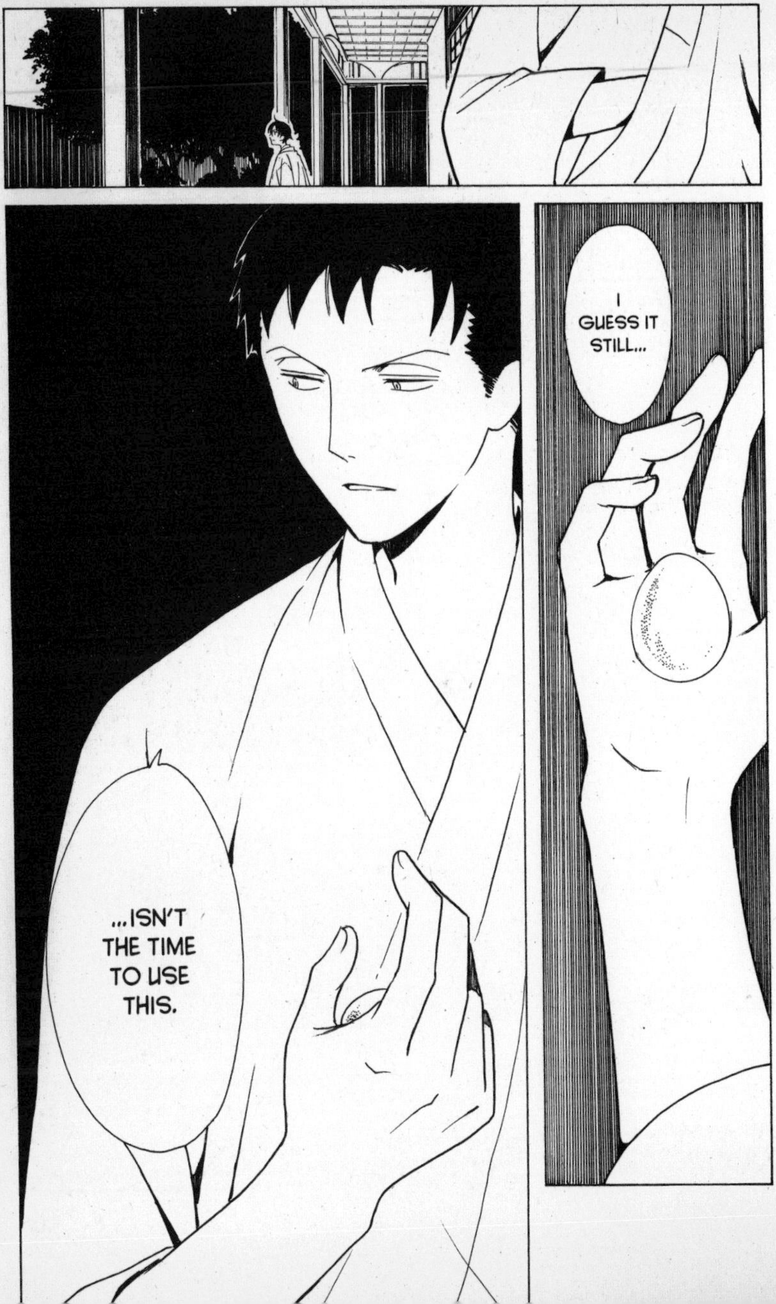
I GUESS IT STILL...
...ISN'T THE TIME TO USE THIS.

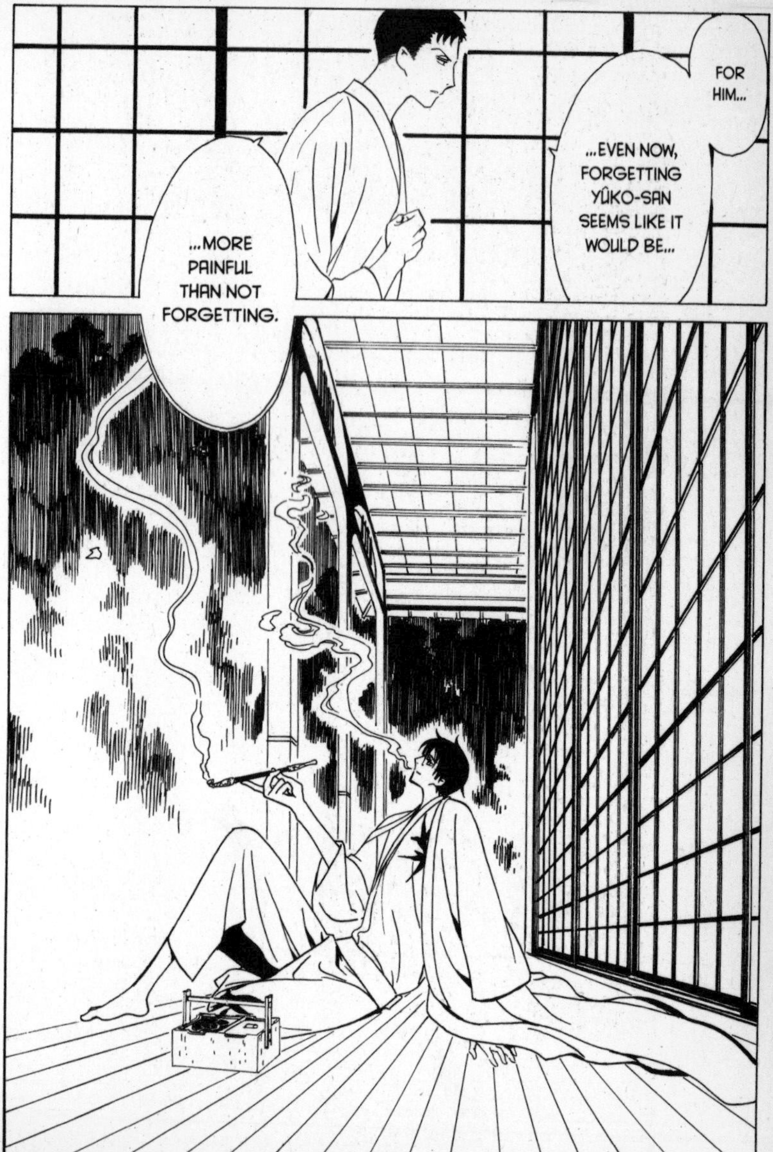
FOR HIM...
...EVEN NOW, FORGETTING YÛKO-SAN SEEMS LIKE IT WOULD BE...
...MORE PAINFUL THAN NOT FORGETTING.

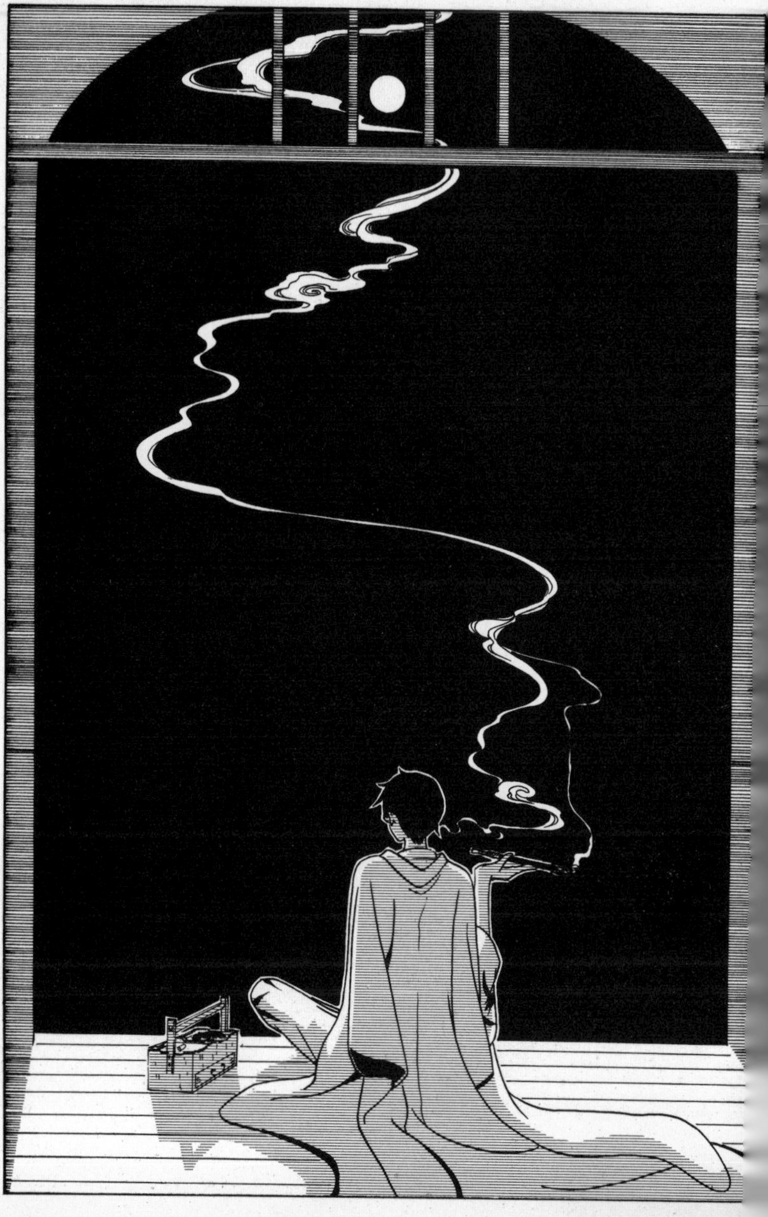

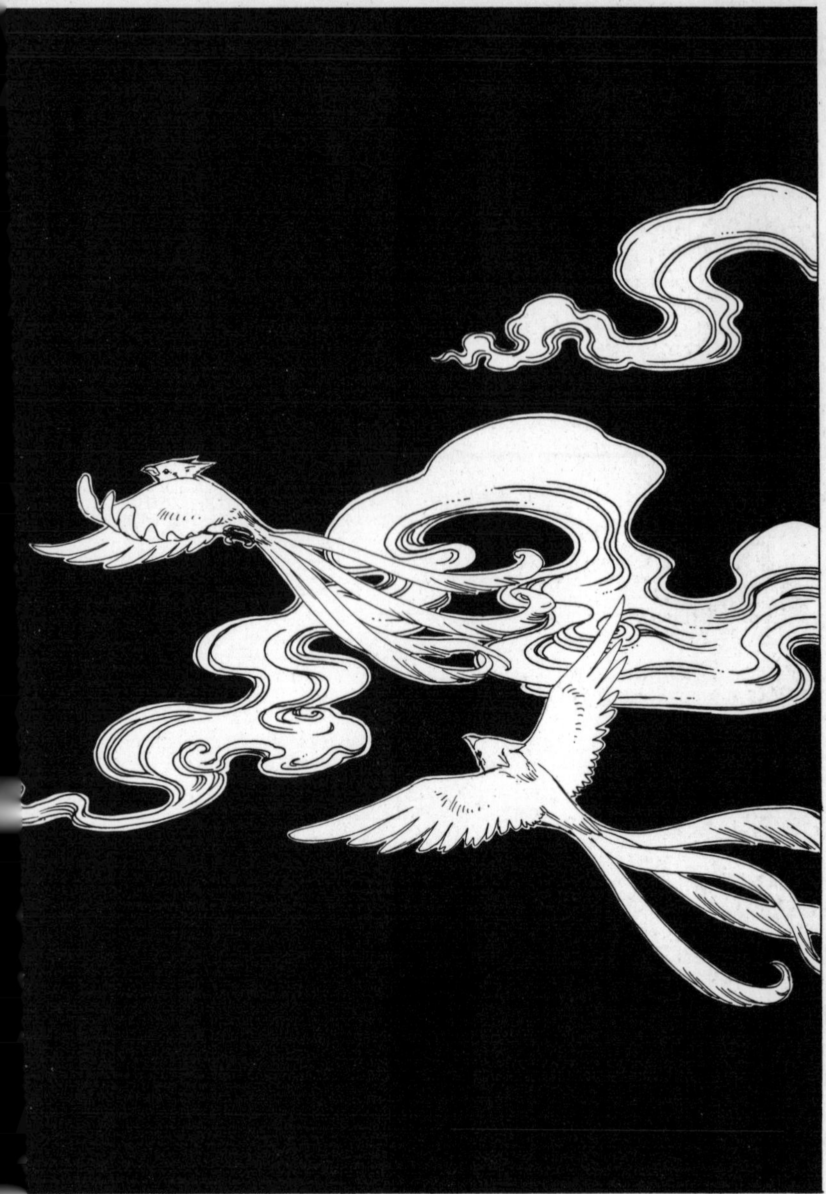

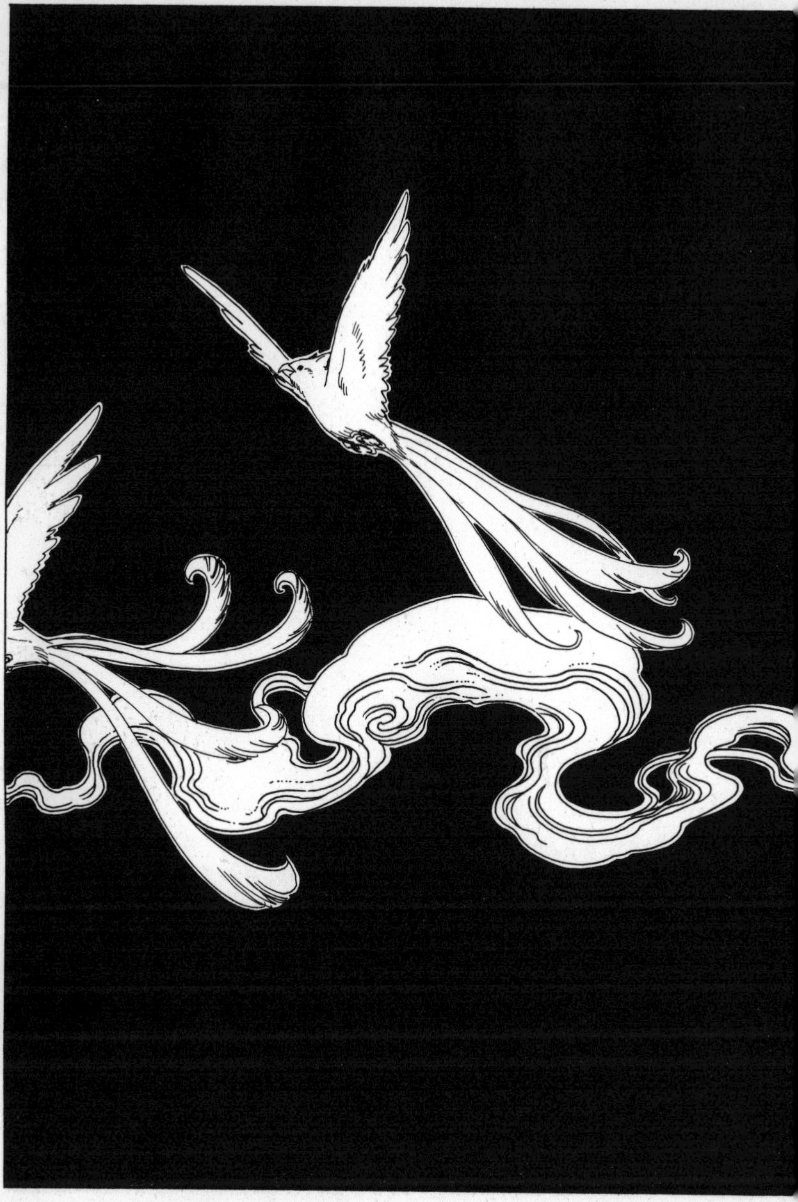

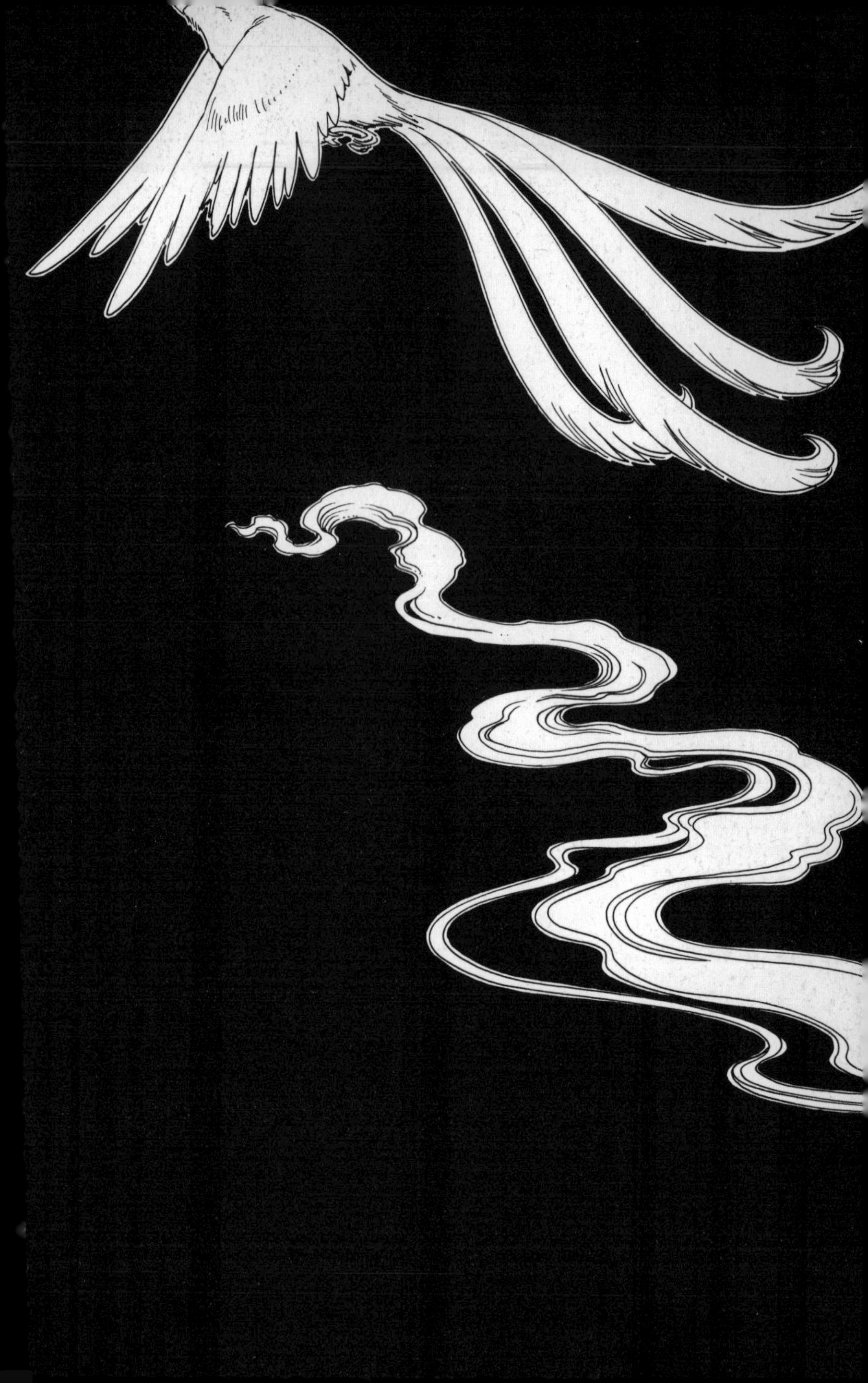

About the Creators

CLAMP is a group of four women who have become the most popular manga artists in America—Nanase Ohkawa, Mokona, Satsuki Igarashi, and Tsubaki Nekoi. They started out as *doujinshi* (fan comics) creators, but their skill and craft brought them to the attention of publishers very quickly. Their first work from a major publisher was RG Veda, but their first mass success was with Magic Knight Rayearth. From there, they went on to write many series, including Cardcaptor Sakura and Chobits, two of the most popular manga in the United States. Like many Japanese manga artists, they prefer to avoid the spotlight, and little is known about them personally.

CLAMP is currently publishing two series in Japan: Gate 7 and Kobato.

Translation Notes

Japanese is a tricky language for most Westerners, and translation is often more art than science. For your edification and reading pleasure, here are notes on some of the places where we could have gone in a different direction or where a Japanese cultural reference is used.

Chapter titles, the kanji for Rô

The kanji Rô in this incarnation of xxxHOLiC can also be pronounced *kago*, meaning "a cage" or "a basket," an enclosed area that prevents escape.

Page 5, Yin and yang and Japanese festivals

Unlike Western dualism, which concentrates on concepts of light versus dark, the Chinese philosophy of yin and yang concentrates on the balance of opposing forces. In other words, a balance of light and dark is preferred, and too much of either extreme is considered bad. Therefore, even though 9 is a "light" number, and September 9 therefore a combination of light numbers, this abundance of light is an ominous thing that throws off the balance of light and dark. The festivals are religious services to help restore the balance.

ALL OF THEM WERE CELEBRATED ON THOSE DAYS ACCORDING TO THE OLD CALENDAR, BUT...
...THE DATES WERE ADJUSTED AND CELEBRATED IN THE NEW CALENDAR.
..... THAT MATCHES WHAT I'VE HEARD.
ALL FIVE SEASONAL FESTIVALS WERE BASED ON THE IDEAS OF YIN AND YANG FOUND IN CHINESE PHILOSOPHY.

Page 5, Human Day

The first seven days of the year were designated as days honoring particular animals: chicken, dog, boar, sheep, cow, horse, and human. In ancient Japan, Human Day was one day of the year in which the authorities could not execute convicts.

Page 58, "At night, from a distance, or under an umbrella"

This is a phrase translated literally from the Japanese. All the possible English translations of phrases like this came out sounding sarcastic, along the lines of "beer goggles" rather than the more romantic way the Japanese think of this phrase.

Page 67, Obi

Obi means "belt," but an obi for a kimono is an elaborate, wide silk wrap that is often tied in a complicated bow in back.

Page 77, Magic square

They say that two thousand years ago, the Chinese had developed what we now call the 3×3 magic square — essentially a tic-tac-toe–style square, in each box of which is placed a number. To make it a magic square, all rows, columns, and diagonals add up to the same numerical sum. In ancient China these were used for casting fortunes and other occult purposes.

Page 77, Ceremony

In Japanese, the word is more vague. Jutsu-shiki is simply a method of performing a technique. For example, a wedding ceremony is a jutsu-shiki for a marriage. In magic, this may refer to words and actions performed while casting a spell. Since Watanuki's "techniques" are very similar to magical rites, the word "ceremony" seemed to be more appropriate.

Page 97, "as the name implies"

The word *kushi* (by linguistic rules, changes to *gushi* under certain circumstances) means "skewer," as in a thin, pointed wooden stick or a long, thin, sharp piece of metal. The *kushi* becomes the backbone of the decoration.

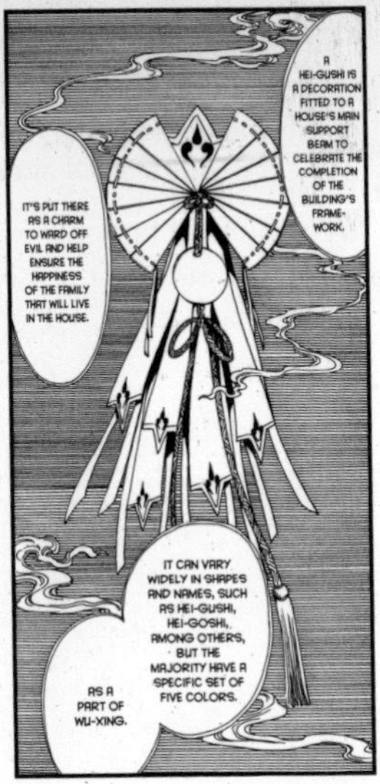
A HEI-GUSHI IS A DECORATION FITTED TO A HOUSE'S MAIN SUPPORT BEAM TO CELEBRATE THE COMPLETION OF THE BUILDING'S FRAME-WORK.
IT'S PUT THERE AS A CHARM TO WARD OFF EVIL AND HELP ENSURE THE HAPPINESS OF THE FAMILY THAT WILL LIVE IN THE HOUSE.
IT CAN VARY WIDELY IN SHAPES AND NAMES, SUCH AS HEI-GUSHI, HEI-GOSHI, AMONG OTHERS, BUT THE MAJORITY HAVE A SPECIFIC SET OF FIVE COLORS.
AS A PART OF WU-XING.

Page 97, Wu-xing-ism

The Chinese doctrine of the five elements—wood, fire, earth, metal, and water—is used in many different areas of Chinese thought, from fortune-telling to traditional medicine. It can be used to determine personality types in love fortunes, but it is also used as a mnemonic device to aid in learning traditional Chinese sciences.

Page 100, Tsukumo-gami

It's said that if tools are well used for a hundred years, they attain a soul of their own and become Tsukumo-gami. According to ancient Japanese legends and folktales, Tsukumo-gami are self-aware and may become vengeful if they are simply discarded after their century of faithful use.

Page 109, Miki

As explained in the notes of Volume 18, miki is saké that is offered up to Shinto gods.

Page 127, Konjac

Konjac (spelled *konnyaku* in Japanese) is a low-calorie jellylike dish made from the konjac potato. It is usually flavored with miso or other sauces.

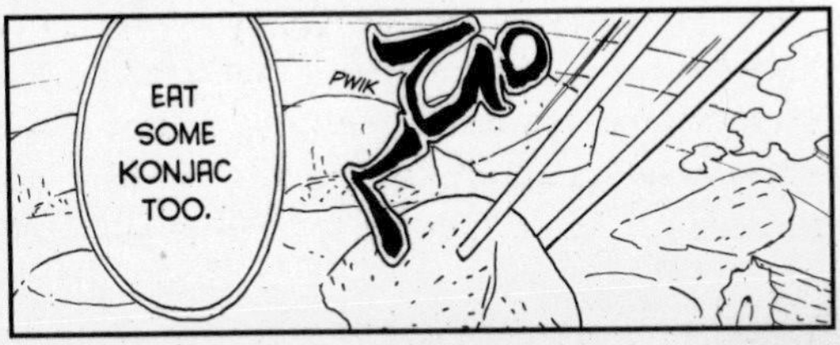
PWIK
EAT SOME KONJAC TOO.

Page 131, Gyoza and Lao Chu

Gyoza (called "pot stickers" in the West) is a Chinese dish that has become very popular in Japan. To go with the Chinese dish is a Chinese drink, Lao Chu, which is a rice-based liquor that can range from a light reddish color to a deep, dark brown.

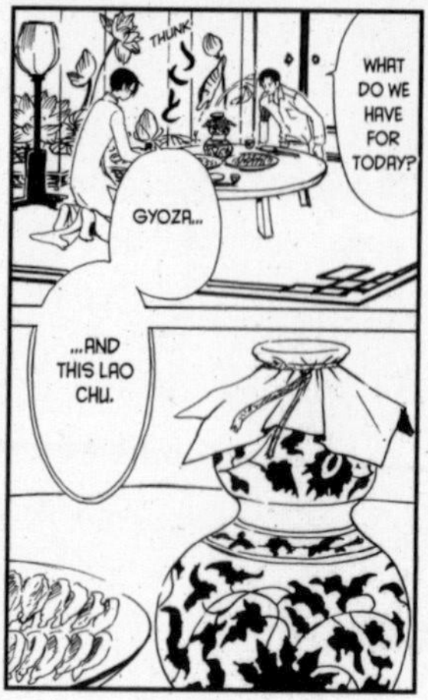
WHAT DO WE HAVE FOR TODAY?
THUNK
GYOZA...
...AND THIS LAO CHU.

Page 161, *Ten Nights of Dreams*

Natsume Soseki is perhaps the most famous Japanese short-story writer, and his stories "Kokoro" and "I Am a Cat" are reputed to capture the Japanese soul. While writing fiction in installments for a newspaper, he wrote *Ten Nights of Dreams*, ten short shorts that describe various dreams. In the first dream, the protagonist agrees to sit waiting on the grave of the woman he loves for a hundred years. He waits for what seems to be an eternity until one day a white lily sprouts from the grave. When he comes to understand that the lily is what he has been waiting for, he also realizes that a hundred years have passed.

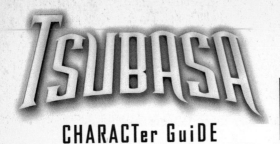
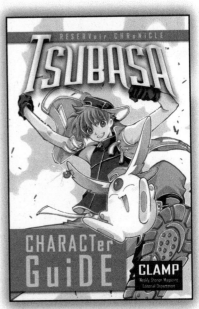

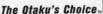

TOMARE!

[STOP!]

You're going the wrong way!

Manga is a completely different type of reading experience.

To start at the *beginning,* go to the *end!*

That's right! Authentic manga is read the traditional Japanese way—from right to left. Exactly the *opposite* of how American books are read. It's easy to follow: Just go to the other end of the book, and read each page—and each panel—from right side to left side, starting at the top right. Now you're experiencing manga as it was meant to be!